D1255202

# Three Generations

Maria Boyle Ewing and Minnie Sherman Fitch
The First and Third Generations

# THREE GENERATIONS

*Maria Boyle Ewing*
(1801–1864)
*Ellen Ewing Sherman*
(1824–1888)
*Minnie Sherman Fitch*
(1851–1913)

*by*

KATHERINE BURTON

LONGMANS, GREEN AND CO.
New York · Toronto
1947

LONGMANS, GREEN AND CO., INC.
55 FIFTH AVENUE, NEW YORK 3

LONGMANS, GREEN AND CO.
215 VICTORIA STREET, TORONTO 1

THREE GENERATIONS

COPYRIGHT · 1947

BY KATHERINE BURTON

ALL RIGHTS RESERVED, INCLUDING THE RIGHT TO REPRODUCE
THIS BOOK, OR ANY PORTION THEREOF, IN ANY FORM

PUBLISHED SIMULTANEOUSLY IN THE DOMINION OF CANADA
BY LONGMANS, GREEN AND CO., TORONTO

FIRST EDITION

PRINTED IN THE UNITED STATES OF AMERICA
BY THE VAIL-BALLOU PRESS, INC., BINGHAMTON, N. Y.

*Dedicated to my native state*
OHIO
*which figures very largely*
*in this narrative*

# Contents

# *Foreword*

EAST TWENTY-NINTH STREET in New York, between Fifth and Madison Avenues, is a thoroughfare where the passer-by hears little save the rattling of the trucks and the horns of passing automobiles. It is lined with inconspicuous old buildings, and, unless attention is called to it, one would scarcely notice a structure little different in appearance from the rest, the Convent of the Sisters of Mary Reparatrix. It is really several old houses made into one, with unexpected levels, where visitors pass up and down little flights of stairs to go from room to room. Here, in their habits of white and pale blue with their insignia of gold, the nuns live their days of prayer and good works, and always some of them are to be seen in the lovely chapel in adoration before the Blessed Sacrament.

With the years all convents accumulate treasures and so with this convent. Some are actual treasures — fine paintings and altar furnishings and beautiful vestments. Some are intangible treasures of prayer and love and sacrifice. One treasure this convent has which combines the tangible and the intangible. It is a monstrance given in memory of three women, the first of whom was born at the turn of the nineteenth century, the third who lived into the twentieth — so that together they represent one hundred years of American Catholic life. At the base of the monstrance are engraved the monograms of Maria Boyle Ewing, Ellen Ewing Sherman, Minnie Sherman Fitch, with a phrase from the Book of Proverbs: *Her children rose up and called her blessed.*

The monstrance has great beauty of design. It has symbolic beauty,

*I*

too, for each jewel, each diamond and pearl and amethyst that was needed to make the shining whole, was once the personal possession of these three women or of their descendants. Now, wrought into this unity, it has become the expression of the love of this family for God.

# 1. Pioneer Families

## [1796–1811]

O<small>N A</small> bright morning early in 1796, young Hugh Boyle came
riding into the Pennsylvania town of Brownsville. Walking
his horse slowly down the road past the sturdy houses, he stopped
in the center of the thriving settlement to look about him with keen
blue eyes.

At his right he saw the river crowded with flatboats, and at its edge
other craft being built. Beyond the town, in the forest where the oaks
stood massed, he heard the sound of axes. A ferry was crossing the
Monongahela toward a smaller town on the other side.

He had been told that this frontier town was of growing importance: in fact, many thought it would some day become the State
center instead of Pittsburgh. Even now Hugh counted on the main
street and the smaller thoroughfares radiating from it close to a hundred houses. Since the early 1760's, when it was called Redstone Old
Fort, Brownsville had attracted settlers, mainly because of the protection offered by the blockhouses along the road, and twenty years
later it had a population of over six hundred people. One overland
route from Baltimore ended there and the trip by flatboat began
down the Monongahela, the Ohio and the Mississippi.

Hugh realized that his uncle in Martinsville had been right when
he told him that Brownsville might be a good place to open a branch
of their business. That had been his reason for coming, and now, as
he rode on through the town, he made up his mind to stay.

Hugh was the son of a well-to-do Irish country gentleman, a high-
spirited lad and a brilliant one. But high-spirited lads and those with
brains got into trouble sooner or later with the English military au-

3

thorities in the Ireland of the day, and such men as Hugh, outspoken in loyalty to their own land, were considered traitors to the Crown.

His father had sent him to France for his education, as so many Catholic families sent their sons during those unhappy years, and when he came home again, his head filled with doctrines of liberty and equality, he could not bear the restrictions and harshness there. At any rate, to avoid possible imprisonment, the eighteen-year-old boy had fled from his country and crossed the Atlantic in a sailing vessel.

He had landed in Philadelphia and gone to an uncle in Martinsville, Virginia, who promptly put him to work. Hugh had not been trained in any profession, nor was he skilled as a farmer or woodsman, but he had a good education and some training as an accountant, so that from the beginning he was able to earn his way in the New World. Before long his uncle had made him a partner in his mercantile business, and, after some years Hugh had gained a certain amount of experience. Now he had been sent to see about opening a store in Brownsville.

Hugh Boyle's first step on arriving into this frontier community was to make inquiries at the inn as to where he would find Mr. Neal Gillespie. His uncle had suggested he see this gentleman, since he was known to be one of the most prominent citizens of Brownsville and would be able to give him good advice.

Hugh followed directions until he reached the stone dwelling which had been pointed out to him. Here he was pleasantly welcomed by a tall smiling man who asked after his uncle in Martinsville, and who welcomed him all over again when he learned from what part of Ireland Hugh came.

"Donegal, you say? County Donegal, that is my county too. Well, it has been many years since I saw its green fields. Are things any better in Ireland now?"

The blue eyes darkened. The smile vanished from the young man's face. "No better," he said briefly. "That is why I am here."

"And welcome you are, my boy. Now tell me what you want and where you are going."

Hugh told him of his uncle's plans, and said he hoped to find at once a suitable place for storing merchandise.

"We'll find you a place to store the goods you bring," promised Mr. Gillespie, "but it is here you must stay for the time at least." And with the young man halfheartedly protesting, he called into the house, "Girls, we have a guest here who is tired and hungry."

Smiling faces framed in dark curls appeared at window and door. "Here's a young man from Donegal, girls," Hugh was introduced, "and he is staying the night."

They came out then and shyly greeted the surprised Hugh, girls with the fair looks of the ones at home, and in a few minutes he was installed at his ease as a guest in the Gillespie home.

During the next few days Hugh met and talked with many of the townsmen, who were favorably impressed with the personable young man and encouraged him to make his home among them. In talking to them he learned more about his host, Neal Gillespie whose first marriage had been a romantic affair — a runaway match in Ireland. The story ran that Eleanor Dougherty had been the daughter of a great county family and Neal a farmer on her father's estate. The two had fallen in love, but her family were violently opposed to the match. So they had been secretly married by a priest and started for America.

Eleanor had died some years before, but the memory of her charm was still alive in the town. A gently bred girl she was, the people told Hugh, anyone could see that, and very beautiful, with a character as fair as her face, and all her life she had remained a fine Irish lady.

But of course young Neal himself had been no country bumpkin. He was a self-possessed, handsome young man and very ambitious. He had become a good citizen of his adopted country, and had done well in America. He had a reputation in the community for generosity and was always glad to help others get a start in life. He was an ardent Catholic and kept one room in his home for the missionaries who occasionally passed through Brownsville, and always he pleaded with them to tell Bishop Carroll of the great need for a priest to be stationed in this town. For not only was it the chief rendezvous of immigrants waiting for the crowded river boats to take them to the West and South, but the few Catholics living in the neighborhood were dropping from the fold because there was no one to give them spiritual aid. Yet, although Bishop Carroll was aware of their need, he had only a few priests and some years were to pass before he could grant their request.

On landing from Ireland the young Gillespies had gone first to Wilmington, Delaware, and had remained there for some years. Then Neal left his wife and children while he looked for another place to settle. But before leaving them on this uncertain and possibly dangerous journey, he and Eleanor had a second marriage ceremony performed, for the Gillespies had not brought with them from Ireland any legal proof of their marriage, since Catholic marriages took place in secret and therefore were not recorded. And Neal wanted this record for the sake of his wife and family.

Hearing so much about the rich Ohio Territory, Neal had planned to find a home there, but when he reached Brownsville, he decided to settle in this historic valley in the western shadow of the Alleghenies where so many pioneers, trappers and traders had passed before him. He had gone back to Delaware and brought his family to their new home. In 1787 he had bought from the widow of a man known only as Indian Pete a fine piece of land on a rise called Indian Hill — three hundred acres on the bank of the Monongahela River, close to the ferry that crossed the stream, and here he had built his home.

In Brownsville the Gillespies had spent most of the rest of their married lives and there Eleanor had died. Afterwards Neal remained in the home he had built, his sons and daughters about him. Some years after Eleanor's death he had remarried and of that marriage there was one daughter, a year old at the time that Hugh Boyle came to the Gillespie home.

Having found, with Neal's help, a good storeroom in Brownsville, Hugh went back to Virginia to bring his wares from his uncle's main

One thing sadly lacking for the Boyles as well as the other Catholics in Lancaster was the presence of a Catholic priest and an opportunity to receive the Sacraments. At the close of the Revolution there had been few white men in the Ohio country, and those few were not Catholics, nor were many of the earlier settlers in that region.

Once, however, there had been Catholicism in the northern part of the country, for it was first settled by the French, and in 1751 the first little Catholic church was built in Erie by Armand de la Richardie, a Jesuit. At the end of the French and Indian wars, the surrender of Quebec in 1759 gave the English these possessions and all claims to the Ohio valley, and the whole of Canada. The Jesuits withdrew from their Lake Erie missions and went to Canada, and for thirty years there was no trace in the Territory of priests or any Catholic activity. Then Pierre Didier, a Benedictine, came to Gallipolis, but withdrew in discouragement. In 1793, Père Pierre Barrière and Père Etienne Badin, on their way down the Ohio had stopped for a few days in the vicinity to baptize, say Mass, and perform marriages for the remnants of the French colony.

In 1803, the year in which the Ohio Territory became a State and larger immigrations began, more and more Catholics were among those who came, and further demands for priests to serve them reached Bishop Carroll. In 1805 one Jacob Dittoe was commissioned by the Catholic group in Lancaster to write to Bishop Carroll regarding the possibility of securing land for a church in the neighborhood.

"There are of our profession in this place that I am acquainted with, about thirty souls," wrote Jacob Dittoe to his bishop. He then asked if one of the newly-ordained priests on his way to Kentucky could stop in Lancaster. He would give directions to any priest who gave them a call. "I live near Lancaster, State of Ohio. Any person coming under such direction from you will not only be directed where to find me, but gladly received by a Mr. Boyle of the said town, who with his family are of the same Church. I hope to hear from you soon."

When Bishop Carroll received this letter he noted on the back of it

a few words on the probability of being able to establish a church
"north of the Ohio."

There was no doubt that he tried his best to aid his scattered flocks
everywhere. But in those days each State and Territory in the Union
was only a parish or a mission of the Baltimore diocese, and for this
vast territory there was only a handful of priests.

All he could then do about such petitions as Jacob Dittoe's, was to
promise to have an occasional missionary stop for a brief visit. Until
he had more priests, he could do no more.

By 1805 Lancaster was a town of almost a hundred houses and
the building still continued. But only as much land as was needed
was cleared at a time. The children picked wild plums from bushes
on the main streets. There was thick timber still standing on many of
the lots. As for streets, now carefully named and numbered, there
were only four which had even a cabin on them.

Then came the rumor that the little settlement would some day
become the seat of State government. This brought more settlers
flocking in — men of various nationalities, Germans, Irish, Scotch,
English, French. Among them were many mechanics, wheelwrights,
cabinet-makers, carpenters, tin-smiths, gun-smiths. There was talk of
starting a weekly paper. To Philemon Beecher's law office, a room in
his own home, came many clients.

Hugh and Eleanor Boyle were very happy in Lancaster. Their life
was a simple one with few luxuries, one where some necessities were
hard to get. But food was plentiful, wood was there for the cutting,
and the climate though vigorous, was not too harsh. They were content with their plain life, their simple home.

They had met with one sorrow. Two years after Maria's birth, a
son was born to them and named Neal for his Grandfather Gillespie.
He was only a few months old when he died of a fever and he was
one of the first to be buried in the little Lancaster cemetery. But Maria
remained a healthy child and her parents found consolation for their
loss in the little daughter who grew prettier every day.

In 1805, Eleanor's sister, Susan Beecher, gave birth to a daughter, and in that same year her own second daughter was born and named Susan for her aunt. She was a fine child and gave promise of the same beauty as Maria's, but Eleanor never fully recovered from this birth. She grew thinner and more frail. Dr. Delano declared he could not say what ailed her, but to some of the women in the town it looked like "the consumption."

Susan Beecher, greatly worried, came often to the Boyle house to be with her sister. One afternoon, when Eleanor seemed especially tired, she suggested taking the little girls home with her for a few days so that their mother could have a complete rest. She did not mention aloud her real fear at sight of her sister's thin face and flushed cheeks. "You've enough to do," she said, "and I'll be glad to have them for a day or so. I'll take as good care of them as ever you did of me."

With her namesake in her arms and little Maria trotting beside her, she walked the short distance between the two homes. That evening after all the little girls were in bed, she told Philemon her fears, and wept the tears she had held back earlier. "She looks too ill to get better, Philemon," she said. "The mark of death is on her."

The plan had been to take the children home again in a few days, but Eleanor grew rapidly worse. Susan, putting a neighbor's daughter in charge of the children, went to help nurse her. One evening she rushed into Philemon's office weeping bitterly: Eleanor had died suddenly. A few days later she was buried beside her baby son.

At Susan's request, Eleanor's children stayed on with her, and Hugh Boyle was content to have it so. With the years two more children were born to the Beechers and named Philemon and Maria. The children of the household seemed to the casual observer to be brothers and sisters of the same family.

Hugh Boyle continued to live by himself in his lonely house with only Eleanor's memory for company. Each evening he came to the Beecher home and spent an hour or two with his little girls. The tall spare figure with the snow-white hair — for it became white when he was thirty — was a familiar sight in the town. He wore a white beaver hat and a flowered waistcoat and carried an ivory-topped cane, and always walked with a very quick step. He was much loved by the people of Lancaster, for he was a kindly man, generous to a fault, and angered only by trickery and meanness.

During these years the Dittoes and Boyles had never given up hope of having some day a church in their town, or at least the regular services of a passing missionary who would spend some days with them each year. In 1808, Jacob Dittoe wrote again to Bishop Carroll: they had land now for a church, and a house could also be erected for a priest. He added that he had various promises from his neighbors to contribute to a priest's maintenance. It was not lonely there at all, he assured the Bishop, for the land was only two miles from the National Road, a busy highway over which immigration continued to the West, and wagons and coaches carried passengers and goods to the new States in the Ohio valley. Perhaps the Bishop had heard someone say the climate was unhealthy but this was not true. It was a fine place and his own family all enjoyed good health.

Bishop Carroll evidently felt that it was now time to do something for these distant faithful of his flock, for in the same year he asked young Mr. Fenwick, the Dominican, to stop there on his way from his Kentucky convent to visit this group of Catholic people in the forests of Ohio. And the young priest promised he would go, learn what were the prospects for a parish, and report to Baltimore.

Mr. Fenwick departed to carry out the mission entrusted to him. Traveling through the deep forests, following Jacob Dittoe's directions, he was at last nearing his destination, but not quite sure how to reach it, when he heard the sound of an axe and turned his horse that way. The sound grew louder and at length he reached a clearing and a large log cabin. At his hail a woman with a baby in her arms came to the door and several children ran up to stare at him.

"I'm seeking Mr. Dittoe," he told her. "I am sent by Bishop Carroll to visit him."

Over the woman's face spread a look of unbelief that changed to joy. Without saying a word she lifted a horn that hung on a log and blew on it. In a few moments out of the nearby forest came two men with axes on their shoulders, and the woman ran to meet them. "Jacob," she called, "it is a priest. The priest has come."

The older man hurried up to the newcomer, his face as alight with joy as the woman's had been. He welcomed the traveler, and his wife hurried to bring fresh water to cleanse away the mud and dust of the journey, while the younger man led the horse away. Then food was brought for the welcome guest.

While Mr. Fenwick was eating, Dittoe sent word to the other Catholic families, and by early evening over twenty had assembled, among them Hugh Boyle and his daughters and Mrs. Beecher. They could not keep their eyes from Mr. Fenwick, for it had been so very long since they had seen a priest.

The young Dominican did his best for them in the limited time he could remain. He heard confessions, he celebrated Mass — his first in Ohio, he told them — and he baptized several children. Then he had to leave them, as much to his own sorrow as to theirs.

"But you will come back, sir?" asked Hugh Boyle anxiously. The young priest nodded. "I will come next year," he assured them solemnly. He would stay longer now, he said, but he had a heavy burden of duties in Kentucky, where he had recently built a convent and a college. "But I shall mention you all and your fervor to the good Bishop. He pities your plight and will do his best to provide for you."

He managed to come for brief visits the next year and the next and the one following, and, though there was no chance as yet for a church of their own, the little Lancaster group no longer felt spiritually alone.

In 1811 Mr. Badin came with Bishop Flaget, who was on his way to Pittsburgh, and they stopped at Lancaster and also at Somerset, some twenty miles away. But in the year following no one came. Mr. Fenwick wrote that his failure to be with them was for one reason only: "I have my hands and my head so full. But take courage and have patience a little longer and you shall be comforted. I will be with you in August or September at latest." He wrote that he had spoken often to Bishop Carroll about the little community in Ohio, and the latter had again promised that at the first opportunity he would provide a priest for them.

## 2. *Early Years in Lancaster*

### [1811–1819]

THROUGH their growing years Eleanor's girls and Susan's children played together in the wide Beecher yard, and Susan gave them all an equal love and care. And every evening Hugh Boyle walked to the Beecher home, talked with his girls for a while and then returned again to his solitary house.

The children grew up with the town, a happy, contented group. No one in the community was very poor and certainly no one was very rich. Food was plentiful enough; there was game, and fruit and berries grew everywhere. People planted vegetable gardens. There was plenty of milk. There was little sugar, but quantities of honey — so much in fact that the children preferred black New Orleans molasses for sweetening on their bread. The honey, Judge Beecher told his own household, was not really an American product at all, for the first swarms had been brought from the Old World and the Indians called the bees "white men's flies."

Schooling for the children of the town had been a real difficulty, until Miss Flora Butler came from New York to open a school for girls in a little log cabin on Main Street, and Mr. James Hunter started a school for boys and girls on Columbus Street. Unfortunately Miss

Butler, whose school the Boyle girls attended, married the next year and went back to New York. But the same year a Mrs. Baker opened a private school for out-of-town boarding pupils in Washington, Pennsylvania, the first boarding school for girls west of the Alleghenies. And there Maria Boyle was sent for her education.

In June of 1812 the American Congress declared war against England, one of the chief grievances being that the British were inciting the Indians to attack the frontier settlements. The results of the war would affect the future of the whole Northwest Territory, and Lancaster men in great numbers rushed to enlist.

A crowd of citizens heard the governor's proclamation read at a public meeting at the court house by Major Charles Sherman, a newcomer from Connecticut. After a patriotic address was delivered, another citizen rose with an offer to raise a company to join the forces arming against the British. A few weeks later the same crowd saw him march his company out of town to the northern frontier where they joined General Hull's army and took part in the ensuing battles.

Not until February of 1815 was there news of the end of the conflict. Word came to the postmaster at Lancaster, in a letter from the postmaster of Wheeling, announcing that peace had been declared between the two nations. Dr. Wilson, president of the town council, issued a proclamation asking that all citizens join in a general celebration of the event. The town was illuminated, there were fireworks, and a national salute was fired.

The children of Lancaster watched it all and only when the salute was fired did some of them show alarm. Susan Boyle clung to her father's hand in fear of the noise, but Maria stood still and straight and listened like a little soldier. After such excitement it seemed very tame to go back again to Mrs. Baker's, but there was to be an exhibition of pupils' talents, with Maria one of the performers, so she returned quite willingly.

Maria was sixteen, when one day her Uncle Beecher brought word that a new student was coming to read law in his office. He said that Judge Sherman had recommended the young man, who had just graduated from Athens College, of which Judge Sherman was one of the trustees. Young Ewing was a brilliant hard-working youth, and had, he thought, a fine future ahead of him.

Judge Beecher smiled when he recalled some of his conversation with Thomas Ewing. "He seems an unusual young man," he said to his wife. "He is older than the usual law student, but that is because he has worked his way through college — in fact, he and one other young man are the first ever to get degrees from Athens. It evidently took him years to get the money together, and he had to leave sometimes to earn more so that he could go on with his studies."

Later that evening he spoke further of the new law student. "I asked him what he had been doing since he graduated, and he said he had been reading Blackstone's *Commentaries* ever since. And then he added, 'My first reading was a mere exploration, sir, to find what was there and to understand what I could.'"

"Is he handsome, Pa Beecher?" asked Maria, who had been listening to the conversation but thought the young man sounded rather boring.

"What is that, my dear? Yes, yes, he is by no means ill-favored." He turned back to his wife. "And then, after that exploratory survey, he said he went back to the beginning and studied the four volumes carefully, and now he feels ready to come into my office!"

Young Ewing came to live with the Beechers. It was the custom of the day that when a lawyer took a young man into his office to teach him the law, the latter boarded with the family and in return helped with the chores — with carrying in wood and building up fires and running errands.

Maria watched from the window of the parlor when the new law student came for the first time to the room which was Judge Beecher's office. Then she ran to her aunt. "Oh, Ma Beecher, he is handsome.

He's tall and has big shoulders and he holds his head high. He is really very good-looking."

When she met him for the first time, she was demureness itself. But it was obvious to Aunt Beecher, and no doubt to Maria too, that she was making him feel aware of his awkwardness and of the fact that his life had left him little time to learn the ways of a man with a maid. The only attention he paid her was to glance at her shyly now and then, as if she were a being from another world than his own.

The shyness gradually wore off as the big young man came to feel himself a member of the family. There was, of course, little time for anything but his work. But at meals and in the evenings by the fire he could be lured into talking. There were moments, too, when reading in the office he glanced up from his Blackstone at sight of Maria picking flowers in the garden or moving down the walk with her light quick step.

During the first few months the Beechers — and their niece — learned much more about the new member of their household than the few facts that Judge Sherman had told them. The elders, and the children as well, enjoyed his stories of his youth, for they were tales of pioneer courage. His father, George Ewing, had held a commission during the Revolution, and had been with Washington's army at Valley Forge. Later he married and made a scant livelihood for his family by teaching school. Soon after Thomas' birth, his father had decided to settle in the Northwest Territory, bringing his family and goods down the Ohio by flatboat, and they landed at Marietta. Young Thomas had never forgotten that trip. "Because," he explained to the Beechers, "when I leaned over the side of the boat my hat — and it was the very first one I ever owned — fell off and floated out of reach before my cries could give the alarm. It was a fine hat of plaited straw," he said sadly, "and it was years before I had another."

After a brief stay at Marietta, the Ewings had moved to a place above Waterford, which was little more than a fortified garrison and where there was constant danger of attack by the Indians. But even had it not been for the Indians it was an exciting life for a small boy.

Thomas remembered the day he and his brothers dug out a walnut canoe together; he could still smell the fresh chips that lay about them as they worked. The children had little freedom; only now and then was the gate of the settlement opened to allow them to go outside. When they heard bells tinkling in the hazel thickets, their mothers told them they were death bells, hoping to keep the children from wandering too far away. It was some years before Thomas realized that the bells were only those tied to grazing cows and sheep.

Once when he was telling them of his boyhood Thomas laughed aloud. "I must have been a funny looking youngster. I wore only a hunting shirt which my brother had outgrown and it came to my ankles. But I was very proud of it and would have chosen nothing else had I been offered it."

When in 1795, a treaty was made with the Indians, life became easier. The Ewings moved to an open farm a half mile from the garrison and led a less exciting life.

When he was six, Thomas' big sister, Abigail, taught him to read and spell. "I had a spelling-book," he said, looking into the hearth fire as if into the past, "that someone in the garrison gave me. And my mother had brought a Bible with her and Watts' Hymns. By the time I was eight I had read the whole Bible through. I read the New Testament first of all; for a time I thought there had been four different advents and lives of Christ and I was disappointed when my father explained away this miracle. In Watts there were some fine hymns and we used to sing them often. I had a favorite of which I have forgotten the title, but two lines ran:

> 'On slippery rocks we see them stand
> And fiery billows far below.'

That was just the way the boys stood on the rock down at the creek. And the brush fires we built used to remind me of pages from Isaiah."

"Was there no chance to go to school at all?" asked Maria sympathetically.

"There was a little. When I was eight they sent me in a canoe down

near West Liberty to stay with my Aunt Morgan, where I was to go
to school with her son Mason. There was an Englishman living there
— an Oxford man — and he taught the dozen of us who lived there.
And that was the year I read my first novel — *The Fool of Quality.*"

He had done well at school, he said, for Abigail's training had been
thorough. When he came, he was at the foot of the class in spelling
and Mason at its head. By the year's end he had reached the head and
ran to tell his aunt about his prowess, but found she was more upset
by Mason's failure than proud of Thomas' victory. "And then," he
said, "I got homesick for the first time."

When he came home again he found that his big brother had made
bedsteads for the whole family and they no longer had to sleep on the
floor, and there were a few new pots and pans to cook in. But the
meat was still put in the middle of the table — his big brother had
made that too — and it was usually racoon or turkey or venison, cut
up by his mother in small pieces. Each member of the family got a
sharpened stick and helped himself.

One evening Thomas told them the story of a book given to him
by a Dr. Baker who lived some miles away from the Ewing farm.
Not until years later did he know it was the *Aeneid* of Virgil, for the
title page had been torn off. "I read it to some of the frontiersmen
who worked for my father. They liked it a lot until we came to the
part about Dido being left in the lurch; they all thought it was a
shame to treat her like that when she had been so hospitable, and
the reading waned. They didn't want to hear any more about those
ungrateful Latins."

When Thomas was twelve years old, he had been taught for a year
by Moses Everett, a Yale graduate. But a bigger event occurred in the
next year — the founding of the Coonskin Library. "Some of the
neighbors got funds together to start a circulating library. Most of
them gave not money but skins which were sold for cash. I contributed ten skins, and so became a member. One of the townsmen
who was going to Boston offered to buy the books. He came back
with a wonderful collection: Plutarch's *Lives; Children of the Abbey;*

*Arabian Nights;* Adams' *Truths of Religion;* Robertson's *North America."*

"A fine choice," said Judge Beecher approvingly.

"Of course," said Thomas Ewing, "it might not seem so according to later standards. We have so many books now, but I think that while we gain much, there is something we lose by too abundant literature."

And Maria thought to herself that she had never heard anyone say things so beautifully as this young man.

Thomas Ewing had been almost twenty years old before he decided he must earn the money to carry out a plan he had in mind: he wanted to give himself an education. He went down the Ohio River in a flatboat to the Kanawha Salt Works, and there he secured the rough job of bringing logs from the woods and replenishing the fires under the great kettles where the salt was being boiled out. He was a powerful youth but even for him the work was hard.

When he went home with his first earned money, he had to use most of it to prevent foreclosure of a mortgage on his father's land. But the next winter he earned the sum of four hundred dollars, most of which he was able to keep for himself. He spent a year at Athens College, and then went back to the mines. He was discouraged, for he seemed to be progressing very slowly, but the president of the college had urged him to return. During the next years he alternated college courses with work at the salt mines, at times working for twenty hours out of the twenty-four and taking his brief rest close to the boiling kettles.

In 1815 he had his reward — a degree of A.B. from Athens College. It had taken six long years to get it, and he was almost twenty-four years old. He had always wanted to be a lawyer, and so, with the aid of Judge Sherman, he had at last entered the study of that profession in the office of Philemon Beecher. Thirteen months later he was admitted to the Ohio bar. He felt certain he had chosen the right profession, but he sometimes smiled when he remembered how little he knew of the law or its phases when he had decided he wanted to be a lawyer.

"I had never but once seen a judge at the bench, never a jury in the box, or a lawyer speaking at the bar," he said soberly to Judge Beecher.

A month after his admission to the bar, Thomas Ewing went with Judge Beecher to Circleville Court where he had been promised a case to argue. It was a suit for slander, and he had prepared an opening argument; however, the case was compromised, much to his disappointment. But later in the day he had another client, whose case he was able to plead, and Judge Beecher went home well satisfied with his protégé whose arguments and questioning had made a very favorable impression on the Court. Later in the fall Charles Sherman invited him to help in the court at Lancaster with a case of trespass and wounding. Other cases followed, and by the next spring Ewing found himself so well employed that he was able not only to support himself but also to help the family at home.

One day when Maria Boyle was visiting relatives in Brownsville someone asked her who was this Thomas Ewing about whom people were hearing so much. "He is known as the first among the younger members of the Ohio bar," she said proudly. "He has a fine practice, but of course his fees are small for his clients are poor. But we know he will do better and better — and very soon."

Her words had almost immediate verification, for the young man was appointed prosecuting attorney for Fairfield County, a hard task at the time, for there was a great deal of trouble with counterfeiters in that part of Ohio. Once Thomas learned that a group of these criminals was to meet at a certain tavern where customers were awaiting them. The sheriff was away and his assistant was found to be too drunk to go along to make a raid, so the young attorney had to manage alone. He had himself sworn in as a special constable, collected six helpers as a posse, and together they rode to the tavern and stealthily surrounded it. After considerable excitement and danger the group was arrested, and the counterfeit money seized. The gang was broken up and young Mr. Ewing went back to less exciting duties.

During these years, the Catholics about Lancaster continued in their attempts to procure a priest and a church. Mr. Fenwick had never ceased trying, either. His duties in Kentucky were still heavy, but he came to Ohio whenever he could, making his long trips on horseback, going from town to town with the necessities for Mass in his saddle-bags. Often before he was back in the Dominican convent in Kentucky he had traveled a thousand miles. Sometimes on these journeys he would receive pressing requests to come to some little settlement off the main road. Frequently he would find only a few Catholics there, but their gratitude was reward enough for his trouble. Once a colony of thirteen families, who had by chance found a Catholic book and had read it over and over, sent word that they wished to be baptized. He went three hundred miles out of his way to find them.

His was a solitary life, riding through tangled forests and over rough trails. Often night overtook him in the forest and he would have to stop and wait for daylight.

"What do you do if you are off the road when night comes, Mr. Fenwick?" someone asked him.

"I fasten my horse, lie down on the ground with my saddle-bag for a pillow and the earth for a bed and commend myself to God," he said. "It is not hard when I have the mighty protection of Heaven."

One day in 1816 the hope that had been long in Jacob Dittoe's heart was fulfilled. Mr. Fenwick was coming to Ohio to stay, bringing with him his nephew, Nicholas Young, as his assistant.

The entire picture changed swiftly now. By 1818 Mr. Fenwick was building a church in Somerset on land given by Jacob Dittoe, and another in Lancaster, on land given by Thomas Frucken. The former was to be named St. Joseph's; the latter called St. Mary's. And plans were being made for another church just outside Cincinnati which Mr. Fenwick said he would dedicate to St. Patrick. They were all very little churches, unplastered and roughly finished, but even so they compared very favorably with the Protestant churches in the vicinity.

St. Joseph's Church in Somerset, was the first to be completed, and was blessed on December 6, 1818. Many people — and not alone Catholics — came from miles around to attend the ceremonies that would open the first Catholic church in Ohio. All the people from Lancaster who by their prayers and their faith had brought this little structure to reality were there, among them the Dittoes and the Boyles. Great though their happiness was, it could not have been greater than that of Mr. Fenwick as he performed the ceremony, his nephew assisting him in the joyous task.

Maria Boyle sat with the others of her family in one of the plain little pews, and afterwards they all examined the new building. It was of logs, twenty-two feet by eighteen, covered with clapboards, and looked little different from any private home. Besides a rough altar the church contained the necessities for Mass and little more — a single chalice and a few vestments brought from St. Rose's Convent in Kentucky. The bare ground served for its floor; the windows were openings in the side walls. The building was unheated, but a tiny log cabin called a warming house was built nearby, so that those who came from a distance could warm themselves before they entered the church and after they left it for the drive home.

Shortly after the dedication, a convent was built beside St. Joseph's, a small building as bare inside and out as the church itself. It had only one adornment: a fine oil painting of the Descent from the Cross, given to Mr. Fenwick by Bishop Carroll and brought by him from Kentucky.

Thomas Ewing liked his life in Lancaster. He liked the men among whom he worked. The Ohio bar in those early days was made up of a fine group of able lawyers with little professional jealousy among them. They all thought that Thomas Ewing was making a good reputation and would go far. "He's a walking encyclopedia and his memory is the index," said one admiring friend, and another thought his speeches were fine because of their "winning metaphors, and well-chosen, sharp pointed Anglo-Saxon words."

Mrs. Beecher was the young man's unfailing friend and adviser, and looked after both his health and his mending. And there was Maria. Sometimes Thomas thought he had loved her from the moment when he first looked out of her uncle's office window and saw her in the garden, and that that day had been the actual beginning of life for him.

Since Maria had finished at Mrs. Baker's, she had become her aunt's right hand, and there was always plenty to do in that busy household. And besides her father liked her to come daily to see and take walks with him, and there were occasional visits to pay to the many Gillespie relatives in Brownsville.

But she was never unaware of Thomas Ewing, or of his courtship, diffident at first, but more insistent as time passed. Maria was sweet but elusive, and when she yielded she did so suddenly. When Mr. Fenwick learned the news, he said with a smile, "Well, at least one thing is true; it is much easier to find a priest now to marry a couple here than it was in the old days."

# 3. *The Ewings and the Shermans*

## [1819–1831]

ON JANUARY 17, 1819, on a day when the garden was bare and a hint of snow was in the air, Maria Boyle and Thomas Ewing stood side by side in her uncle's parlor and were married by Mr. Fenwick. Thomas was not a Catholic, but he was entirely in agreement that the wedding be performed by a priest.

As Hugh Boyle stood beside his pretty black-haired daughter, he

MARIA BOYLE EWING
Wife of Thomas Ewing of Ohio

found himself wishing her mother could see her. She was very like his Eleanor, he thought — the same thoughtful look, the tilt of the head. He wondered if the twelve years' difference in Maria and Thomas' ages was perhaps not too great. But he knew that his girl was marrying a good dependable man, a brilliant one with a fine future, and he knew his Maria had the makings of a splendid wife and mother. That ought to be enough to satisfy anyone.

There was no wedding trip; the newly married couple merely walked the short distance to their new home, a comfortable little house which Hugh Boyle had given them as a wedding present. As a special gift he had added his own tall grandfather's clock. Her aunt had helped Maria furnish the house and given her instruction in some matters of housewifery and her best receipts. But Maria did not need much advice: she was already a good cook and homemaker.

She took to the new house with her books which she had ordered some months before from Peter Dittoe of Somerset. They were very pious books: two volumes of the *Sufferings of Christ, Pious Lectures, Elevation of the Soul, Garden of the Soul,* and *Spiritual Combat.*

In March the young Ewings received a letter from Thomas' father in Indiana. As soon as he had been able, Thomas had arranged for the purchase of a farm for his parents, and they were now comfortably living there with their son George. Mr. Ewing now wrote of his happiness at hearing of his son's marriage: "The account you give of her amiable qualities by no means exceeds what I had previously heard from some of your neighbors who some months ago called at our house. I send you both a father's blessing and sincere wishes for your happiness in the married state."

Maria was much touched by the politely worded references to herself. "He must be a man of fine manners, Thomas, to write like that."

Thomas nodded. "My father was always a very polite man, far more so than most of the settlers about us. But I remember once when he was not. One day when I was about fifteen he and I were working in the cornfield when a finely dressed rider stopped and asked if we could entertain him for the night. My father agreed, but very coldly, and told me to show him to the cabin. I took his horse and tried to be very polite to make up for my father's unusual rudeness. We had a wonderful evening and the visitor told many interesting stories, but my father would not unbend. Next morning he asked me to go with the stranger the mile that courtesy required of a host, and when I came back he told me who the visitor was. It was Aaron Burr, who had killed the great Alexander Hamilton."

The one regret Maria Ewing had in her heart during the early days of her marriage was that her Thomas had to be away from her so much. He traveled the circuit of Ohio towns, for it was in the larger of these — Circleville, Columbus, Zanesville, Marietta, Mount Vernon — that a lawyer's income was best sought; in fact, he had sometimes to go as far as Washington City on legal matters. Thomas liked these separations no better than Maria, as his letters to her made clear. "Although, my dearest girl," ran one, "circumstances may detain me from you, nothing can divert my thoughts from my beloved home and its dearer inmate, and however desirable public estimation may be, however flattering their applause to me, they derive half their charm from the reflection that they will afford pleasure to her whose tender endearments sweeten my leisure hours, spread a charm over even the toils and labors of my life."

Maria depended on her husband to bring home all sorts of things which she could not get in Lancaster. He was very patient about fulfilling her commissions, from shawls and bonnets to thread and garden seeds. But she would have preferred to have him at home with her and do without the things he brought her.

Maria, with time on her hands during his absences, spent most of it with Ma Beecher; sometimes she went to see Mrs. Charles Sherman whose house was not far away. She liked to hear Mary Sherman reminisce about her young days in Connecticut, when she was dashing Mary Hoyt, going to the Poughkeepsie Female Seminary on the Hudson River. The brood of young Shermans ran in and out as the two women talked. The eldest, Charles, was a boy of nine, the youngest was Julia, a toddler of two, and there were four between. Charles and his younger brother went to school at Mr. Howe's academy, where there were classes in reading, mathematics, history, and a little Latin, and where in the English class Mr. Howe used his own grammar as textbook. The rooms were large, there were desks, and even an improvised theatre where the boys enacted plays and made speeches.

The Shermans had come to Lancaster just before the War of 1812, although both the Sherman and the Hoyt families had been in America almost two centuries. Charles Sherman had come to Ohio because his father, Judge Charles Taylor Sherman of Norwalk, Connecticut, had been given, as indemnity for property lost in Connecticut in the Revolutionary War, title to two sections of land in the Western Reserve. Admitted to the bar in 1810, he had married Mary Hoyt and shortly thereafter had left her to go to Ohio to seek a home. He came to Lancaster and liked the town immediately; young though it was, it had the air of an established society. He was certain Mary would not be lonely here, and that he would have plenty of legal work. He went home to find that their first child had been born during his absence. As soon as possible he and his family made ready to trek by horseback and covered wagon to the new home in the distant West. Charles was fourteen months old and a second child, Elizabeth, was born ten days after they reached Lancaster.

Maria listened with deep interest to the story of their travels, for, although they must have been difficult, Mary told the story as if it had all been high adventure. "But how you must have hated to leave your home. I can't imagine ever leaving Lancaster."

"Well, I wasn't very anxious to come," admitted Mary Sherman, "but in any event we had quite a leave-taking. The morning we left Norwalk the town turned out to see us off. Charles had bought a two-horse wagon without springs, and sheets I had spun myself were spread over the hoops that spanned the wagon's top. There were other travelers in our group and several wagons full of household goods, driven by hired wagoners. The rest of us rode on horseback on broad pillions that were really very comfortable. Some of our neighbors came all the way down from the Hill to see us start for the Connecticut Reserve, and they called goodbye and godspeed until we rattled out of sight. And I looked back as long as I could see the slightest bit of them. I know my own people felt I was moving to what was a howling wilderness infested with wild beasts. And to tell the truth I was a bit nervous myself even though Charles kept reassuring me."

"You must have been terribly tired before you reached here," said Maria sympathetically.

Mary nodded. "I was — it took over six weeks, and they were very long ones, and sometimes I cried because every mile took me farther away from everything I had known all my life. But most of the time I looked forward and not back, and we were both happy. Yet all we had for our patrimony, except a few horses and a wagon and a little furniture and one young baby, were hope and ambition."

In February of 1820 Mary Sherman had another son. On hearing the news, Maria went over at once to help with the other children and to see the new baby, a healthy boy who was screaming with anger, his hair almost as red as his little puckered face.

"What are you going to name him?" she asked.

Mary Sherman shook her head in comic despair. "Charles says I promised that if this was a boy he would be named Tecumseh."

Maria's eyes widened. "Tecumseh! After an Indian?"

Charles Sherman came into the house in time to hear her amazed remark. "My dear girl, he was much more than 'an Indian.' He was a very wonderful man and I'm glad Mary is going to let me name this little red head after him."

"He wanted to give the name to one of the other boys," laughed Mary, "but the first one had to be named Charles for him and the next James for my brother. Then came the three girls. Now this is a boy — and I have no more brothers. So I shall have to keep my word."

They smiled at each other with the happiness of people deeply in love.

But Maria still puzzled over the name. "Who under the sun was this Tecumseh the Shermans are naming their baby for?" she asked Thomas when he came home.

Thomas, who seemed to know all about the matter, smiled at his wife. "He was a wonderful man, a chief of the Shawnees, Maria, and a true organizer of his people. He tried to bring all the tribes from Lake Erie to the Gulf of Mexico into one great union so that they could work together for the Indian nation he envisaged. He argued his case like a trained lawyer and he almost succeeded, but a few tribes went back on their word and he had to give up. Then he joined the British and led their Indian allies against the Americans. They made him a brigadier general but he would not wear the uniform — just his Indian hunting dress."

"But he fought the Americans, didn't he?"

"Yes, more than once. But when he led two thousand warriors in the siege of Fort Meigs, he saved many of our men there from massacre. However, it was not his fighting that was important. It was that idea he had of Indian union. He had a real power of organization, eloquence and self-control, and I think it is fine to name the little boy after such a man, Indian or white."

But Maria, though Thomas had convinced her that Tecumseh was an important Indian, still did not see any reason for loading that name on a little white baby. It was certainly no Christian name and it was really too bad Mary Sherman did not have at least one more brother.

In November of that same year Maria Ewing's own son was born and there was no hesitation about the name he was to be given. She knew her father would not care if she named her first child after the man who had been so good to her and to Thomas. The baby was christened Philemon Beecher Ewing.

Two years later another son was born to the young Ewings, and named, at Thomas' request, George for his father. No one could have been happier than Maria was with her treasures. But this second child, although he was a healthy baby, fell ill of some childish ailment, and died when he was not quite a year old. Her Aunt Beecher and Mary Sherman tried to console Maria's grief, but Thomas himself was so saddened at the baby's death that he too needed a great deal of comforting and in so doing Maria gradually was able to forget her own sorrow.

She was certain that one thing which had caused the baby's illness and death was the fact that their home was damp, and she persuaded Thomas to build a new house in a dryer spot. He bought a good site on the Hill close to the Sherman house and building began.

In 1823 Thomas Ewing was a candidate for the State legislature. There seemed little doubt at first about his election, until some of the wealthier holders of valuable lands who were opposed to any change in the system of taxing property, asked him to support this opposition in his platform. He declined to do so, and, because he was young in politics and too busy to do much stump speaking, he was defeated.

The Ewings were still in the old house when their third child was born, this time a daughter. She was born on a sunny day in early October 1824 when the leaves were turning red and gold and the air was full of the sweet spiciness of autumn.

Mr. Boyle had been very anxious about Maria before this child was born. Maria must not do this nor that, he insisted. She listened patiently to her father, but when he objected to her going out to the little farm the Ewings had recently purchased, and where she loved to go, she rebelled. "This time I wanted to go out and dry peaches while you were gone," she told Thomas, "and he came right over when he heard it and made a big fuss. The wagon would be upset and we would be killed, or we would get sick and not be able to get home. It was so very certain that something serious would befall us that we simply stayed home."

Her father was very sure that it was due to his efforts to have Maria take care of herself that this baby was so healthy and that Maria was too, and he said so very plainly when he came over for the baptism.

Their old friend Mr. Fenwick was no longer with them at St. Mary's: he was now Bishop Fenwick, head of the recently created see of Cincinnati. Another Dominican came from the convent at Somerset to baptize the baby. They named her Eleanor, a favorite name in the family, but from the first she was called by the affectionate shorter name of Ellen.

The new house had been slow in building, both because Thomas wanted it large enough and of the best materials, and because sometimes he had to wait until he had amassed more funds. A fourth child was born to the Ewings before the house was entirely ready for occupancy — another son, named Hugh Boyle for his grandfather. When the new baby was only a few weeks old, the Ewings moved into the house on the Hill. It was a roomy place of white brick, and its wide hospitable front door delighted Maria every time she entered it. Thomas was happy to see with what dignity his young wife presided there. She looked no older than the day he had married her. He was proud of her and of his fine family — Phil, his eldest, a sober, handsome lad; plump little Ellen, who sat on his lap and tried to tell him, on his evenings at home, about her busy days; little Hugh, lying asleep in his mother's arms.

The weeks when Thomas could stay in Lancaster were Maria's really happy ones. When he was away, she wrote to him often, sending him accounts of all Lancaster marriages and births and deaths, accounts of parties and of the children's activities. When she did not hear from him she was uneasy, even though she knew it was poor postal conditions which were to blame. Her letters were still full of requests for items hard to get in Lancaster but which could be bought in the larger towns: plants — a monthly rose or a passion flower — gold paper to ornament a fire screen, new mantle ornaments, spectacles for Grandfather Boyle, a book on cookery, one on gardening. There was no end to the things she wanted and for which Thomas obligingly shopped.

Once, when he had been away unusually long, he brought her from Columbus a fine new-fashioned cape and an elegant bunch of feathers. "Oh, they are beautiful, Thomas. They will put a dash in my bonnet, won't they?"

When she had admired them sufficiently she told him about her cousin Susan Irvin's new furniture. "I have been feasting my eyes on it for two days now. It is very evident they will outdash us all." But the affectionate voice in which she spoke of her cousin's elegant purchases held only pride and not envy.

"How is the new stove working?" asked the practical Thomas, interrupting her rapture.

She shrugged her shoulders. "Well, it is in full operation and no doubt it is a good makeshift, and it does save the trouble of always having wood brought in, but just the same give me the old way of cooking with plenty of good wood and not this new-fangled coal."

There was other news, more exciting than new stoves. A dancing teacher had come to town and Maria planned to have Phil go. And the Clark girls, Abby and Rachel, who were Thomas' nieces and lived nearby, had promised they would come whenever they could and help with the children.

Last of all came the most important item of news. "Thomas," Maria began, "yesterday morning a gentleman called here from Philadelphia, and he has three elegant pianos for sale. He said he heard that I had taken lessons when I was younger, and that we have nieces who stay with us often, and a daughter who ought to learn to play."

"But, Maria," he remonstrated, "Ellen is only three years old."

Maria put that aside as unimportant. "Well, in a few years she will be old enough to take lessons. He tried to leave one with me but I said no, that I would have to have your approbation first."

Thomas' face showed his relief. "Then you haven't really bought one?"

"Oh, no," said Maria righteously. "I wanted to see first if you had the money to spare. The uprights are cheaper, of course, but he says we could trade it in later for a little grand piano. And you know I did play some when I was a little girl," she added hastily, to forestall refusal.

Thomas looked sorry but firm. "Maria, wait just a little longer and I will buy you a finer one than these. And I'll even stay home all the time to hear you and Ellen play it," he said.

At this Maria forgot the piano. "Oh, Thomas, that is what I really want most of all. Sometimes I am almost dead of loneliness. I never in my life felt an absence so much as this last long time you were away."

During the latter days of the 1820's Lancaster had a considerable number of distinguished visitors, many of whom were the guests of the Ewings or Beechers or Shermans. In 1825 the Duke of Saxe-Weimar came and was asked to carve his name on the rock of Mount Pleasant, as were all distinguished guests. He was introduced to Judge Sherman, who invited him to his home for tea and there he met many of the town's citizens. "Very agreeable society," the Duke was reported to have said later.

Henry Clay often passed through Lancaster on his way to Washington City. He was the idol of all the old Whigs and they were always ready to honor him. Governor De Witt Clinton, father of the Erie canal system, also paid a visit to Lancaster and was the guest of Mr. Sherman.

Daniel Webster always stopped at Judge Ewing's house on his way through Lancaster. Once the two drove together to Chillicothe, and in crossing a forest found the way blocked by a big fallen tree. Ewing borrowed an axe from a farmer and cut a log off to its proper length from the tree. Then the two statesmen rolled it off the road and continued their journey.

In 1826 a branch of the American Colonization Society was formed and joined by all the leading citizens; its purpose was to buy slaves and colonize them in Liberia, since that seemed the best, perhaps the only, remedy to slavery, against which institution Lancaster sternly set its face. When Mr. Peck, the Lutheran minister, learned he had inherited slaves, he promptly freed them, a sign of the spirit which animated the community.

Each year the militia held an annual muster in or near Lancaster. The military demonstration consisted mainly of roll call; the rest of the day was given over to fun, with gingerbread and watermelon the most popular refreshments. In 1829 a Captain Witte, who had been an officer in the German army, attended one of these musters and he could not believe his military eyes. One officer wore a white coat and a black necktie. One, mounted on a horse, carried a rusty sword and an umbrella, and one wore an epaulette on only one shoulder. But Captain Witte had to admit the marksmanship was superb. He settled in Lancaster and tried to organize the militia into his idea of a regiment. They were all proud of him and cooperated, for after all he had won a medal for bravery at Waterloo; but they really liked him best because he was such a wonderful host.

Best of all Lancaster's celebrations were the ones that took place on the Fourth of July. First the Declaration of Independence was read and then there were fine orations by the town's own orators, followed by a big dinner. There were always toasts, and one which Horace Biddle, a young law student, offered proved so popular it was repeated in following years: "To the Tree of Liberty, planted by the sword of our fathers, pruned by the wisdom of experience of sixty and more years."

The need of pinching pennies was past for the Ewings. By 1829 Thomas had become a well-known lawyer even outside Ohio, and his earnings were as high as any man's in Lancaster, where one thousand dollars a year was considered an excellent income. And that year he went to Washington City to argue a case before the Supreme Court.

When a letter arrived from her husband, Maria undid it carefully. "And now to see how he is enjoying himself in the midst of the great and mighty folk of the nation," she said unfolding the sheets of paper, very thin to save the costly postage.

Thomas had written very fully of his stay at the capital. First of all he had called on President Adams, one of the plainest little men he had ever seen, with ungainly manners and as diffident and abstracted as a law student. But there was a blunt honesty in him which appealed to Thomas. "I like him well," he wrote. Then he had been taken by General Harrison's son to a levee at the British Minister's. He and General Beech had dined with the Postmaster General. He added that he did not think so much of the ladies at these parties: "There were about ten or fifteen, as ugly old things as you ever saw, and the fashion of the day which they follow most punctiliously renders them hideous." Thomas also told of his visit to the Senate to hear the debates. He had renewed old friendships and was making some new friends — "but all I want to do is to come home."

Only a side lawn separated the Sherman and Ewing homes, and in that pleasant yard the children played together, although by the summer of 1829 some of the Sherman children were too old for play. Charles was eighteen and ready to study law, Elizabeth a lovely girl of seventeen. The rest — and there were nine of them — ranged in age from fifteen-year-old James to the baby of less than a year.

Four-year-old Ellen Ewing's particular playmate was Susan Sherman, just her age, while Phil's was Cumpy Sherman, "Cumpy" being what the lordly name of the Shawnee chief had become in the affectionate nomenclature of the family. Ellen was no longer the baby of the house. In 1827 another son had been born to the Ewings and named Thomas for his father.

Maria was busy with sorting her yarns one morning in June, when Elizabeth Sherman ran across the yard, her hands tight together, her eyes tear-stained. "Oh, Mrs. Ewing, my father is dead."

Maria looked at her as if she had not heard her rightly. She had seen Charles Sherman only the week before as he had started out to ride the circuit, and he was in his usual excellent health. "Oh, Elizabeth, it can't be true!"

But it was true, although it seemed impossible that hale, smiling Charles Sherman could be dead. He had been on his way to Lebanon to hold court, when he was taken with a fever and had died the very next day. Partly, no doubt, his death was due to overwork, for he always worked too hard, making the circuit continually for distances that included even such far places as Detroit.

"Oh, Thomas, what will they do?" asked Maria.

It looked like an insuperable problem. There were eleven children between one and nineteen years old to be cared for; in addition Charles Sherman, due to his honesty, was greatly in debt. The President had appointed him Collector of Internal Revenue, and later the government demanded payment from its deputies in gold or bank paper. Since the northwest region used mostly local banknotes, the collectors were burdened with sums of depreciated currency. Judge Sherman took it on himself to pay as much as he could, and when he died his home was still mortgaged from his effort to meet these debts of honor.

Everyone in Lancaster and many from other towns came to his funeral. The First Brigade of the National Guard, in which he had been a colonel, marched in their long blue uniforms with muskets reversed. "He never succumbed to any enemy but death," said the Norwalk paper in chronicling the story of his death.

The courage which had carried Mary Hoyt Sherman from Fairfield County, Connecticut, to her new home in the wilderness was with her now. But she had only a small pension, and her husband's mother, who lived with them, had a little income — not enough to bring up so many children, even according to the simple standards of the time. Charles, the eldest, was reading law in Mansfield, and Elizabeth, the family beauty, was engaged to a young lawyer, William Reese, who was beginning to practice law in Lancaster. But there were nine others.

Thomas Ewing told Mrs. Sherman that he would like to bring up one of the children, to repay the debt he owed Charles Sherman for help given him in his young and difficult days. When a few days later he stopped at the Sherman house, Mrs. Sherman was away and he talked to Elizabeth.

"Well, Elizabeth," he asked her, "which of the boys is going to be mine?"

Elizabeth did not hesitate. "Oh, Mr. Ewing, take Cump. He's the brightest. Wait a minute and I'll call him."

The little boy was out in the backyard making mudpies and there were marks of them on his cheeks and his hands. Thomas Ewing smiled down at him. "Well, Cump, you're going to be my boy now. Want to come along?"

Without hesitating, not even waiting to get his jacket or put a cap on his red hair, Cump confidingly put his dirty little fist into the big hand and together they went up the hill to Maria.

From the very first Maria Ewing treated this charge of hers as her own child. Cump never called her "mother," because that would not have been fair to his own mother who loved him dearly, nor Mr. Ewing "father," because the Ewings wanted him to keep his own good name.

But affection the child found in plenty. Perhaps it was because Maria had herself been brought up in a family not her own that she was so understanding of Cump. He went to school with the rest of the Ewings and Maria had him join her two older children in their private French lessons.

As for the Ewing children, they took Cump for granted. Phil simply added one more brother to his collection. Four-year-old Ellen had so often seen Cump in her home that it did not cause her any excitement to find he would be permanently there.

Every month a priest came over from Somerset to say Mass in the little church at Lancaster, and then stayed for several days in order to instruct the children in religion.

Maria Ewing, having discovered that Cump was not baptized, had asked his mother if she minded having Mr. Young, when he came to the house, baptize him. Mrs. Sherman gave her consent and preparations were made to make Cump a child of God.

They all went to the parlor. Mr. Young in his white habit, Cump and Maria, who was to be his godmother, stood in a little group at one side of the fireplace. Ellen, though she was too young to know exactly what was happening, was an interested onlooker. All went well until it came to the name to be given in baptism. Mr. Young looked taken aback when he heard it. "Tecumseh?" he repeated in surprise.

"His father named him so," explained Maria.

Mr. Young nodded. "I'll name him that too, but he must have a Christian name besides."

They considered for a moment, then Mr. Young spoke. "This is St. William's Day, so perhaps that would be a good name for him."

So the little red-headed boy who stood wide-eyed and uncomfortable during a ceremony he had never seen before, was named William Tecumseh Sherman.

"But we'll keep right on calling him Cumpy, won't we?" asked Phil anxiously afterward, and Maria, catching an equally anxious look in Cump's own eyes, told them that Cump's name would remain what it was. It was only that the fine name of William had been added.

# 4. *Senator Thomas Ewing*

## [1831–1834]

IN 1831 Thomas Ewing was elected by the Whig party as United States Senator from Ohio. By this time he had become an important man in the party, and was on terms of personal friendship with Henry Clay and Daniel Webster. When these two men came to Lancaster to consult Mr. Ewing, the children, from unobserved positions, would try to hear what the gentlemen talked about as they sat at the long dining-table over their wines and cigars.

One word was used over and over, and finally Ellen was moved to ask what it meant. "What is a Union, Cumpy? They say it a lot and they talk so loud when they talk about it."

"I asked your father yesterday," said Cump, "and he said it's all of us. It's all the people, only we have to be grown up before we count. He said it means that it is the country that counts and not just the States like Ohio, and that when the States stay together you have a Union, and so he and Mr. Clay and Mr. Webster keep on talking a lot about a Union because they want to keep on having one."

Ellen nodded her head wisely to show she understood, though she did not. But there was no doubt that eleven-year-old Cump Sherman was very sure about what these big men meant. Mr. Ewing had made it quite clear.

It was difficult for Maria to join her husband in Washington City, but she had promised she would visit him there as soon as possible. There was a very large family now to care for; even with good servants and Abby and Rachel to help her, there was much work to do. There were Phil and Hugh and Ellen and Cump and little Tom. She hated to leave them and yet that was too many to take along. So they all remained in Lancaster, and Maria managed as best she could the entire household until the times between Senate sessions when Thomas could come home and take the reins for a while.

While he was away she wrote long letters and kept him well informed on home matters and regarding "the place" — the little farm on the outskirts of town which was being farmed for them by help which proved hard for Maria to control.

She wrote about the children. Tommy had grown so fat his father would hardly know him: "He can scarcely waddle across the room." Hugh, strong and hardy, wanted his Pa to hurry home and bring him a little colt. Ellen was so bright and so pretty. Phil did so well at school, and Cump was standing so high in his studies that they were as proud as was Mrs. Sherman herself.

The first Christmas in Washington City Thomas found it impossible to come home and he sent gifts instead — mostly books. For

Tommy there was a toy; when Hugh opened his package there was a toy also. He was offended. "When you write," he told his mother, "tell Pa I read you a lesson every day out of the Infant School Book. I ought to have a book too."

Among the Christmas books was one big set — the works of Peter Parley in nine volumes. These, her husband wrote Maria, would furnish matter for evenings' amusement and recreation for the children: "After the work is done, set out the lamp table and gather them all around it and the fire — Phil and Cump and Ellen and Hugh, and let Tom have a place too." The Geography, he thought, would be best to start on. They could all look at the pictures and then let Phil and Cump take turns reading the stories for the general information of the company. The Parley maps were small, but the boys could take their school atlases and point out to the audience such places as Peter Parley spoke of. And he added: "The happiest evenings I recollect ever to have spent were in a poor log hut by my father's fireside, reading to my mother and sisters on matters not much more profound than this childish narrative. But to give the proper effect you must become a hearer too and seem interested in the stories and mingle an occasional expression of approbation and praise of the performance of the reader — though it may be none of the best." And at the end of the letter he cautioned his wife not to make the readings too long: "A half hour or an hour an evening would be long enough but you must be sure to make it a privilege rather than a task."

So, evenings at eight, after the children had spent an hour with the writing teacher who came at seven, some time was spent in reading. "I assure you," Maria wrote Thomas, "I keep pretty steady watch over them; they do not show that disposition to run abroad that they did last winter. They have not spent any evening from home since you left but one."

On Christmas Day, Maria and Abby went to Somerset for the night in order to attend Christmas Mass while Grandfather Boyle stayed in charge at the Ewing house. Some days later more books came from Washington City and a letter from Thomas which made Maria sigh and smile. "I hesitated for some time this morning (he had written it on Christmas morning) which I should do: go to church or stay home and write you a long letter. I have at last resolved to stay at home and write you a long letter. Am I right?"

That was just like Thomas, propounding something as if for her to answer — and then answering it himself. He knew perfectly well she would have wished him to go to church, just as he knew she wanted to hear from him. She sighed again and went on with the letter.

He had dined with President Jackson the week before. There were many gentlemen and a few ladies, including two young ones — "neither of them remarkable for beauty or accomplishments." He had a half hour's chat with the ladies before dinner — "the two married ones. You know I let the girls alone. Then at dinner the President took me under his wing and allowed the old Senators to take charge of the ladies."

The President's manner, thought Thomas, was exceedingly fine. He was a good talker, familiar yet dignified, although he had no gift of chit-chat. There was fine wine at dinner, a Madeira of ancient vintage and some champagne, first rate enough almost to make a Jackson man out of Thomas, "but not quite." The same beautiful table service was used which he had seen during President Adams' régime.

Someone sent Maria a paper from Portland, Maine, and in a column called "Washington Chit-Chat" were remarks about the new Senator from Ohio: "He is not only a new senator but a new man in Cicero's acceptation of the phrase. He is emphatically a sound man, an able lawyer and will by and by, I venture to predict, be a distinguished statesman. That hackneyed topic, the Tariff, he has already clothed in a new dress. He has started in another orbit and developed many points of political economy as well. He is a big man, over six feet, with black hair and light blue eyes."

Maria sent this to Thomas, as she sent him everything. She gave the family gossip to keep him in touch with them all. She told him how well Ellen was reading now, and how many poems she knew by heart; about Tommy's fine repertoire of songs, taught him by the older boys, his favorite being one which began:

> "Where are you going, Mike?
> Going down to Zanesville to work on the Pike."

Cump had tried to darken his red hair but very unsuccessfully and Phil was attending court as page, and very proud of his work. One day when the weather was stormy and his mother asked if he thought it really necessary for him to go every day, he looked shocked. "I must go, for I belong to the Court," he said sternly, and each day he proudly brought home his pay for calling, "Silence" for the Judge.

She was glad to have Tommy at least still with her all day. She wished sometimes that Thomas could see his namesake sitting pretending to write letters to his father, and reading them aloud to her. They were nearly always alike, the refrain being, "Oh, Pa, I wish you was home. I want you so bad."

And Maria echoed the words in her heart.

In the spring of 1832 Maria Ewing planned a visit to Washington. Thomas had been urging her to come and she was eager to join him, but first she had to see how many children she would take with her and how she would dispose of the rest of them. She wanted very much to see the capital, but she wanted especially to see her Thomas in the company of important men.

Thomas suggested that Ellen be left at the Somerset convent school, which was finished now and taking boarders, an excellent school in charge of Dominican Sisters, where both Catholic and Protestant families were sending their daughters. Hugh was hurrying with learning to read, hoping that he could go. He had even learned a page of Peter Parley by heart to impress his mother, and he recited it with nods and gestures until the rest fled when they heard the opening words. Little Tom was certain he was going to Washington City to see his Pa, and was waiting impatiently to start.

One thing that delayed Maria's going was the condition of the Lancaster roads. Even in late February the streets were like a bed of mortar and it would be a month before a carriage could travel over them. Mr. Tallmage, whose stages ran to Wheeling and Columbus and Cincinnati, and this year for the first time to Lancaster, sometimes had trouble in getting them through at all.

Besides, though Maria was no timid soul, she disliked setting out on so long a trip with no husband to protect her. But his coming home in the summer seemed an age away and she was willing to face any perils just to see him. Sometimes the voice of duty said to her: Stay home and take care of all your children. Attend to your garden in the spring and have everything in order by the time your husband returns. But after all it was his voice urging her to come: was that not a duty too?

As for expenses, Rudoply at the stables would take them to Washington City for eighty dollars, counting four dollars a day there and back, and the Ewings would pay their own road expenses. She thought it too much but Thomas wrote in every letter that expense was no consideration at all. So Maria started out with Phil and Tommy, and Abby to help her, while Ellen departed unwillingly to the convent school.

Ellen bore with convent life in Somerset but she found it very different from the freedom of Lancaster; a restricted life for a child used to a school where boys and girls were together and where there was home at the end of each day. Her mother wrote her from Washington City, letters that were supposed to cheer Ellen up but which did not have that effect, for there were accounts of parties and dinners and walks and rides, in at least some of which Ellen knew she would have shared. But the names in the letters she could mention to her schoolmates, and that helped — names like President Jackson and Calhoun and Marquis de Barcourt, the French minister.

The letters did not make her homsesick, for she did not really want to be in Washington. She wanted to be in Lancaster, and, when Mrs. Ewing decided she would stay in Washington until late May, Ellen knew she had to see her home before that. The shrubs were blooming in the school-yard and they carried the aromas of the yard at home. There was only one difficulty: how was she to get away?

Then one day the opportunity came. She had been given permission to accompany the girl whose duty it was to get the mail. While her companion was busy in the post office, Ellen, waiting outside, saw the stagecoach standing in front of the tavern across the street. She walked over to the coach, climbed in and sat down in the corner of the back seat, making herself as small as possible.

The passengers came out and took their seats in the coach. Several looked slightly surprised to see such a little girl traveling alone, but evidently regarded her as merely another passenger. The coach started and for the first time Ellen felt dismay, which increased when one of the passengers leaned forward and looked at her closely. "Is that you, Ellen?" he asked in surprise.

The new passenger nodded, not sure whether she felt relief or alarm. It was her uncle Judge Irvin, and to him she poured out the whole story — the homesickness, the fact that her mother would not be home for another month. He patted her hand and told her not to cry. Since she was on her way to Lancaster he would see she got there, but he was certain she would be sent back.

That didn't matter. All that mattered was that she was soon getting out of the coach in Lancaster, walking through her own yard, and looking at her own shrubs and flowers. There was the brick walk of home, the front door that opened at her touch and creaked with its lovely remembered noise. The delight she felt was greater than any she had ever known.

Rachel Clark, who had stayed at the Ewing house with Cump and Hugh, was as surprised to see her as the Judge had been, but she was philosophical about it. And after a few happy days at home — for the grown-ups had talked it over and decided to let Ellen stay and had made arrangements for this with the nuns at Somerset — she went back again, quite content this time.

She reached the convent during the recreation hour. Everyone was in the garden, including the sister in whose especial charge she had been placed, and who was a bit haughty in her manner toward the runaway. But evidently she was not to be punished for her escapade, and as a matter of fact Ellen was not aware that she had done anything wrong.

When her visit came to an end, Maria found it very hard to leave Thomas in Washington instead of having him come home with her. But she left Philemon with him for company, since her husband insisted he could not be entirely without his family. She went back to Lancaster in mid-June with Tommy by stagecoach. Abby was to remain in school at Georgetown Academy.

The return journey was much harder than the trip to Washington by carriage. The gentlemen in the coach insisted on having both windows open; there was a bad fog over the mountains and icy air poured in all night. Maria had heard people call this a pleasant journey. Well, if there was any pleasure in flying over the mountains day and night without time enough to eat one full meal the whole trip — then it was pleasant.

They stopped for tea at Cumberland, and hardly was it poured when the stage horn blew and the driver sent in a messenger to say they must come in one moment or he would leave. Maria went out to the stage herself, thinking to beg a moment's delay. But the driver started right off, leaving her standing there, and she had to shout to him to stop. He did, but only after several gentlemen on the pavement called after him.

When they reached Somerset, Maria ignored the driver waiting for passengers and hurried over to Mrs. Dittoe's where Ellen was to meet her. "Tell her to hurry," she asked breathlessly and flew back.

The driver knew that he was to wait for another passenger, but he was already mounted and blowing his horn and cursing at Maria for detaining him. Half the town, so it seemed to the mortified Mrs. Ewing, gathered around to see what was wrong. The minute Ellen came up Maria pushed her into the coach, hardly waiting for the baggage to be added, and not even stopping to greet the daughter she had not seen for so long.

"Deliver me from riding in a coach again," she said when they were safely at home again. "I feel as if nothing on earth would ever induce me to get in a mail coach again except for a one-day journey."

She and Ellen had reached home in time to take part in the celebration for the Fourth of July. They all went to hear the oration, this year delivered by Mr. Henry Stanbery, but Maria kept thinking how much better was Thomas' delivery. Henry's voice was weak and his delivery hurried in contrast to Thomas' deep thrilling tones.

A few weeks later Thomas himself came home, and life became again what it should be. He straightened out matters at the farm, got trees planted, examined the boys to see how they were progressing in their work and settled happily into his home. But Maria was amazed at some of the extravagances he had acquired in Washington, such as reading with two candles. When in October he went back to the capital, he took Philemon with him to go to school there.

He had but barely gone when sad news reached Lancaster: Bishop Fenwick was dead, a victim of cholera, contracted on his way from Canton to Somerset. Maria wept at the loss of this old friend. "He really sacrificed his life for his flock, didn't he?" she said to her father, "exposing his valuable and useful life to that dread pestilence."

That winter Maria had a good many repairs made to the house. When the work was done, it was very comfortable with coal fires in all the rooms, for Maria was now a complete convert to coal. It kept a room so warm, and when they went to bed, they threw a little coal in the stove, covered it, and if at night they had to be up they had a good fire in a minute.

Then late in December a letter came from Thomas announcing his purchase at auction of some fine pieces of furniture which had belonged to Madame Iturbide who was returning to Mexico. Especially, there was a piano of rosewood. He had also bought a center-table and chairs and a dinner-set of china. Maria's first thought was that it must have cost him a good deal. Her second was that, after all, Thomas must be the best judge of the extent of his funds. And her third thought was that at last they were to have a piano!

When Henry Stanbery came home from a trip to Washington he said he had seen the furniture, the grandest pieces he had ever laid his eyes on. Henry had bought some things at the auction also, but his ladies were disappointed at what he had secured. In explanation Henry said Thomas had gotten there ahead of him and had the choicest pieces.

Thomas had sent a shawl by Henry Stanbery, so handsome a one that it took Maria's breath away. She and the girls looked at it, and tried it on over and over. "It is the richest one of its kind I have ever seen," she said happily. "I wonder what he gave for it. High I am afraid, for everything in Washington is extravagant."

On January 16, 1833, the furniture finally arrived. Maria had just taken care of Tom and Hugh through a ten days' siege of chicken-pox, and she was sitting down at last to write a long letter to Thomas when Mr. Crisworth came to the door. "Your goods has come, Mrs. Ewing."

So the letter had to wait while Maria supervised and sometimes lent a hand to the uncrating and unpacking. The chairs came first; they were very fine and very genteel, and in good condition except that the leg of one was unglued and Maria's careful eye saw little rubbed places on two of the others. In the boxes were also a pair of candelabra, and a dinner-set with nothing broken except two little custard cups. She looked in vain for the wonderful center-table, but Mr. Crisworth said it would come later. But the piano was there. And what a piano — of dark gleaming rosewood and utterly unmarred. Everyone who came to see it during the next few days — and that was nearly everyone in town — said it was the most delightfully toned, the richest and the sweetest they had ever heard.

Thomas wrote that he hoped Maria would take lessons herself along with the girls. "Isn't that kind of him?" she said to Susan. "But it is really joy enough for me to hear others perform."

She told her sister Susan something she had told no one else. "A handsome brass fender came too, but Frances Stanbery claimed Henry had sent it to her. It was marked 'Hon. T. Ewing,' but I gave it up to her."

"How is Philemon?" Susan wanted to know, for this oldest nephew was her favorite.

"I had a letter from him last week from Philadelphia. Thomas has been taking him about a great deal this winter to different cities and even to parties and the theatre. I hope he won't be saucy when he gets home. Oh, Susan, I wish they were home. This year was harder than last to have Thomas away. I don't know what will become of me before six years are up."

"Well," consoled Susan, "he'll be home in a few months and will stay a while anyway."

When Thomas came, in June, there were gifts for everyone, and for Tom there were all the things he had asked for in a painfully worked-over letter he had sent his father: "a little sword and a little drum and a box full of sugar candy."

# 5. *The Children Grow Up*
## [1834–1845]

I N THE late spring of 1834 news came that the new Bishop was on his way to Lancaster. After the death of Bishop Fenwick, Bishop John Purcell had been appointed to succeed him, and he was now paying his first episcopal visit. Father Dominic Young came ahead of him to prepare for Confirmation those who were to receive that sacrament.

When the Bishop came he brought with him a gift that made glad the heart of every Catholic in Lancaster: his promise to the little parish of a priest of its own, Mr. Martin. And before he went away he said that he realized now what he had more than once been told: before long Lancaster would need a larger church to care for its congregation.

In mid-September of that year cholera struck Lancaster and nearly every house, except those high on the Hill, had some sickness. The weather was responsible, said Dr. White; it was unusually sultry and hot for September; the water had been let off the Canal, and the slimy refuse caught in the rushes and reeds at its bottom helped spread the disease.

Maria guarded her family as best she could. When the weather turned the least bit cool, they had fires morning and evening, and dressed in winter clothes. Her father was taken ill with the disease, and Tommy and Hugh were quite sick, but none of them had the true cholera, which remained confined almost entirely to the neighborhood of the Canal. By the time Thomas came home in the fall the epidemic had subsided.

He could stay only a few weeks, and then he had to go back to Washington. When Frances Stanbery came over to ask Maria what she thought of her staying in Lancaster for the winter while Henry went to Columbus to set up a business, Maria looked depressed and shook her head. "Oh, Frances, I find keeping house without a husband during the winter season a doleful business. I wouldn't encourage you in doing it."

In March 1835, another son was born to the Ewings and named Charles. When Ellen saw how cunning this newcomer was, she became resigned to one more brother, although she still sighed in secret for a sister among so many boys. Maria was in poor health for a time after the birth of this child, and so he became the special charge of his sister Ellen, who at eleven was a very capable young person and well used to handling babies. When her mother was better, she went back for a time to the Somerset convent.

This time Ellen was content to go. She was older now, and she settled quickly into the routine of lessons in reading and writing and geography and religion, recited in the big sunny classroom. It was a simple life of rising at six-thirty, breakfast at seven, classes until noon, and then a long recess, the afternoon almost a repetition of the morning. By evening she was very ready for her bed in the big dormitory under the roof.

Ellen was very busy that term preparing for a grand concert in which she was to perform on both harp and piano. She was taking dancing lessons too, and studying French diligently. When she came home at Christmas her mother enlisted her aid in arranging the church for the holidays and also in collecting funds to build a larger church. There was a strong hope that by the next year the cornerstone could be laid.

In every way the Ewings regarded Cumpy Sherman as their own son. One day a strange lady asked Mrs. Ewing how many children she had, and she replied, "Four." But Tommy spoke up promptly, "Oh, Ma, you forgot Cumpy, our oldest boy."

Once, while Mrs. Ewing was reading a letter from Washington, she called to Cump. "Here is a special message for you. 'Tell Cumpy I want him to learn fast so that he may be ready to go to West Point or college soon. Kiss the little fellow for me.'"

Cump had nodded seriously. He was studying very hard, but if Mr. Ewing wanted him to he would study even harder. He was eager to go to West Point and hoped to pass the examinations when the time came.

In the autumn of 1835 he had his first job. He went with a surveying party to help in the laying out of a canal not far from Lancaster. He said he liked the work, but what most impressed Ellen was not so much his industry but the fact that he actually liked to get up early and go to work before daylight. For Ellen loved nothing better than to sleep late, even though that was not encouraged in the Ewing household.

Early in 1836 word came from Washington that Cumpy had been appointed to West Point, and a month later he left Lancaster. As he stood waiting for the coach, a tall, slim lad with red hair and a nice smile, he looked very boyish indeed. His mother, Mary Sherman, had come all the way from Mansfield to say goodbye to him, and he had spent a long time with her in the parlor alone before the coach came. She would miss him very much, they all knew, even though for years she had not lived in her Lancaster home. On the Sunday before he went away, he went to church with her, carrying her prayer book, and it was evident that her pride in him was great. With the others she stood now at the Ewing door and waved as he went from sight. At her side was John Sherman, Cumpy's brother, still at school, but hoping to enter his brother Charles' office soon as a law-student.

Very shortly after Cump had gone, a letter came from Washington where he was staying for a few days with Mr. Ewing. He wrote, he had had a pretty fatiguing journey; and Maria nodded her head in sympathy: she knew well how hard those trips were. There had been eight passengers in addition to Cump in a very small stage, and it had rained all the time so he could not see the beauty of mountain and lowland. Mr. Ewing, he reported, looked very well.

Ellen continued at school during part of that year and the following, still with the Dominicans at Somerset.

In the autumn she had begun to prepare for her First Communion, along with her schoolmate and cousin, Eliza Gillespie from Brownsville. The priest who instructed them, Mr. Richard Miles, was a gentle kindly man who understood young people, and knew how to explain doctrine so that a twelve-year-old could understand it. That Christmas Ellen Ewing made her First Communion in the little church of St. Mary's in Lancaster. In the summers she was a great help to her mother, especially when, in 1837, another child was born to the Ewings, this time to Ellen's delight a little girl, named Maria Theresa; the long name was soon shortened to Sissie. Charley was still Ellen's charge; she would sit in a rocker, busy with embroidery, telling stories to the flaxen-haired child or hearing him recite his letters; sometimes when he was especially mischievous she would stand him in the corner for his misbehavior.

As soon as he was old enough for pantaloons, he began climbing trees, and even Ellen could not stop this. His especial favorite was a black cherry-tree where in the spring he got himself well stained. Once, high in the branches, he heard a deep voice below him, and there stood Grandfather Boyle, shaking his yellow ivory-knobbed cane at him and ordering him down. But next day, on his morning stroll, Mr. Boyle saw amid the dark leaves the almost hidden yellow head of his grandson, and like Ellen he gave up trying.

Some day Charley, too, would be going to school, and Maria planned to send him to the Dominicans in Perry County, where the young priests of the order brought Virgil and Xenophon and Caesar to the peaceful seclusion of a countryside still very rural.

Mr. Martin, who had often to take a hand with the teaching as well as with other duties, was hard at work for the new church. A fine lot had been secured for four hundred dollars in 1837, contracts were drawn, and a draughtsman was being sought to draw up the plans. The little chapel was much too small now and Mr. Martin was asking the aid of the Bishop to hurry up the building of the new church.

In 1838 Cump Sherman came home for his first vacation from West Point, looking very different in his uniform. Fourteen-year-old Ellen, somewhat in awe at first of this former playmate, soon found Cump as boyish as ever and that he had lost none of his fine propensity for teasing.

Mr. Ewing, though his term as senator had ended in 1837, still went often to Washington on business. When, in the summer of 1839, he traveled there, Ellen went with him, for Thomas and Maria had decided that she was to enter classes at the Visitation Convent that fall, and this was the only time it was possible for her father to take her. The Sisters agreed to board her until the school term began.

In other years it had usually been Philemon who took this trip with Mr. Ewing, but for the past few years he had been taking his father's place at home during his absences. He was a steady and trustworthy boy. Once, when his father mentioned sending a blank check to him for household expenses, Henry Clay said he wouldn't send a blank check to anyone, but Mr. Ewing answered he ought to make at least one exception, and that Philemon.

The whole family felt badly at seeing Ellen go so far away from home, and it was a doleful group that saw her and her father off on the stage. Little Charley kept throwing his arms around her, and trying to keep her at home by sheer force of their small pressure; her own eyes were full of tears as she turned to wave to her mother and brothers and little Sissie, who was standing on a chair by the window the better to see her big sister going away.

There was of course one great compensation: she was traveling with her father. But the journey itself across the Allegheny Mountains was long and wearying. The passengers wrapped themselves in their shawls — blankets really, of coarse blue cloth with zebra-like stripes, called "western shawls" — and sighed for the dawn, since it was at least less dreary when one could see a little scenery instead of merely being bumped around in the dark.

Then, while they were still in the coach, Ellen developed a bad toothache which grew worse with every hour. As soon as they reached Washington, Mr. Ewing took her to the dentist, who gave it as his opinion that four of her teeth were in bad condition and would have to come out immediately.

Mr. Ewing took one glance at his daughter. "While you are with Dr. Lunnell, I'll get you some books to take with you to the Academy for your recreation hours," he said and forthwith departed.

When he came back the teeth were out and Ellen looked white and weak. But the pain was gone, and gradually she began to feel better. It was not until later that Ellen realized why her father had gone away: it was because he could not bear to see her undergo pain. He had, however, bought the books which had been his excuse for leaving, two fine volumes — Landor's *Poems* and Frost's *Selections from British Poets*. Ellen treasured them and read from them whenever she felt homesick which, big girl though she was, happened more than once in those first days after her father left her at the Academy.

Ellen was especially lonely because there were no other pupils as yet. But before she could mope too much an invitation came to her from Mr. Young's sister-in-law, who lived near Washington, inviting her to spend the rest of the vacation at her home, Gisboro, an historic mansion on the Potomac River, the family seat of the Young and Fenwick families, who had given so many sons and daughters to the Church. The picturesque house stood on the banks of the Potomac, and one could catch glimpses of Washington from its windows.

Everyone was kind to the homesick girl. Mrs. Young and her sister, who was Ellen's age, treated her as if they were her mother and sister, and there was a delightful little boy who made her think of her own Charley. When it came time to go back to the Academy, Ellen did not mind at all, for she was already invited to come to Gisboro for the Christmas holidays.

A note from Cump awaited her at the Academy. She had written him about her new school and he opined it sounded like a very dull place to him, though he knew different people had different tastes. But was she really pleased with that nunnery?

West Point, he said, was all right but a little boring, too. He had three room-mates; he and two of them were Buckeyes, so they all wanted the Whigs to win. So Mr. Boyle was married again — that was a surprise. And Abby married, too — another surprise. West Point had had a fire. The loss was about twenty thousand dollars — "but Uncle Sam is rich and the loss will not be felt." You had to go to church there on Christmas Day instead of celebrating each in his own way. But you always got a good dinner that day anyway, and three out of four of his West Point Christmases were over — that was one consolation.

A few weeks later another letter came, this time to thank her for a pair of slippers she had made for him — too fine, he wrote, for use, just as the knife and the pencil the Ewings had given him were too fine, so he had put them all at the bottom of his trunk for special occasions. But the candy they sent had been eaten, and quickly too.

Why didn't she pay West Point a visit this summer? There was fine scenery — old Fort Put with its gloomy cells — Kosciusko's garden with its water works — a new army building. Maybe Mr. Ewing would bring her. Then, at the end of the letter, he mentioned the two people who had taken such care of him for so many years. He wrote very solemnly now: "Time and absence serve to strengthen the claims and increase my love and gratitude to those who took me early within their care and conferred the same advantages as they did on their own children. Although I have rarely spoken of it, yet I assure you that I have always felt deeply grateful and hope some event may occur to test it."

There was a postscript: "Direct your letters to *Cadet* W. T. Sherman, if you please."

From her mother came frequent letters, full of news from home. The Sewing Society missed Ellen; they were busy, stitching along together, mostly at rug work. Eliza Denman had just finished working a portrait of General Washington on one, and it was greatly admired. Several of the ladies thought it so fine it ought to be framed and taken to the city, and they wondered what price to set on it if it were decided to sell it. Ellen might look at work like it in Washington and price it for them.

Maria said she often took her work and went to sit with Aunt Beecher who was very poorly. When she was well enough, she took her to church on Sundays, and she visited her often. "It's all the comfort and happiness she has left," she wrote.

When Ellen came home in the summer she would find the new church on High Street ready, and she wanted Ellen to buy — or rather get her father to buy on some occasion when he brought her to Washington — an antependium pattern for the altar, with silks and braids for the ladies to embroider it — "and any little ornament besides if your father has the funds."

In 1840 Maria Ewing had exactly the kind of summer she loved best. Her family was at home. The house was full of people — "where does she put us all?" her children often wondered. There were so many visiting cousins that sometimes beds were set up in the upstairs hallway.

Others besides relatives came. It was a very exciting time politically, for the presidential elections were to take place that autumn, and General Harrison, the Whig candidate, came to see Mr. Ewing and brought others with him for consultations. "All I hear is election talk," said Maria. "From the first thing in the morning until late at night."

Cump came home too. He had written Ellen a few months before, "I will, fortune willing, exchange the cadet's gray coat for a sword and pair of epaulettes, and better still have three months furlough and come home." He was very happy at having at last finished his education and becoming a full-fledged officer, and looked forward to receiving an assignment for army duty in October. Mr. Ewing was very proud of this foster child of his, and it was evident that the boy reciprocated; his letters to Mr. Ewing usually ended, "affectionately your son."

The election campaign was a very personal one, for General Harrison was a favorite son of Ohio. There were long processions in Lancaster; banners decorated with drawings of 'coons and kegs of cider and buckeyes waved everywhere. There were big free dinners in the grove and speeches galore. Girls as well as boys knew all about the campaign for Harrison. When little Mary Gillespie, one of old Neal Gillespie's great grandchildren, saw General Harrison standing with Thomas Ewing on the latter's porch, she told her mother she thought Mr. Ewing would make a much better looking president. And when she saw her grandmother getting things for a picnic, she said sorrowfully, "Oh, if it were only in honor of our noble Henry Clay I would be much better pleased."

In the fall with the election of General Harrison as president, Thomas Ewing was asked to become a member of his Cabinet as

Secretary of the Treasury. When he left to take up his new post, Ellen went back with her father to continue her studies at the Visitation Academy.

Maria did not attend the inauguration, saying it was enough if her husband and Ellen and Philemon represented the family. But she wrote Thomas a letter saying she supposed he was having a grand time, "now Old Tip is in possession of the White House. How happy you Whigs must have felt on the great occasion." But under the gay words lay a great pride in her husband, and Thomas realized it.

Cump wrote, too, before Ellen went back to Georgetown, a letter full of pride in Mr. Ewing. He was still waiting at Fort Columbus in New York Harbor for an assignment to duty. He hoped he would be sent south: "I have a natural curiosity to see strange places and people, both of which exist in Florida."

The letter was addressed to Mrs. Ewing and it began very formally "My dear Madam," but near the end the old Cump was writing: "Assure Ellen that a few lines from her would be exceedingly welcome. Kiss little Sister for me and believe me, to be, Yours affectionately, W. T. Sherman, Lt."

Mrs. Ewing read the message to Ellen. "And when you write to him, remind him of his Faith. Tell him his godmother tells him to hold to that at least if he abandons everything else."

She then told Ellen she had heard that Mr. Blaine was coming into the Church. "What happiness for his wife and children that would be! Oh, Ellen, if only that might be our joy some day — to see your dear father kneeling before the same altar with his family — to hold in his heart like Job the hope of a glorious resurrection from the tomb."

They were both silent for a moment, then Maria added hopefully, "The Bishop speaks so highly of your father in his last letter and he said he was going to write to him."

During the winter of 1841, Ellen, back in Georgetown, was continually asked by her mother to make purchases for the new church. It needed so many things and had so little money to buy anything.

"I'll get Ellen to help us," she would promise the ladies when there was an especial need of furnishing or vestments. "Beg something of anyone you think has something to spare," she wrote Ellen, "and ask the Archbishop, too, if he visits you before you leave. Or Mr. Ryder or Mr. Donda."

And Ellen did. Often people came to see her, visitors passing through Washington, many who knew her father or mother and called to pay their respects. Of all of them she asked for something for the little church at home. She even approached Archbishop Eccleston, who was delighted to give her a fine offering. In fact, so many such gifts arrived at Lancaster that Ellen's mother was moved to remark that she had not expected Ellen to collect enough money to finish the church. Then, afraid this might stop the fine flow of charity, she added, prudently, "But tell each one who in the future contributes, that they could do no greater act of charity than send our poor church something."

Cump, now at Fort Pierce in East Florida, was often mentioned in Mrs. Ewing's letters to her daughter. She said she found so little time to write any letters except to Ellen and her father that Cump had had none; but Ellen was to say in one of her letters to him that they all thought as much of him as ever, and loved him as much as if they wrote to him every week.

In April of 1841 President Harrison died, only a month after his inauguration as President. By the first of the year Mr. Ewing had resigned as Secretary of the Treasury, not being in sympathy with President Tyler's views on the banking question. The entire Cabinet felt as he did and resigned in a body, with the single exception of Daniel Webster. Henry Clay's bill for rechartering the Bank of the United States had been vetoed by the new President on grounds, said Secretary Ewing, that had "no reference to the public good."

Mr. Ewing wrote a long public letter, detailing his reasons for resigning and giving a full account of exactly what had taken place in the Cabinet meetings where the matter was discussed. The Democratic papers assailed him promptly and said he was guilty of breach of confidence, but the Whigs of Columbus and Zanesville and other Ohio towns welcomed him home enthusiastically as a great patriot.

Ellen heard with joy the news that she was to go home with him. In February, 1842, the two left for Lancaster. To be home with the family was wonderful, and it was better still to know she was there to stay. She fell back quickly into the old ways of home, helping her mother, taking Charley and Sissie as her charges, and devoting herself especially to the education of the former. This was a somewhat mixed pleasure for Charley, who often looked more eagerly out of the window at the delights of the yard than he did indoors at the delights of learning spread before him by his big sister.

Mrs. Ewing had been made very happy over the results of Ellen's final shopping in Washington, especially the lovely design for an altar piece for festivals of the Blessed Virgin, and she hurried to share her riches with the ladies of the church. She showed Ellen some of her own needlework — the antependium of white velvet in the center of which the Lamb and the Cross was quilted. "But the design is not so well cut," she said, contemplating it with some irritation. "The workman was a Protestant and did not understand the matter at all."

Ellen had brought the fruits of her own accomplishments home with her: a prize in drawing, a book for her skill with the harp, and best of all, the gold medal given for superior excellence in the senior circle.

Often Ellen woke up in the gray mornings of that first spring at home to find her mother lighting her fire, so that she would be warm before they went together to early Mass. Together they acted as sacristan for the church, but often all the work devolved on Ellen, for now that she was at home her mother sometimes went on a trip with Mr. Ewing when he was called out of town on a law case.

It was a happy and united family that lived in the brick house on the Hill, a larger house now than the one to which a young Thomas and Maria Ewing had come twenty years before. Wings had been added, and there was a high brick wall protecting the yard from the street.

The Ewing family was a congenial group, quick with sympathy, hearty with laughter, willing to help each other. Philemon was almost twenty now; Hugh shooting fast into young manhood, and Tom not far behind him. But Sissie and Charley kept actual childhood still in the house.

One person still missing from the family circle was Cump. They heard often from the young officer at Fort Pierce, letters full of the problem of the Indians and of the warfare being waged against them; Cump said he really admired them a good deal even though he knew they were enemies of American culture. He was bored with his post and hoped he would go somewhere else soon. He was weary of seeing so much drinking and gambling, and hoped he would have something better to look at before long.

"I'll see what I can do for him," said Mr. Ewing; and at the year's end Cump wrote he had been transferred to a post near St. Augustine, and also that he was now a first lieutenant. There was plenty of society at the new post, a few English and Southern and many Spanish planters. Cump wrote Ellen that the Spanish ladies were certainly ready to play a game of hearts at every meeting; they were very pretty: "Many here have captivated officers who married them. The 'aspirantes' are left playing a desperate game that the least penetrating can perceive."

"Do you think he ought to stay in the army, Mother?" asked Ellen when she finished reading her letter.

"Well, I think that would depend on what Cump wants," said her mother judiciously.

Ellen waved the letter. "He says it's the only profession he is educated for. He says he thinks he will stay in the army, for he is sure there will be real work soon and not just barracks duty."

Maria looked thoughtful. "What he needs is a family around him, and not to be always and only with strangers."

Ellen smiled reminiscently. "Do you remember what he used to call it here — 'best home of all.' "

During the next few years the Ewings grew used to receiving letters from Cump from many places, for he was transferred often. For a while he was in Charleston where the landscapes were so lovely that he decided to lay in a supply of water-colors and to paint some of the vistas. "I have a great love for painting and find that sometimes I am so fascinated it amounts to pain to lay down the brush."

He was evidently often homesick for Lancaster. "It is near midnight," ran one letter to Ellen. "The winds are howling terribly. The surf roars as it dashes against the ramparts. A bright fire is on my hearth and my fancy is regaled with the picture of your bright smile as you penned the note now before me. . . . The army is a first-rate place for the single man but no place at all for a married man, that is unless the wife is willing to forsake and often lose the comforts of civilized life."

Ellen had asked if he ever went to church, and he answered that on Sullivan's Island there was no church whatsoever: "Charleston is near with its churches of every denomination, but our custom requires on Sunday forenoon a thorough inspection of the quarters, clothing, arms and accoutrements of our men and that usually takes nine to twelve, making it impossible to take advantage of the invitations of almost every congregation."

A priest came to the fort sometimes to preach to the Catholics there, but the sermons though good were suited to the capacity of the audience and "therefore not interesting to us. I can say little else than that to be a soldier and a regular professional Christian is somewhat incompatible."

In the autumn of 1843 came word that Cump would soon be home on furlough. Ellen knew when he was expected but stagecoaches did not often arrive just when they were supposed to. Maria was amused to see how often during the afternoon her daughter took her embroidery to the window which looked on the street where the coach passed. It was almost evening when Maria heard the sound of an embroidery frame falling to the floor and saw Ellen running to the door.

Perhaps the next move was unexpected to both the young people. It was decidedly so to Maria. Cump opened his arms and Ellen flew into them. A moment later they turned in alarm, but Ellen's mother was smiling. She had not realized that these two were in love, but she accepted the fact and later her husband also gave a half-hearted approval.

Mr. Ewing's misgivings were many. He knew that Cump had to give some of his small salary to his mother, but chiefly he hesitated because he did not want his Ellen to live the nomadic life of an army wife.

"Of course they can't marry for some time," he said to his wife.

"Oh, they know that," she said reassuringly. "Mrs. Sherman needs the money Cump gives her, and the salary is pretty small anyway."

The financial situation troubled Mr. Ewing more and more, until finally he offered a suggestion to Cump. "Look, my boy," he said, "why don't you leave the army and study some profession instead?"

"But then we would have to depend on you for a while," said Cump, "and I want to be entirely independent, Mr. Ewing." The older man could understand this feeling, and it pleased him, but he managed to extract a promise from Cump to think it over.

The wonderful two months' leave ended only too soon and Cump went back to Charleston, to Fort Moultrie. It was hard for him to go this time, for there was Ellen to leave behind — a different Ellen, for she belonged to him. Before he left he told her that he had decided to take her father's advice, at least part way. "I'll read Blackstone down there all summer and I'll study instead of running around all the time."

"Oh, Mother," said Ellen after he had gone, "I wouldn't mind traveling all the time. It makes father uneasy but I wouldn't mind at all. I hope Cump and I can go abroad some day. To England,

Cump says — but I hate England for the way she treats the Irish. But surely to France and Italy."

She often dreamed about these voyagings, of the long trip through Europe she and Cump would take. She decided she was even willing to go to England, since Cump admired its people so much, and she was reading the books by English authors he had left with her — *Lallah Rookh* and *Barnaby Rudge*. In fact, she meant to read all of Dickens — everything but the terrible *Notes on America*. And they would go to France and Italy, and last and best of all, they would go together to the Green Isle — to the land of saints where her deepest sympathies lay.

Once in a letter to Cump she asked him seriously to consider the doctrines of the Church, and he promised he would. But there was little immediate chance to consult libraries, he wrote, since he was even now being ordered to Northern Alabama and Georgia — "where religion is never found." It was on Ellen herself that he must rely — "on your more pure and holy heart and faith to intercede for the divine protection during the few years that may be allotted to us on this earth." Yet she was not to consider him a perfect heathen in religious matters, but rather one who "assures you he cannot fathom the mysteries of many Christian institutions but endeavors to strict adherence to honesty and the general rules of morality — a pretty safe guide to the Destination."

Ellen had spoken of a serious cold from which she was suffering and Cump suggested a cure. "Tell Mr. Ewing to send you to a Southern climate, say a trip to Havana. Should you pass this way, I would go with you. Don't think this quixotic."

Mr. Ewing wrote Cump late in 1844, again urging him to study for a profession in civil life, and Cump asked Ellen once more what she thought about it. As a matter of fact, what he really wanted to do just then was to be with her — or even better have her there with him in Charleston. They would go to hear Mrs. Keys sing, have a social chat with Mrs. Hawkins, eat of her mince pie and drink her wonderful whiskey punch and play euchre — "and afterwards stand on the ramparts and see the moon rise slowly from her watery bed and throw a gentle light over the calm sea and quiet scenes so different from the storms and gales of the North."

This was an unusually flowery letter for Cump to write, and Ellen read it over and over, especially the ending — "that you are and may continue happy is the sincere prayer of one who loves you dearly."

## 6. *Ellen and Cump*

### [1845–1852]

Cump came home on furlough in February of 1845, and he and Ellen spent a happy fortnight together. After he had gone and Ellen was feeling very lonely, Sissie said suddenly, "Elly, it seems as if Cumpy is in this room now, and sitting right there," and she pointed to a chair.

Ellen had to smile at that. "Well, then, why don't you get on Cumpy's knee?" she asked. But it was true that his stay had been so brief, his going so hurried, that it seemed as if he were actually still there with them.

Ellen had a letter from him soon after his return to Charleston. "Mother," she said after reading it, "he plans to leave the service. He says there is nothing but peace ahead for years and he is very tired of barracks duty. And listen to this," and her eyes were shining. " 'On Sunday last I attended both church and vespers at the Cathedral. Father Lynch preached and his sermon impressed me profoundly.' "

Maria hoped this letter meant an interest in the Faith. "He told me when he was home that he didn't think the Christian doctrine was necessary to assure peace and good will among all. I hope he learns much better than that."

In November 1845, St. Peter's new Cathedral in Cincinnati was consecrated. Mr. Ewing had promised his wife that he would take her to this celebration when the time arrived, and he kept his word. He carried on some legal business during their stay, but to many of the functions he went with Maria. She attended every one of them and wrote lengthy and admiring accounts back to Lancaster. At the consecration, Archbishop Eccleston of Baltimore presided "in all his glory," and Bishop McCloskey of New York gave the sermon. The venerable Bishop Flaget was also present and Bishop Miles, who as a young priest had instructed Ellen in the Faith and prepared her for her First Communion. Maria sat and feasted her eyes on the beauty of the new building, listened with all her heart to the heavenly music, the fine sermons, and missed not one thing of the grand and imposing dedication ceremony.

On Saturday she and Thomas went to the old Cathedral and heard the celebrated Dr. Spaulding, Bishop of Louisville, preach a sermon that moved even Thomas by its brilliance and clear arguments. Bishop Purcell of Cincinnati paid the Ewings a call at the Dennison House, and invited them to come to see his new residence just back of the Cathedral. The day before they left they went to call on Archbishop Eccleston of Baltimore who inquired about Ellen.

"I have a message from her for you, Your Grace," said Maria.

The Archbishop laughed. "What is she collecting for this time?" he asked. "If we had her working for us still, we could soon build all the churches we need in the United States."

There was also the important matter of looking over the shops of the city. Maria found the women's clothes not very superior to those in Lancaster, but with a greater use of flounces. She liked the long sleeves trimmed to the elbow and those cut with scallops or laced together with a cord over a white undersleeve.

She had planned to go to the mantua-maker's too, but there had been so much to see in the churches that she came home from what she called the "city of faith and piety" without a new mantle. "There wasn't time, Elly. Three Masses every morning and sermons every evening since Sunday. Oh, it was riches for one who has had so little for years. I didn't have time to buy anything but a bonnet for you and get a relic for myself, and candy for the children and a special book for Charley because he studied his catechism so well."

Very soon, Cump's picture of "nothing but peace" had changed, and war with Mexico was threatened. The following year it had begun and he was ordered to report to Pittsburgh for recruiting service; from there he was detailed to open a sub station, and when Ellen saw where she could hardly believe her eyes. "Cump is going to be stationed at Zanesville," she announced to the family.

He came briefly to Lancaster from Zanesville, but the plans changed again almost immediately. Taylor had won the battle of Palo Alto, and Cump asked immediate active duty. He told Ellen that he had done this. "I'm hoping for a chance to go West now — perhaps to California. Wouldn't that be wonderful?"

Ellen tried hard to share his enthusiasm, but her heart was heavy. California was so very far away. When Cump saw her hesitation he tried to reassure her. "Oh, Ellen, it will be a great thing to be a pioneer in such a move, to precede the flow of population there, and be one of the pillars of the land. And I'll move at last from my tiresome work. I'll become an active part in the profession for which I've been trained."

Cump's first letter to Ellen after his return to headquarters told her he had his wish: he was ordered to California, by sea around Cape Horn. He was so sorry he had not had time to go to Mansfield to see his mother before he left, but would Ellen go in his place? And now he hoped she regretted she had not had that miniature made for him which he had wanted so much. He had no token of her at all — "nor any memento save a small lock of hair that has been guarded when all else has been neglected."

That summer Maria and Thomas Ewing worried a good deal about their Ellen. She sewed as usual, making fine linen shirts and stocks for her father, but she looked thin and pale and was without her usual energy. She did not even want to join in picking the peaches at the farm, but got Charley and Sissie to do it alone. She did make the damson jam, and put three glasses away in a corner so that they might be there for Cump when he got home again.

How could Ellen be happy and carefree when she worried so much about Cump? Every time a letter came from him, she ran to the map she kept on her table to look up Rio de Janeiro or Valparaiso or San Francisco — all the strange places where he had gone.

From Monterey came the longest letter she had ever received from him. "Twenty sides of paper, Mother — five full sheets. But the day he wrote this — in July — he said he hasn't heard from me since October of last year."

"Is he as devoted to California as he was before he saw it?" asked Mrs. Ewing.

Ellen leafed through her letters. "Well, here is what he says: 'I wouldn't give two counties in Ohio or Kentucky or Tennessee for the whole of California.'"

But he had been promoted. He had been quartermaster and now was promoted to the rank of adjutant-general.

Two long years passed for Ellen while Cump was in California. Although his letters were often homesick, there was never in them one word of transfer to the East. They were full of his work, of the country, of his anxiety to see Ellen again, of his love for her and his eagerness to set up a home with her soon, but that was all. Then one morning in 1848 a letter came from him with very exciting news. Only forty miles away from his station Cump said he had himself seen valley beds of gravel mixed with gold, and he was sending specimens to Washington.

Before the year's end Hugh Ewing and his cousin Hampton

Denman, decided they, too, would join the rush of the thousands who were beginning the trek West.

"If I were a young man I would go with you," said Thomas Ewing, his eyes alight and he agreed to outfit his son for the trip.

The women of the house spent busy days getting Hugh's bags ready. Ellen was taking full advantage of the fact that the boys would be very likely to see Cump in California, and in his old trunk she had found some good pantaloons and socks which she put into a bag she was packing for him, with all manner of gifts, cakes of good soap, a fine toothbrush, a black silk cravat, a pair of slippers worked by herself with a lily embroidered on each, a housewife complete with needles and buttons and thread and pins, a watch-guard with a gold catch. Charley wanted to send Cump something too, and he chose a little pocket ink-stand.

Ellen had had a picture of herself taken to put in it — "correct but not flattering" she said. She studied it before she packed it, and decided she wasn't really very pretty; and so of course if Cump ever found a prettier girl than this picture showed and preferred her — well, Ellen would always try to be a fine sister to them both all their lives. Maybe there was such a one in California. But of course, she told herself quickly, there were probably not many very pretty girls in such an outlandish place.

She asked a favor of Hugh before he left, but a favor that had nothing to do with Cump, only with Hugh himself. "Don't forget your prayers, will you? At noon every day let's each of us say a Hail Mary." And he promised, feeling very serious, for the family had the day before been suddenly summoned to the Boyle house: the old man was dying. Children and grandchildren knelt about his bed as Father Young administered the Last Sacraments. Hugh Boyle lay placid and happy, entirely conscious during the whole recitation of the last prayers. Only a few moments after they were finished he died so quietly that those watching thought he had only fallen asleep.

In February of 1849 the boys started for the gold fields, their carpet bags overflowing. There were six in the party, one of them a son of the Dittoe family. As Maria Ewing stood in the doorway watching the stage take Hugh away her heart was full of fear. He was so young and so beloved — and he was the first of her children to leave home. Not for a good dependable position either, but for mere adventure. She thought of the risks of exposure, of the rough elements with whom he would have to mingle, of fevers and cholera and even of starvation. And then she said a little prayer and commended Hugh to God and His Mother and felt better.

"I hope Cump gets his bag all right," said Ellen beside her.

"Hugh will manage," her mother said confidently. "But it is certainly a very heavy bag, Ellen."

Ellen smiled. "Hugh asked me what under the sun was in it and I gave him a list of the items. But I told him what probably made it extra heavy was all the prayers and love and hopes I had tucked in between the packages."

They went back into a house that was, for Maria and Ellen, quite empty. For Mr. Ewing had gone to Washington for the inauguration of President Taylor and taken Tom with him, and the summer before Philemon had married Mary Gillespie, and he and his wife were living in a small house some distance away. That left only the two women and the two small children.

Suddenly came amazing news! Mr. Ewing was to enter the political scene again. In 1848 the Whig National Convention had nominated him for Vice President, a member from Pennsylvania proposing him and a member from Tennessee seconding the motion, but a disgruntled member from Ohio refused to accede, acting as if he spoke with the authority of Senator Ewing himself. "We want no sugar-plums," he shouted, angered at the nomination of Taylor for president when he felt a son of Ohio should have had that honor. So Millard Fillmore was nominated instead as running mate for Taylor.

Ellen had been indignant when she heard it and so was Maria, but Mr. Ewing had taken it philosophically. The vice presidency was not a position to which he aspired, and he was doing well where he was, he said. But now came word that he would not be returning to Lancaster after the inauguration of President Taylor, for he had accepted a post in the new Cabinet.

"Ellen," Maria called to her daughter, after she had read the letter carefully, "we are going to Washington to live. The President has appointed your father Secretary of the Interior, and he has accepted."

Ellen was breathless with excitement. "Oh, Father will love that. When they created that department last year he wondered who would be the first Secretary."

"But, Ellen, it means we must move to Washington. We must leave Lancaster!"

Nevertheless Ellen was delighted at the prospect and so were the children. But Maria was not happy; she feared lest events might so shape that they would not come back to Lancaster at all, and for her here were her home, her roots, her kindred. Washington was fine for a visit, but this was a better place to live. And this year the fruit was going to be so abundant — peaches and plums and cherries and currants — and all these would be enjoyed by strangers.

Her letter to Thomas was one expressing her mixed feelings. "As one of your particular friends, I must congratulate you upon the honor conferred by President Taylor. Although the consequences of your elevation will bring upon me many trials! Nonetheless the will of God be done in all things. But oh, that the Home Department were in Lancaster!"

"We'll see a lot more of Father this way," said Ellen consolingly.

It was suggested to Philemon that he and Mary take over the Ewing house, but the very thought of being saddled with so large a place made Philemon melancholy, and it was finally decided to rent to Mr. Slade. "And just as well," opined Ellen, "or Phil would be troubled by Mother's host of traveling acquaintances who have always preferred her house to taverns. I don't mean friends," she added, "but that other sort whom it is no charity or pleasure to entertain."

In the middle of May the Ewing family moved to Washington. Thomas had given Maria three days to get ready to come and she had actually made it in five, and was still moaning about the move. "Washington is a great trial to me," she told Ellen. "It may be a forward step but I think it a sad thing."

Her husband had found a good house for them — the Blair house, a roomy mansion of four stories. There was a small greenhouse; the grounds were well landscaped, and when the long windows from the sitting-room were opened one had the feeling of living in the country. Mr. Ewing liked it because it was close to his office, and Maria liked it because it was as near a church as had been her own home on the Hill. Ellen loved her room on the third floor and she hung the walls with pictures she had brought from home; on the mantle she put Cump's and Hugh's pictures side by side.

Even the reluctant Maria was soon swept up into the new life and was so busy she had little time to lament the old. There were few chances for idle moments, for this way of life meant housekeeping and entertaining on a larger and much more fashionable scale than Lancaster had demanded of its first citizens. The calls she had to pay soon became a heavy duty, for there were at least three hundred during the season. Ellen and her mother divided them, going about in a fine Washington carriage with good Ohio horses, dark brown and high-spirited; some people said they were the handsomest span in the city. The summer carriage was very nice, but the winter one, sent from New York was, according to their own coachman, "nobler looking than the President's."

The younger children were at school, Charley with the Jesuits, and Sissie at the school of the Sisters of Charity. Tom was busy studying law. Maria thought often of her Hugh, from whom no word had come since he had left for California with the little group which Ellen had named the Lancaster Mining Company. She worried about Ellen, too, and insisted on having her see a physician. When he said the girl was in sound condition, Maria still worried.

She knew of course what really ailed Ellen. It was the separation, the hopelessness of the long absences from Cump. There were months when she did not hear from him at all, and when word did come it was apt to be a letter full of woe because he had not heard from her for an equally long time. Each such letter made Ellen more despondent. Even the carefully packed carpet bag had not reached him, nor had Hugh seen him.

When she was certain no one heard her, Ellen cried bitterly in the quiet of her own room. If only Cump could come home to marry her. It was lasting so long, this engagement; even hopes of future happiness were growing dim as were the dreams they had shared.

Suddenly after a long period in which no word had come a great accumulation of mail arrived from the West. Letters from Hugh, who had seen Cump and turned over the carpet bag. He said Cump was well and no one was to worry about any of them. Cump's own letter was a happy one. Mail had come for him, loads of it, his first letters from Ellen in a whole year. Surely he would be home soon now, he wrote; surely very soon they could set up their own home. They had waited long enough.

Ellen's spirits immediately lifted. Of one thing she was amusedly certain: Cump would be delighted to find her in Washington. His opinion of Lancaster was that it was a boring place; it was the one thing she and Cump did not see eye to eye about. For, like her mother, she loved the town passionately, and said that in Washington she was frequently taken ill with *mal de pays*. If someone blindfolded Ellen, picked her up off the ground and whirled her around and then set her down, said Cump, "she'd not hesitate. Like a homing dove she'd head straight for Lancaster."

Now that Ellen felt more cheerful about Cump, Maria was able to draw her into the younger social life of the capital. Tom took her sometimes to the Saturday concerts on the White House grounds, when the Marine Band played. Sometimes she and other young people went for picnics along the Potomac banks. But to her all these things were only makeshift ways of spending the days. Life's reality was far across the continent.

In November more letters came. Cump wrote that he might be at home any day. Hugh reported finding actual gold, and sent a package to his mother containing a little bag of the metal to be made into a cross for herself. A nugget came for Ellen and she had it made into a breast pin for her father. Mr. Ewing was delighted with this and wore it on every possible occasion. "He wore it to the President's house," Ellen wrote to Hugh, "and he boasted of it as your 'first washing.'"

Maria was happy to see how much her husband enjoyed his work in the new Department. It gave him an opportunity to use his judicial knowledge and to effect reforms he could only have talked about had he no official position. He had a chance to do the thing he wanted above everything to have the power to do — to place able men in government positions. He had offered the commissionership of the General Land Office to Abraham Lincoln, just retiring from a term in Congress. Lincoln at first for political reasons declined, but later he changed his mind and wanted to accept. Mr. Ewing had to tell him regretfully that the appointment had been given elsewhere.

On hearing this, Lincoln had sat dejectedly in Ewing's office for a few seconds. Then he got up and ambled away. "Well, I reckon they'll find some use to put me to," he said to a friend later that evening.

One morning in mid-February 1850, Ellen was in the little conservatory giving her favorite canary a bath when she heard steps that sounded familiar. She turned to see who it was — and then she quickly fastened the door of the gilt cage and sped out into the hall. For the first time in four long years she felt Cump's arms about her.

He told her he had asked for a six months' leave and it had been granted. In New York, despite his rough, unpressed uniform he had gone directly to Delmonico's on Bowling Green and reported to General Scott, who allowed him to stay in New York until he could get new clothes and then sent him to Washington with dispatches for the Secretary of War. After delivering them he had hurried straight to Ellen, declaring that this time they would delay no longer. The wedding must take place very soon.

"Let's get married on May first and then we can write our day of joy with all nature," he suggested, and so that day was set. Dr. Ryder, the President of Georgetown, promised Mrs. Ewing that he would perform the marriage ceremony.

This time even Mr. Ewing could not counsel further delay. But he had several serious talks with Cump on the subject of his future. He still hoped Cump would leave the army, and he regretted to hear of the possibility that he might be stationed in St. Louis. He would rather have them in some entirely northern state if the threats of secession continued.

Cump went to Mansfield, Ohio, to see his mother. During this brief absence he wrote Ellen every day, very different letters now from the mournful ones of other years. "Perhaps in the uncertainty of our destiny there may be more true happiness than to be bound down to a certainty," he wrote blithely. "The present is ours; let us make the most of it."

"Just now I am as free to go and come as though I wore not Uncle Sam's livery," ran another letter. "If a fair prospect comes I'll resign, but if not it would be prudent to wait a year or two — a suspense, not change of purpose."

Soon he wrote that he was on the way back "to her to secure whose happiness is now my chief and only aim." He was very weary when he arrived in Washington, for the stage route from Mansfield to Cumberland was a hard one, and he had been packed with eight passengers in a small coach. But he forgot his weariness, for he was immediately swept up in wedding preparations.

In mid-April Washington received cards, small and lace edged, engraved: "Mr. and Mrs. Ewing request the pleasure of your company on Wednesday evening on May 1 at 8½ o'clock." Enclosed were the cards of Miss Ewing and W. T. Sherman, U.S. Army.

The first of May was a beautiful day, warm and sunny. The marriage was to take place in the bride's home, but early that morning Maria and Ellen drove to Mass and Holy Communion in St. Matthew's Church. Maria prayed long and earnestly that this daughter of hers might have a happy life and that her marriage would be a blessed one.

In the evening a bright moon was shining as the guests arriving for the ceremony entered parlors bright with tall, white candles and shaded lamps and flowers. The assembly was a distinguished one, with guests high in government office as well as friends and relatives. President Taylor and his entire Cabinet were there; Sir Henry Bulwer, the English envoy, came in court costume. Some of the statesmen present were men whom Ellen had known in the old days at Lancaster when she listened with Cump to the political talk of the men gathered around the Ewing table. Daniel Webster was there, and Senator Benton of Missouri, and Senator Corwin of Ohio, and so was Henry Clay, whose gift, a silver filigree bouquet-holder, was carried by the bride.

Ellen looked utterly happy and lovely as she came down the wide hall on her father's arm. Her satin gown shone in the lights; her little feet were clad in heelless kid shoes, laced at the sides; her curly black hair was half hidden in the shimmering folds of her lace veil.

Cump with his red hair and a serious look in his hazel eyes came towards her. They met before Dr. Ryder, and looked at each other for a long moment before they turned to face the priest who was to make them man and wife.

On Thursday the young couple left by carriage for Baltimore.

"It doesn't seem possible Elly is gone," Thomas Ewing kept repeating to Maria during the first days after the wedding.

"They'll be back soon," she consoled him, but he would not be comforted. A young married couple would be back; but the girl Elly and the boy Cump were gone forever.

Maria was very busy with callers — forty-eight of them in two days, who were enthusiastic about the lovely wedding and the pretty bride, and who praised the beauty and elegance of her costume. Maria sent pieces of cake to friends who had not been able to come to the wedding; to Mr. Vespre at Georgetown College, who had been Ellen's spiritual adviser since her school days, she sent a mould of charlotte russe and three bottles of wine to drink the bride's health. She found time to drop a note to Ellen, saying she hoped she would write frequently, at least every few days, and that when she got to Lancaster she would give *them* a brushing up about writing. She sent a message to Cump: "Tell him I thank him for his kind assurances, but they were unnecessary, for my confidence in him is unlimited and I trust it will ever be so."

The young couple's day in Baltimore was spent in sightseeing, quite as though Ellen had not been in that city many times. Then they took the cars for Philadelphia, and there Cump bought for his wife a fine present: a trunk large enough to hold all her clothes, with a closed box on one side for her bonnets.

They reached New York the following day, a Sunday, and went together to High Mass at the Cathedral where Archbishop Hughes was confirming a group of children; and after Mass they called on him. They paid a visit to West Point where Cump played host and showed Ellen all his old haunts. They went to the Brooklyn Navy Yard and aboard a man-of-war, where they met a Captain Kilbourne who had seen Hugh in California only the month before and reported him in good health.

It was Ellen's first visit to New York and she went shopping with some of the Hoyt and Stanbery cousins who lived there. She bought presents for everybody at home, from Sissie to her father, while Cump was off on a different sort of shopping expedition. He had a wager with Ellen that he could find homemade sugar, as Ohioans called maple candy, somewhere in the city. But Ellen won the bet.

The big house in Washington was more and more lonely as the weeks passed. Mr. Ewing was restless without Ellen. During the day he was busy, but it was at its end that her father realized most the loss of his daughter. The bright face that smiled at him from across the dinner-table was no longer there. When he took his evening ride, there was no Ellen to enjoy it with him. "A vacant seat in house and coach, Maria," he said. "And all these roses that want picking. I wish," he added energetically, "that Cump could be stationed in Washington during our time here."

Maria brightened. "Oh, Thomas, that would be wonderful."

"Of course Cump's feelings and judgment would be of importance," said Mr. Ewing. "But St. Louis is such a sickly place — all the old inhabitants say so. In fact," and he spoke gloomily, "I know people there who have buried all their children and are alone in their old age. And there's plenty of cholera there."

Maria said nothing, but her emotions were mirrored in her face.

On Ascension Day a letter came from the young couple. "Why, Thomas," said Maria in surprise, "they are still in New York. But of course it *is* such a beautiful place."

"They'll never get to Lancaster at this rate," observed Mr. Ewing.

That week a present came for Maria from the travelers: a lovely cape and cap. "I'll wear them at the very next dinner to which we are invited," she promised Ellen in a letter which ended, "I have to tell you, dear Ellen, that the house seems deserted; that we are sad and lonely at your loss would be useless to say, for you know it. We have told you so. But the will of God be done."

The young Shermans were next heard from at Niagara Falls, and then from Mansfield where Cump's mother and many relatives still lived. "The family here is so large," wrote Ellen, "and they must all be visited, so we can't get away very soon." In June they reached Lancaster and were guests of Philemon and his wife. Here there were parties and many calls on old friends. Tom joined them there and brought with him a letter from his mother with a bewildering list of things to do in Lancaster. He and Ellen were to call on at least a score of people — the Ainsworths, the Denmans, the Rodmans, and many others — "above all be polite and friendly to dear old Aunt Beecher, go out and see Cousin Louise whether she invites you particularly or not. Young folks must not stand on ceremony." They were to look at the garden and see if the house was all right. If Ellen saw Mr. Young she was to give him Mrs. Ewing's regards and ask his prayers for her father: "Dr. Ryder of Georgetown speaks quite confidently of his becoming a Catholic. God grant it."

When the Ewings heard that the young Shermans had reached Lancaster they half decided to go too, but Mr. Ewing could not leave until July when Congress adjourned. Maria was weary of Washington, and what she wanted most in the world was to be in Lancaster with Ellen and Cump, seeing all the people she loved best, superintending the picking of the fruit and putting up jams and jellies. When the young people returned to Washington after a brief visit in Brownsville with the Blaines, they had to give a full story of their travels and a very exact account of how things were in Lancaster.

Before many days had passed Cump began to get restless. "Perhaps I ought to quit this loafing and get back to the regiment before the furlough is over," he said, but Ellen persuaded him to stay a little longer.

In July, President Taylor died suddenly and Secretary Ewing handed in his resignation to the new President, Millard Fillmore. He was immediately appointed by the Governor of Ohio to fill the unexpired term of Senator Corwin who in his turn became a Cabinet member. Maria did not know whether to be glad or sorry, since they would still have to stay for a time in Washington. Then a thought suddenly struck her. "Thomas, if they had nominated you for Vice President you would be President now!"

Thomas Ewing smiled at her excitement. "You remember I told you how much trouble it would be to be Vice President. Think how much more trouble it would be to be President, Maria."

Soon after President Taylor's funeral the Ewings turned over Blair House to Senator Corwin and went to Lancaster, the Shermans with them. Later the Senator returned to Washington to lodgings on Capitol Hill. Cump had expected to take Ellen to St. Louis as soon as his furlough ended, but he agreed that, since she was expecting a baby the early part of the next year, she stay in Lancaster until the child was born and then join him.

He came from St. Louis to spend Christmas with her and found her well but restless. It almost seemed to her that the old days of separation were beginning again.

After Christmas Cump went back to his bachelor's rooms in the hotel in St. Louis, but, when word reached him that on January 28th a daughter had been born to them and baptized Maria Ewing, he decided the time had come to establish his family in a home. "I'm coming for the two of you right away," he wrote.

For all her eagerness to be with Cump, Ellen was aghast, for this would give her only ten days to get ready. Cump, eager to see his baby, came even sooner than he was expected and did not want to delay for the few days the doctor and Mrs. Ewing thought necessary. Meanwhile Mr. Ewing, then in Washington, wrote urging Ellen to stay until he came back — and Cump too — "but if he can't, tell him I'll see Ellen gets to St. Louis safely. I'll be responsible for their safe delivery there within a month."

"Man proposes but God disposes," said Maria when she read the letter, for the young Shermans were on their way before it arrived.

To go to St. Louis was a complicated matter for travelers had to take the stage from Lancaster to Columbus, then the cars to Cincinnati, and from there a water trip down the Ohio River by steamboat. When they reached St. Louis, Ellen liked at first sight the house which Cump had rented for his family. Some distance out from the city, it was set in a grove of oaks, a quiet and sunny place. Cump had selected simple furniture, for their money was limited, but it was their own and they loved it. Ellen wrote home that she was not a very efficient housewife nor a very amiable woman, but she seemed to suit Cump. She had a cook and a boy for odd household jobs and to drive her in the horse and buggy, and Catherine, who had come from Lancaster with her, liked the city and promised to stay as nurse.

The following April the Ewings arrived in St. Louis for their first visit, Thomas for the ostensible reason of handling a case for a client there, Maria openly saying she wanted to see her new granddaughter again. "The most sprightly, prettiest, most amiable, interesting little creature I ever saw," she told Thomas after a few hours of watching the baby.

Thomas laughed and said she was partial, but she dissented. "I was never charged with blindness to the faults and imperfections of my own children and I would not be partial to my grandchildren," she said firmly.

She brought Ellen all the news from home. She had taken Sissie to the Ursulines in Brown County, fine women, ladylike and accomplished, English, French, and Irish. Fanny O'Neil, a young woman who had spent some years as assistant to Maria in the Ewing home, was recently professed a Dominican Sister at Somerset and her name in religion was Sister Aloysius. Aunt Beecher was so very frail now that she could hardly get her home from church sometimes after she had insisted on going. Mrs. Ewing reported to Ellen that she had recently heard from a friend in Washington that the French Minister, who had written home a letter of bitter criticism of the manners met with in the American Capital, had also mentioned, as showing the picture was not entirely bad, "the cultured hospitality of Thomas Ewing's home where his lovely wife presides."

The Shermans wanted to take their visitors about St. Louis but Mrs. Ewing cared little for sightseeing. All she wanted to see of the city was her grandchild and namesake. "I have been kissing her in my dreams every night until I could kiss her again in reality," she said, "and now I want to stay here and see all I can of her."

The Shermans' first years in St. Louis passed pleasantly. There was quite a bit of entertaining, for Cump loved to bring officers out to show them his pretty wife and baby. In the fall Mr. Ewing came again, this time bringing Philemon with him. A letter from Mrs. Ewing likewise arrived: Ellen was not to fuss while her father was there. He liked best of all a simple diet, and that should be little trouble. And she hoped that perhaps when he came home he would bring Ellen for a visit.

Her father had a list of things to bring back to Lancaster with him
and Ellen shopped for him: piccalilli, walnut catsup, a cake of honey
soap, a rice mould, a patent ice cream freezer.

But he did not bring Ellen back with him; she sent word she could
not leave Cump. Maria cried a little, and even the lovely cap Ellen
had sent her did not at first assuage her disappointment. But when
she tried it on, she was delighted to see how well it became her. Then
she looked it over more carefully, and removed some of the flowers —
"a bit gay for Lancaster," she said regretfully.

She had news for Thomas. Some of the Forty-niners were beginning to come back, among them Samuel Stambaugh who had brought
back a lump of gold weighing eighty ounces, and worth some sixteen
hundred dollars, and who had fifteen thousand in gold deposited in
the Hocking Valley Bank. "And no doubt at this moment his wife
is dreaming, with her eyes open, of marble halls," added Maria.

## 7. Early Married Years

### [1852–1854]

THE winter of 1852 in St. Louis was bitterly cold. Ellen, though
accustomed to brisk Ohio weather, found this very different.
She and the baby sat before a roaring fire, wearing a profusion of
sacques and shawls, and still their fingers were cold and their feet like
ice. Even in the bedroom, where there was a good fire, the towels
would freeze shortly after they had been used.

Little Maria — the Shermans usually called her by the affectionate
diminutive of Minnie — sat at table with them now. By the New Year

she was walking; Ellen could count six steps before she toppled. To Ellen everything the baby did was a joy, and during her first year her mother said Minnie was such a perfect and pure source of happiness that she could regard any future suffering for her an easy thing to bear.

One day she and Cump took the baby to the College Church of the Jesuits to have her dedicated to the Blessed Virgin. They were afraid she would cry, but Minnie was fascinated throughout the ceremony by the statue of Our Lady and the lovely lights.

Busy though she was, Ellen found some time for church work, for that had been an occupation for so many years that she would have felt lost without it. Cump often went to Mass with her on Sundays to the near-by Jesuit church, especially when Father De Smet was the preacher. When Orestes Brownson, the well-known convert, came to lecture in St. Louis, the Shermans went to hear him. The hall was crowded, the applause loud and frequent, and Ellen was delighted with the fearless way he defended and exalted the Church.

One day Cump brought Ellen an ivory crucifix which he had seen in a shop window on Fourth Street, and she put it on the mantle between the miniatures of her parents. She was glad that thus she could make a public declaration of her faith, and doubly glad that it was Cump who had given her the opportunity.

In the spring of 1852 there was great bustle and preparation in the house on the Hill in Lancaster. For Hugh was coming home at last from the gold fields, not wealthy, he wrote, but very healthy. And Ellen was coming to visit with the baby, because Cump had to go for a few months to Leavenworth to inspect cattle for the government. Sissie would soon be home from school, and so would Charley who was close by at St. Joseph's in Somerset.

Mr. Ewing had bought a new carriage and team of horses, and when it was time for Ellen to arrive he sent Tom to meet her with the fine new outfit. In the old home Ellen had a jubilant welcome. As for Minnie, she was the cynosure of all eyes, and her proud grandparents agreed that there had never been such a baby.

A few weeks after she came home Ellen kept a promise she had made to Cump: to take the baby to his mother in Mansfield. Mrs. Sherman considered her grandchild an extremely pretty girl. "She is a Ewing," she told Ellen, "all but her hair and that is certainly Cump's," and she fluffed the baby's soft red curls.

She told Ellen gaily of her visit to the State Fair in Cleveland the month before. "I stood the trip better than the girls. Some of our folks gave out the second day but not I. I saw old friends there I had not seen for years and it was a comfort to talk with them."

She was as pleasant and smiling as ever, and to look at her one would never have guessed the hard life she had led — the loss of her husband, the debts with which she was left, the separation from one and the other of her children. She had carried all her life with her an air of hospitality and charm, and that she still wore.

Her children had all turned out well, the entire eleven. The girls were happily married. The older boys were lawyers, businessmen and one a soldier — all successful men.

She told Ellen, she wished for just one thing — to have a quiet home of her own for a little while. "All my clothes are scattered around in relatives' homes and I scarcely know from day to day where I will be."

"Why don't you come and stay with us for a while?" said Ellen impulsively. "It won't be exactly quiet but the change might be nice."

Mrs. Sherman's face lighted. "Perhaps I will — and I'll help you keep house. I am still very strong. But," she said regretfully, "I wish this visit of yours were not so short."

"The one you make us will be much longer," promised Ellen.

She and the baby had been back in Lancaster only a week when word came from Mansfield of Mary Sherman's sudden death from a heart attack. Ellen, writing the sad news to Cump, wept to think it happened just as she was planning to visit them and that now Cump would never see her again. She was buried from the Ewing house and laid in the old cemetery in Lancaster beside her husband.

When Cump received the sad news he wrote Ellen of his grief, and of his sorrow at not being at his mother's funeral. "Poor mother! She has had hard times and nothing but the kindest, most affectionate and simplest heart could have borne her up under her varied fortunes." He ended this letter by saying he had been transferred to New Orleans. Since he would remain there for some time, he wanted Ellen to come to him as soon as he could find a house, but he agreed that she stay at home until after the birth of her second child.

When Sissie, at school in Somerset, learned this from Ellen who wrote her that she was sorry poor Cump would have to be without his family for a while longer, she dashed home an indignant note to show Cump was not the only lonely one. It was she who had the better right to be, for she heard her parents had been in Cincinnati and had not stopped to see her. She did not write to the cruel grown-ups but addressed her letter to her small niece Minnie. "Darling Minnie," it began, "this is the second time my mother has served me that way, but if she and Pa go to Cincinnati next month I hope they will remember they have relatives in the adjacent county who are not sorry to see them and friends occasionally."

Minnie went about the house, delightedly carrying her letter; the contents did not matter at all; the fact that it was her letter and written to her gave her deep satisfaction.

Ellen's second baby was born in November, 1852, and named for her grandmother, Mary Elizabeth Sherman. She was baptized and dedicated to the Blessed Virgin by Archbishop Purcell in Cincinnati. When she was six weeks old, Ellen left Lancaster with her and two-year old Minnie and faithful Catherine, to go to Cump in New Orleans by way of Columbus and down the Ohio River.

In New Orleans Cump met them, and with great joy he took them to the house he had found for them; all the way he admired the new little daughter, a tiny baby with thick dark hair like her mother's. Minnie at first called her father formally "the man," but later was induced to change this to "Papa," although sometimes she hailed him companionably as "Tump."

New Orleans was a delight to the girl from the North; it was so very different from the prosaic midwest towns she knew, different, too, from Washington and St. Louis. Cump, who knew the South well, rejoiced in Ellen's pleasure over the sunny days, the bouquets of bright flowers for sale in the streets, the delicious fruit displayed at every corner, the French Market, the Creole way of living, the little Catholic church of St. Patrick's where they went to Mass together. Everything had an Old World flavor which the northern cities lacked.

The house on Magazine Street was so small that housekeeping was sheer fun. Cump's work gave him considerable leisure time, and they took walks about the city. And one day Ellen took the children by boat to Biloxi, Mississippi, to visit her Aunt Jane Latimer, one of Thomas Ewing's sisters.

On Minnie's second birthday they all went in the cars to Lake Ponchartrain, had dinner there, and came home late in the evening. Minnie had been allowed to eat regular food instead of the usual bread and milk for which she cared little. Cump always watched with sympathy her efforts to eat this dish. "I never liked the stuff myself. It isn't really food at all. It's nothing but a poultice."

As a matter of fact, Minnie was the only one who ever grew dissatisfied with life in New Orleans and who now and then wept a little to "go home to Grandma." But usually she was happy and already had a favorite spot in the town — a little candy store at the foot of Magazine Street, where her father took her to buy toys and sweets. There was one bad place in the paving where he had to lift her over to the curb and this became a regular ritual of their walks.

It was a pleasantly normal life, and the Shermans would have felt completely settled in it had it not been for the uncertainty of army life. However, in the end their stay in New Orleans proved very short.

Soon after Ellen had arrived with the children, Cump received a visit from Major Turner, a friend recently retired from the army. He had become a member of a banking business in St. Louis and he wanted young Captain Sherman to go to San Francisco to establish a branch of the firm. He spoke very persuasively and made Cump a handsome offer of four thousand dollars a year and a share in the profits. When he went away he left partnership papers in case Cump decided to accept.

He had been half inclined to do so, but Ellen was so happy in New Orleans that at first he put aside any thought of accepting the Turner offer. Later he began considering it seriously; perhaps he ought to take it up. He was thirty-three years old; he had a wife and two children; it was time for him to be settled in life.

He talked Major Turner's offer over with Ellen. "This would be much pleasanter work, Ellen, and there is a fine chance for quick advancement, and commissary work is tiresome. Commissaries are not fighting men, and I'll just get one job after another like this because I do it well."

Finally they compromised: he would ask for six months leave of absence from the army and go to San Francisco. So in March Ellen found herself headed north again, sad at heart to be leaving the home just set up, but at least with the happiness ahead of a brief return to her beloved Lancaster.

Mr. Ewing picked them up in Cincinnati and took them to the cars, for one traveled to Lancaster by rail now. "Only one small line," said Ellen's father, "and not very noisy." There were signs of building going on at the house on the Hill. "An ell, to take care of my grandchildren," Mr. Ewing told his daughter proudly.

Those were happy days for Maria Ewing, with Minnie beside her, her tiny thimble on her finger as she pretended to sew and solemnly rocked in her little chair, while Lizzie looked on and chewed at a piece of bread and butter which she, though still toothless, much preferred to milk. Ellen alone was sad at heart as she recalled the happy weeks in New Orleans, and hoped the lure of a fine salary would not pull Cump too hard. She would go with him wherever he decided to go, but she hoped it would not be so far away. When she told her father about the new scheme, he said in his slow wise way, "Well, Elly, I have confidence in his judgment and the coolness of his decision," and Ellen decided that was really just how she felt too.

Her mother asked her when she first came if she and her father had gone to call on the Archbishop in Cincinnati and Ellen said yes, her father had gone willingly, but it was just a social visit and no one had mentioned religion.

Maria's eyes filled with tears. "I wish you had, Ellen; it seemed like such a favorable time. It wouldn't take him long to come into the Church if he made up his mind. No one need know about it except his family and the Archbishop. I have an idea he would really like to take the step if it were not for the noise and clamor of the world."

"Perhaps he will receive the gift of faith before long," said Ellen, gently.

"Oh, if only he would, Ellen. It is the hope of my heart."

When Cump came back to Ohio in August 1853, he told Ellen that Major Turner had offered to make the salary five thousand dollars. "Ellen, I shall leave it to you. Shall we stay in the army or go West?"

It was a hard choice, for it seemed as if California lay on the other side of the world. But without hesitation Ellen chose California; it was what Cump wanted and it pointed to a better future.

The decision upset her parents much more than it did Ellen. They would be too lonely, they said; they would never see the babies, and they would lose Ellen too. Perhaps, Mrs. Ewing said, with only a small hope in her voice, they could let them keep Minnie for a while; later when they were settled the Ewings would take her to her parents.

At first it seemed an impossible thing even to consider, but after long thought Cump and Ellen realized it would soften the pain of separation for her parents, and after all Minnie could be brought to them before very long. So they agreed. And then Captain Sherman sent in his letter of resignation to the army.

With Ellen and Cump and Lizzie went Mary Lynch as nurse for the little girl. As they settled themselves in the carriage that was to drive them to Columbus, Ellen suddenly realized fully what it meant to leave Minnie. She looked back as they drove away, and saw her father holding the child high in his arms. "Elly," he had said to her, "I'll never be homesick for you as long as I can take a good look at Minnie." But what of herself, her heart was now demanding.

They went by the cars to New York, and were two nights on the way, sleeping on long seats, Cump keeping a soldierly watch most of the time. For their meals they ate the tongue and bread and grapes Mrs. Ewing had put up for them, and whenever they stopped at a station Cump bought ale.

From her hotel Ellen wrote a short note home, saying she was going to buy for Minnie the bonnet and the dishes and spoons she wanted. "And have her always say her little prayer: Holy Mary, pray for us."

Tom Ewing was in New York and helped with the shopping, not only for Minnie but for the many things the Shermans must take with them. "Honestly, Cump," reported Tom, who had spent most of the day with Ellen, "I think we have today dealt with fully a third of the storekeepers on Broadway. We went as far as Thirty-second Street — only because that was as far as the omnibus ran."

While in New York the Shermans went to pay calls on the Hoyts in Brooklyn and the Shermans in Norwalk, and on the surface everything was gay and pleasant. But when a letter came from her mother Ellen knew how shallow her gaiety had been. The letter was meant to be cheering but it had the opposite effect. The Archbishop had come to see them and remarked that Ellen had not taken herself away: she had left half of herself behind in Minnie. Then Ellen's tears fell. Half? Just now she felt as if she had left all of herself back in Lancaster.

On September 19th Ellen Sherman sat repacking for the voyage they would begin next day. There was no pleasure in the task. Rather she had the feeling that someone she loved was dead. Worst of all the

promised telegram of farewell from her mother had not come; she
kept hoping it would until the very moment the ship left. She knew
it would have told her only that Minnie was well and happy, but
even that would have been something to take with her — the tangible
statement of a fact.

It was a hard and an unpleasant trip. The meals were poor; the
decks were crowded. Most of the food was in cans and tasted of them.
There was only a small allowance of washing water daily and they
drank the condensed water from the boilers. When they reached San
Juan del Norte at the mouth of the Nicaragua River they transferred
to another boat, large but with no cabins, so that they had to sleep
on the floor. Mary Lynch was by this time in what she herself termed
a state and heartily wished herself at home.

A skiff took them ashore at Virgin Bay, and from there they began
a twelve mile trip overland on mule back. Mary gingerly mounted
one, Ellen another, and Cump took Lizzie with him on a third. "I
like it," called back Ellen, "and anyway it is a lot better than that
awful boat."

In the afternoon they reached the San Juan del Sur where they were
to take a steamer for the rest of the way to California. The boat had
to anchor some distance out in the harbor and the natives made a
chair of their hands to carry the passengers through the surf. Ellen
landed safely and looked back to see Mary behind her being borne
along with Lizzie in her lap. Suddenly Mary began to scream with
fright, and the noise so alarmed Lizzie that she became convulsed
with fear, and it took hours for Ellen to quiet the terrified child.


They were all glad indeed when on October 15, 1853, they reached
San Francisco. It had been a long weary trip — down the Atlantic,
across the Isthmus, and up the Pacific coast, with all travel lacking
any sort of comfort.

Ellen was not greatly impressed with the city which was to be her
home. The sunlight was lovely but it showed up cruelly the dirty
streets, the rough huts. "Even so it has grown a lot since I was here

six years ago," said Cump. "There are some brick houses now and there were only shacks then."

He had found a house for her even before they came, rented from a friend of his. But Ellen was thoroughly dismayed at sight of her new surroundings. There was no yard at back or front of the little house. The street was narrow and full of sand, and high winds whistled through the thin, unplastered walls. Fleas and flies were swarming. And there were, a neighbor told her, many wanderers and tramps in the city, brought by the lure of gold. The one delight was the climate with its bright sunny days and cool nights.

"I'll feel at home in a little while," Ellen promised Cump, but in her heart she wondered if she ever really would. It was as though they were in a far-off country with no familiar objects about. Minnie was a thousand miles away and it would take weeks, perhaps months, to hear any news of her. But before she had been a week in the city Ellen realized she had less complaint to make than many other women: many here had been obliged to leave their children with strangers in the East, while her own little girl was surrounded by loving relatives.

A lesser difficulty was that they had been able to bring so little from home to furnish the house, and there was not much to buy in San Francisco except at exorbitant prices. Then one day Cump gave her a wonderful surprise: he sent home a piano. So in the evenings she played gay bits from memory, as well as from the sheet music he found for her. Sometimes Cump danced about the room to some tune with Lizzie in his arms, or he and Ellen sang old-fashioned songs together to her accompaniment.

But what Ellen really lived for were the mails from Lancaster and the news in the Lancaster *Gazette*. The mail steamers came only once a month and left that often, so when they did arrive there were always many letters. And always they were filled with stories about Minnie. Mr. Ewing wrote that she was as fat as a little pig and in motion all the time: "You may consider her a kind of mythic personage by this time but she is a loving, romping, laughing reality and a very substantial one." She had been very naughty in church one morning and Sissie had to take her out; as she hurried her along the aisle, Minnie smiled sweetly at the congregation, telling them in a high voice about the little girl in the pew next to hers who had been bad.

Not a single day went by that Ellen did not think of Minnie. When she saw a little girl of her daughter's height, she had to control the impulse to put her arms around her and pretend it was Minnie. Sometimes a fit of crying came over her, a yearning for home, a fear that she might never see the child again, an indefinite dread of the future.

She asked Mrs. Ewing to send her scraps of any new dresses she made for Minnie. Often she looked at the clock and added three hours to the time, and tried to figure out just what they were doing in Lancaster at that moment. She read every letter from home over and over, and whether it were grave or gay, it made her cry. And every night before she slept she placed her little girl in the care of the Immaculate Heart of Mary for safety and protection.

She wrote long letters to the absent daughter, closely written pages, for it cost a great deal to send mail so far. And each month in one of her letters was enclosed a gold dollar which was to be saved or spent on toys and charity as Grandma decided. Minnie, wrote Mrs. Ewing, was all for spending it according to her own ideas: "I tan do it. I'm most a young woman," she declared.

Housekeeping in San Francisco was a complicated matter. Servants were hard to get and Ellen and Mary Lynch had to do nearly everything themselves. The first cook who came to them could not cook at all and asked seventy-five dollars a month. The next one got up when she pleased and drew sixty dollars. The third could do little because she had hurt her hands in some way before she came to them. But the fourth, to their relief, seemed a very competent girl.

"How is the new girl?" asked Cump after a few days of her services.

Ellen looked gloomy. *"Nous verrons,"* she said, out of the depth of past experience.

The cost of living was exorbitant. Every Monday Cump gave Ellen seventy-five dollars for the week's expenses, for wages, food, coal, and wood. By the end of the week it was gone, even though Ellen, the usually extravagant, made a great effort to economize. Mutton was fifty cents a pound, good butter a dollar and a quarter. Apples were a dollar each, and so was a small can of apple sauce. A two-sack bucket of coal cost two dollars and a half. Even though they lived simply it cost them six thousand a year.

The rainy season came and brought new problems. The stores were only a block from the house, yet by the time Ellen got home her shoes were full of mud, her dress splashed to the knees. Rubbers were useless, so she bought high boots instead. "I'd rather live in old Granny Weeks' cabin at home than here in any style," she thought rebelliously. "Is this what they call the Promised Land of Eldorado?"

But she asked such questions only of herself, never of Cump. He was working very hard and the asthma from which he had suffered from childhood troubled him that winter. Lizzie too caught cold for the nights were chilly and damp, and the house was thin and unplastered and had no fireplaces. They could talk all they wanted about their mild climate, thought Ellen. She preferred the winds and snows of Ohio, and the good bright fires, with apples and nuts to eat in front of them.

The evenings were lonely, even though they had each other, and it was pleasant when a visitor came. Cump's friend, General Hitchcock, was in the habit of coming over with his flute, and Ellen played his accompaniments. Archbishop Alemany came sometimes, and that was like seeing someone from home, for at one time he had been priest at the Somerset church and sometimes stayed overnight at the Ewing house. Ellen often sent him jellies and cakes and mended his church linen, and often his clothing, too. On the previous July he had laid the cornerstone of Saint Mary's Cathedral in San Francisco, and his extensive diocese ran from the Pacific to the Rocky Mountains. A Spaniard by birth, he was a good prelate for a State which had only recently passed under American rule and which still had many Spanish citizens. When he had been made a bishop he had insisted that he continue wearing the white habit of his order, and he adhered as far as possible to the Rule of St. Dominic.

Sister Aloysius of the Dominicans, who had been Fanny O'Neil, was not far away in Monterey, and Cump promised Ellen he would drive her there as soon as the roads were in good condition. Meantime Ellen sent her by Archbishop Alemany, when he went to Monterey, many things she knew Fanny would like — letters from home, daguerreotypes, patterns and dress materials for the orphans cared for by her community.

On Christmas Eve Ellen went to Mass at midnight with Mary Lynch, and she prayed with all her heart for the dear ones at home. She had kissed Lizzie in her crib and prayed over her before she left the house, and now, in the little church of St. Francis of Assisi, who loved children, she prayed again for her and for Minnie, the darling absent one. And she prayed, too, for the child stirring within her. When she started for home again in the darkness, she felt comforted, thinking that even if she and Minnie were so far apart, they were together with the Child Jesus on this night in a holy region of purity and truth.

Presents came from home, only a little delayed — a beautiful à Kempis from her mother, for Lizzie a big box of toys well wrapped in many papers to keep them from damage. One bit of paper fell to the floor and when Ellen picked it up she found it was a memorandum in her mother's hand: "Fix the church. Presents for Lizzie, Sis, Charley. Aprons. Turkey."

Suddenly she had a vivid picture of their last Christmas at home. Her father had insisted Lizzie be brought to see the table, though she was only a month old, and Minnie had stared at her first Christmas tree with the little colored tapers. Every family in town had come to see the tree, and one old man said it made him feel as if he were back in Bavaria again.

On New Year's Day Ellen and Cump kept open house, and the table was loaded with pound and jelly cakes, wines, brandies, eggnog, champagne. She was surprised to find in her book that night more than sixty names. "And they slighted everything but the eggnog and champagne," she reported to Cump.

A few days later Ellen had what she called a delayed Christmas present, for a Miss Lizzie Fall from the East came to see her. She had seen the Ewings only recently, and had promised she would call on Ellen when she reached San Francisco.

"Did you see Minnie?" asked Ellen eagerly.

Miss Fall nodded. "A few days before I left. She played and sang *Katy Darlin'* for me and told me to tell you she is a good girl."

Miss Fall had brought additional presents, and Lizzie's eyes glowed when she saw the big doll with its cape and cap. But Ellen thought her own best gift was to talk to someone who had seen Minnie lately and could tell her about her.

That same month Ellen heard from Lancaster of the appointment of Father Young as Bishop of Erie. Ellen decided to have her wedding dress, which she had left at home, made into vestments for him, and Mrs. Ewing promised to take care of this for her. She wrote she would have them made by the Ursuline Sisters in Brown County, because they had so many lovely trimmings and ornaments sent them from France.

In February Cump came home with good news. He had found another house, one with a backyard and which was plastered throughout. It was the half of a double house, the other side being occupied by a Navy captain and his wife.

This move brought a welcome change. For one thing, their new home was on higher land, and this brought relief to Cump's asthma. Once during that winter, in the midst of a bad attack, he had said dolefully that he promised himself very few more years of life, and Ellen, though she laughed away his fears, had her own.

The house was built on a wide quiet street, and from her upper windows Ellen could see the Bay and the steamers coming in. There was even a side-door in this house, and wood and coal no longer had to be carried in at the front. She bought a new rug for the living-room, new chairs and a table, and over the mantel she hung her parents' pictures. But there was no picture of Minnie except the baby one, and she wrote her mother begging to have one made at the Daguerre room of herself and Minnie together.

Every morning after she had bathed and dressed Lizzie, Ellen went to the nearby church for the nine o'clock Mass. She liked the little church, which was always crowded, many of the worshippers Spanish women who knelt on mats in the aisles and wore crepe shawls, often beautifully embroidered, their faces almost hidden in the folds. When Ellen went to the church to make a visit, there were always people before the Blessed Sacrament, men as well as women, and for Ellen this was one of the redeeming features of the ugly city.

Ellen received a letter from Father Young thanking her for the vestments which were being made for him. He wrote sadly of being made a bishop, for all he wanted was to stay where he had been for many years, in the town they both loved. Tears filled Ellen's eyes; she could sympathize with him for they were both exiles from home. "Be brave, be patient," he had told her when she left, and now he would have to follow that advice himself.

Later Mrs. Ewing wrote that he had choked up during his sermon when he bade his parishioners goodbye. He had asked them to meet in the church every evening and say the rosary for him.

All through May, her grandmother wrote, Minnie was taking flowers to Our Lady's altar for herself and her far-away mother, and she enclosed in the letter a few petals from a rose that had been on the altar. Ellen put the fragrant blossoms carefully in her missal.

In June 1854, Ellen's first son was born, and Dr. Hewitt said he had never seen a sounder child. With this physician, the brother of the well-known Redemptorist convert in New York, she had long and interesting talks on religion. Dr. Hewitt said he, as a High Church Episcopalian, hated the word Protestant applied to his sect. "It sticks to us though," he said sadly.

The day after his birth, the baby was baptized by Archbishop Alemany, William Ewing Sherman. He was plump and red-haired and Ellen thought him every inch a Sherman.

When she wrote this to her mother, Mrs. Ewing replied, "unless he could be like your dear father in disposition and character, he had better be Sherman than anything else. I trust and pray he may be as fine, as noble a man as his grandfather Sherman."

Lizzie was completely fascinated by the new baby and made herself his immediate champion, even interfering during his baptism because the water had made the baby cry. Ellen thought Lizzie was getting much prettier, but Cump, who adored her, said she was still ugly enough, though he admitted she had very lovely eyes — so dark and sparkling that one day the cook said, "Oh, Lizzie, it wasn't for the good of your soul that those eyes were made."

That year Ellen was saddened by news of the death of Aunt Beecher. Her mother wrote it had been a very happy death; Mrs. Ewing, to whom the dying woman had been a mother for so long, had heard her murmuring little prayers as she sat by her bedside as the end drew near. When the priest began to give her the Last Sacraments, she was unconscious, but she roused for a moment as if listening, and then fell asleep.

In July came the picture of Minnie and her grandmother for which Ellen had begged. It was thoroughly charming, Minnie leaning confidingly against her grandmother, her round little face very solemn and looking exactly as when Ellen saw her last. Mrs. Ewing gazed out of the picture with her own motherly air, her cap framing her face, her cross bright against the dark dress front.

Cump was delighted with the picture, and for days they carried it upstairs and down, so they might have it with them wherever they were. With it had come a picture of the Bishop of Erie in all the glory of his episcopal dress. Poor Bishop Young, thought Ellen. To both of them home was like a Paradise with the gates closed against them.

One day Hampton Denman, one of her Lancaster cousins, came to San Francisco and called on Ellen. He brought her an apple. "I bought it for memory's sake, Ellen. Remember the old tree of summer sweets? This one is as near a summer sweet as I could find."

They divided the apple and ate it gravely. Ellen shook her head and so did he. It did look just like an apple from home but it lacked the flavor, the fine crispness of an Ohio apple.

In August the Shermans at last made the long planned trip to Monterey. Ellen, who had been housebound for a long time, enjoyed the drive through the summer country, the smooth dry roads, the fields of flowers bright under the warm sun. They stopped for the night at a clean neat house where a kind old lady made them welcome, and in talking with her, Ellen found she came from Muskingum County in Ohio. "I'm from Lancaster myself," she told her.

"Then perhaps you know Judge Ewing there?"

"I'm his daughter," said Ellen.

"Well, my dear!" said the old lady in delighted surprise. They agreed it was a small world and she asked about the Beechers and the Irvins and the Boyles, and had a fine evening of reminiscing.

In the convent parlor at Monterey, Sister Aloysius warmly greeted her old friends and kept repeating that it did not really seem possible this was the Cumpy and Elly she used to take care of in the Ewing house. She laughed with them over incidents of the old days, and before they left Ellen brought out a present she had long wanted to give Fanny — a fine shawl to wrap about herself on cool days.

The winter of 1854 saw the rising of the Know-Nothings against the Catholics in San Francisco, and there were threats to burn down the church of St. Francis, near Ellen's home. Ellen was very irate but had to restrain herself, because Cump advised it. "No use lending dignity to their cause by showing anger," he said sensibly.

This crisis passed but another did not. There were several serious business failures and runs on various banks including the one in which Cump's firm had an interest. Lucas, Turner and Company were better prepared than some and managed to weather the storm, and the heads of the firm said it was due in great part to the wise management of young Mr. Sherman.

That winter the Shermans moved again. This time they bought a house, one large enough for their growing family. They had a horse now and a cow and chickens and a fine secure yard where the babies could play.

# 8. *Lancaster Again*

## [1854-1855]

FOR SOME months the Shermans had been talking of a visit home for Ellen, and Cump wanted her to bring Minnie back with her to San Francisco. Ellen agreed with this plan, for it was time Minnie returned to her family. Mrs. Ewing's letters were no longer enough to console her for the absence of her child.

It was true her mother tried to tell Ellen everything about Minnie. She even wrote letters sometimes at Minnie's dictation; she sent beads — the joint gift of Minnie and herself. She described how Minnie could sing little songs in a very true voice; how she loved to cook and worked for hours over a biscuit dough and molasses combination which she called pound cake. She carried her own private purse like a lady of fortune — "something few of the Ohio ladies can boast," commented Maria drily. Then she said it would soon be time for dancing school, and Minnie was practicing dancing all the time. She also told how they had taken the child on a trip to what she called "Washing City," and they had all had a good time.

Sometimes Ellen found herself resentful that Minnie had so much and Lizzie so little. When Mrs. Ewing wrote about the wonderful new playhouse built for Minnie, Ellen felt rebelliously that Lizzie ought to be enjoying it too. But Lizzie out in the yard was happily and unconcernedly calling, "Ticky, ticky," to her two pet chickens, and evidently wanted nothing more than she had. She was beginning to talk now, but in a language of her own and difficult to understand. She imitated very clearly the huckster's cries of "charcoal" and "fresh fish," but nothing else was intelligible. She was still a very little thing, much smaller than Minnie at her age, and not much bigger than her brother Willy, who was a big, eager, almost a violent child. When he wanted something he plunged for it, very much, thought Ellen, like his father, who was addicted to sudden movements. He and Lizzie had the same unruly hair and Ellen was using stick pomatum to keep it back and out of their eyes. "I only wish there were as easy a remedy for taming stiff wills," she said to Cump.

The discussion about the trip home went on. Cump encouraged it, for it meant Minnie would come back to them. Ellen found an excellent nurse to take care of the children during her absence and Cump promised to be at home every evening. And the trip was much easier now, for the Isthmus railroad was completed and it would take only two weeks to go by the Panama route.

On April 16, 1855, Ellen set sail in the *Golden Age,* and many friends went with her to the wharf to say goodbye. As the boat started out of the harbor Cump stood with Lizzie in his arms, while the nurse held up Willy; then the figures of the children and Cump grew dim and vanished from Ellen's sight.

The *Golden Age* was a fine ship, with pleasant cabins and good decks. Ellen sat at the Captain's table and enjoyed the talk, and at night played euchre or listened to the music of voices and guitar. But all this she did with only half her mind; the rest was back in San Francisco. She hoped Biddy was airing the rooms well and not covering the children too warmly at night, and that she had plenty of clean dresses for Lizzie. Already she missed them terribly — Lizzie's voice with question marks at the end of almost every sentence; Willy's sweet smile that was reward enough for anything. Mornings she thought of them having their baths, Willy splashing gaily in the tub, Lizzie half afraid to be put in. "Oh, don't," Ellen could almost hear the little voice saying.

The last night on shipboard was clear and moonlit, the sea like a mirror. On the next day — the 28th — they expected to be in Panama and change to another ship. But that night the passengers were awakened by a crash, and Ellen heard at her door the excited voice of Patrick Egan, a lad who was traveling alone and to whom she had been kind. He was shouting her name, and when she answered he told her, "The ship has struck a coral reef and ripped her bottom from bow to stern. But don't be alarmed, Mrs. Sherman, I'm a good swimmer and I'll save you."

By the time she reached the dining-room, the ship's fires had been almost put out by the flooding water. Orders were given to beach the ship, and life boats were lowered. Signals had been sent up, but no help had come.

Another day passed; salt water had got into the drinking water tanks, and there were several terrible tropical storms with violent lightning and thunder. Still their signals went unseen until the third day when the *John Stevens* hailed them and the passengers were transferred to that ship. Transferred once more, they docked at New York on Sunday, May 13th.

The first thing Ellen saw on the wharf was Charley's yellow head and his arm wildly waving his hat. When they met she asked, "How is Minnie?" and in the same breath he asked, "Are you all right?" and then they both laughed and began to talk one at a time.

"You won't know Minnie, she's grown so," he told her. And Ellen reassured him that no harm had come to her on the wrecked vessel. What she wanted though first of all was something to eat. Because of the increase in the number of passengers on the steamer there had been no food at all left for breakfast, and very little the night before for tea. And Ellen thought she ought to stop to buy a few presents.

"For Pa and Ma if you want to," said Charley, "but don't get anything for Minnie. She's got too much now."

A wire was sent to Mrs. Ewing telling her the time of their arrival, for she was sending the carriage to Columbus for them. All the way on the cars Ellen felt that Charley was trying to tell her something, but that he hesitated to do so. Finally when the carriage was halfway to Lancaster, he managed to come out with it. "Look, Ellen, please don't try to take Minnie back with you. Honestly I don't think Father could live without her."

She had faced this possibility more than once on the boat, and she wanted to say now that Cump, too, wanted his little daughter. But she could not say so to Charley who, for all his eighteen years, was still only a child in knowledge, so she merely smiled at him. "Oh, Charley," she said, "before I talk about leaving her again I want to see her first."

When the carriage stopped before the brick house in Lancaster and Ellen saw her family waiting for her, she could hardly see for the tears in her eyes. When she saw Minnie she could not believe that she was the baby she had left two years before. Minnie was now tall and very pretty, but she greeted her mother as if she were a stranger to whom a little girl must be polite. Later she unbent, but it was to her grandmother that she turned if she wanted anything. This hurt Ellen, although she told herself that it would take a little time to get reacquainted with her daughter.

Ellen thought her mother looked well, but her father seemed ill and infirm, although he stoutly declared he felt as well as ever. "I am not so fleshy as formerly," he admitted, "but I have more capacity for business than I have enjoyed for ten or twelve years." He even insisted that he liked his diet — a bowl of boiled milk and crackers three times a day. "You can hardly imagine how perfectly it satisfies me, and how well it agrees with me," he said.

There was so much for Mrs. Ewing to tell about Minnie, and Ellen had so much news about the other children, that it seemed the days of her visit would not be long enough for it all. When Ellen said to her mother that Lizzie was slow in learning to talk, Mrs. Ewing merely shrugged. "All the children who resemble dear Pa are like that. But when they talk, they talk well."

Minnie, at four, always had a book or two under her arm and was asking someone of the household to read aloud to her. When no one had the time, she tried to spell out the stories herself from the pictures. Her favorite bit at that time was "The Boy Stood on the Burning Deck," and Mrs. Ewing thought this very unusual. "I would expect her grandfather to admire that, and perhaps drop a tear; but would you believe a child of four could admire such a piece?"

One day when Mr. Ewing, who, despite his insistence on fine health spent much of his time resting, was asleep, Mrs. Ewing began to discuss her husband with Ellen. "The Archbishop has had many talks with your father and he thinks he will surely come into the Church some day."

"Does he show any actual signs of it?" asked practical Ellen.

"Well, no," said Maria. "Last winter when he was so ill I prayed hard, but when he showed no signs of coming in, I knew he would recover. I know he will not be taken away until he enters the Ark of Safety. Let us hope, Ellen, hope on and hope ever."

Ellen told her mother about their visit to Fanny, and of Archbishop Alemany who always spoke gratefully of the Ewings' hospitality when he was in Lancaster. His new cathedral in San Francisco was finished now, but it had little equipment. She had helped all she could.

Mrs. Ewing was not very happy about their own new priest in Lancaster. He was a fine, good man, she admitted, but he was also very progressive, too much so, some of them thought. "He wants to change the inside of St. Mary's. He says that Lancaster is behind the times, and the town is so quiet and dull the church seems to him a monastery in the woods. How do you like that?"

Ellen laughed. "Cump would like him. That sounds just like his opinion of Lancaster."

Maria sniffed. "I wonder what Father Young — I can't remember to call him Bishop — will say to that. This town always suited him until they took him away and made him a bishop. And another thing," Mrs. Ewing went on with her grievance, "Father Lange doesn't like the candlesticks on the high altar. 'Doleful' he says they are. And they were made to order for Father Young. Now we are going to have a new set from Cincinnati, if you please, and they are going to cost sixty dollars."

Ellen, despite her mother's strictures, admired Father Lange's efficiency, and his efforts to improve his church. He had called a few days after Ellen's return, on a begging errand for an order called the Passionists. He brought a member with him, an Italian just come from Rome who was asking for aid in building a monastery in Pittsburgh. Everyone gave him something — Ellen and Maria five dollars each, and Minnie brought him one of her hoarded gold dollars.

Father Lange had ideas about teaching children their faith, and he discussed them with Ellen. "In this country," he said, and his blue eyes were very serious, "people do not begin early enough to teach their children to know and to love God. They can understand something of their Faith as soon as they are old enough to talk." And Ellen agreed.

Sooner or later all Ellen's talks with her father or with her mother, came back to one subject — Minnie. Her father was always telling her of something Minnie said or did. He himself sometimes seemed aware the stories were not very exciting or amusing. "Elly, it isn't so much her words as the manner and the show of feeling and intelligence with which they are spoken," he said. And once he remarked, "She has been the bright link between her dear mama and papa and the loved ones here. Our home would have been desolate indeed without her."

They had not spoiled her for all their affection. Minnie was generous with her store of toys whenever her little cousins came to the house, and she was sweet and loving with her mother. But it was the grandparents to whom she went with her joys and her troubles. She still slept in the room with them, although Mrs. Ewing had suggested the trundle bed be moved into Ellen's room. At that Minnie's face had clouded over, and Ellen hastily suggested they leave it where it was for the present.

She began to wonder if she ought perhaps to be careful not to get Minnie attached to her too much, for it was being borne in on her that it would be almost cruel to take the child away with her. "I can't take her away," she thought despairingly, "when Papa is so sick and infirm." And then she thought, "But what will Cump say?" Surely Cump would be willing if he could only see the situation. He would not be so selfish as to refuse to her father this one child of their three for a while longer. Surely later Minnie would learn to love her parents just as much as if she had spent all her life with them.

This hope sometimes became fear, for Minnie herself had evidently no desire to go with her mother to California. Once when they went to Somerset to see Charley take part in the exhibition, Ellen said smiling, "What if we were on our way to California now?" Minnie burst into tears and begged, "Don't say it. Don't say it."

After that Minnie was afraid that any trip to a nearby town meant going West and she could hardly be coaxed into a carriage unless her grandparents were in it too. Still she loved to hear about her father and was anxious to see him. It was only when Ellen suggested that they go together to him, that she would not agree.

The child seemed, in fact, to have her relations with her parents and her grandparents twisted. She had the idea that Cump was Ellen's brother, that Mrs. Ewing and Ellen were sisters, and one day she even told Ellen she wished she would go away soon — "then Grandma would be my only mother."

In June, Ellen received from Cump a daguerreotype of the two children at home, and a sketch he had made of the house with Willy and Lizzie looking out of the window. He assured her they were both well, and that she need not hurry home.

Ellen was glad of reassurance, of course, but she worried just the same. Was Willy having trouble with his teething? Would Lizzie become really ill if she had one of her fits of holding her breath? Foolish little fears, and if she were with the children they would evaporate, but now their importance was magnified. Must she always be lonely for one or the other of her children, she wondered? Then she put away the thought. She must put it away, for she realized by now that she could not take Minnie back with her. She wrote Cump the unhappy facts and waited for his answer.

The last week in October, Ellen Sherman was preparing to go back to San Francisco. And she was going back without Minnie. Cump had written that he understood the situation and agreed to let the child remain in Lancaster, but with the understanding that on her next visit home Ellen was to bring Minnie back. The Ewings were so relieved and grateful to hear that Minnie could stay with them a time longer that it was almost worth the pain Ellen felt at leaving her again.

Minnie too seemed to realize that her mother was going away. She began following her from room to room, and one day she took her medal from around her neck, wrapped it up carefully and gave it to Ellen to take to her father. She even asked to go as far as Columbus when Charley took her mother to the cars, but Ellen felt she must leave the child in her own home for her last sight of her or she could not leave her at all.

On the last day of October she was in New York again, and spent a day shopping for a blue sacque for Minnie and a muff and a locket. She bought a breast-pin for Philemon's Mary, a shawl for her mother, and collars for the maids. She sent a short note to her mother before she sailed; "with a last kiss to Minnie," it ended, "and dearest love to all, I say once more, dear mother, farewell."

The *John Law* was a steady steamer and the sea at first was smooth. But in Ellen's heart was storm and dreariness as she looked out over the wide spaces, and the emptiness between sea and sky. The weather grew rougher as the days went on, and finally came a storm worse than any she had endured on the *Golden Age*. The Commander laughed and said it was just the ship shaking her feathers after a dip in the water, but the passenger who sat next to Ellen at the Captain's table murmured that it was more like an elephant trying to get rid of an unwelcome burden. She ate little on the trip and was thankful for the brandied cherries Charley had given her as a parting gift.

After the transfer to another ship at Panama, the weather improved. The ship was late in reaching the San Francisco wharf and Ellen felt so weary and worn after a sleepless night that she wished Cump could not see her until she was more presentable. But Cump, who had been pacing the wharf for hours, was too happy to see her at all to pay any attention to how she looked.

He had the carriage waiting and they drove back home. Ellen did not wait to be helped out, but flew ahead of him into the house, through the parlor and up the stairs into the sitting-room. And there stood Lizzie in her petticoat, just out of her bath. She was in Ellen's arms when Willy, hearing the commotion, appeared too, toddling from behind a trunk. When Ellen caught him up in turn, he took one look at the strange woman and held out his arms, weeping, to Biddy.

When Cump went to his office, Ellen settled to unpacking and the distributing of gifts. One, Cump's special gift, she put on the parlor table so that he would see it as soon as he came into the room — it was a picture of Minnie which she had had Beard paint for him in Columbus.

When he saw it the look on his face was worth all the trouble and expense. He carried it from room to room trying to decide where it looked best, and when anyone came to the house he was shown the picture, even before Ellen could invite the guest to sit down. "This is our little girl," he said, and when Ellen heard the pride in his voice she thought again how unselfish it was of him to allow her parents to keep Minnie in Lancaster.

Ellen thought Cump looked far from well. His asthma was worse, and he had an alarming cough. The children, however, were very well. Lizzie was a little taller and much prettier, and she remembered her mother and clung to her. When on her first night at home, Ellen was hearing her prayers and she came to "Holy Mother, pray for Mama and bring her home to me," a phrase she had been repeating for months, she looked up puzzled, then smiled: her mother *was* at home.

But it took some time for Willy to get used to her. For weeks he regarded her as an intruder, clinging instead to his nurse. The latter had taught him that when anyone asked him where he came from to say, "fra Donegal, God help me," which was amusing, but he had somehow learned other things too — to kick and even to swear, which was rather advanced for nineteen months, and Ellen set to work to cure him.

## 9. San Francisco and Fort Leavenworth

### [1856–1859]

IN THE summer of 1856, trouble broke out in San Francisco. It began with a quarrel between two newspaper editors, one of whom — James Casey, by name — shot the other man, James King. Rioting broke out and there was great danger that Casey might be lynched. Sherman, recently appointed major general of the State militia, went to the mayor of the city asking him to act, since the jail where Casey was lodged was not mob proof. But nothing was done, and the Vigilance Committee of earlier years was revived and grew until five thousand members were enrolled.

King died, and the city broke into turmoil, for it was now entirely in the hands of the Committee. The sheriff was unable to defend the jail, and the governor of California who came from Sacramento to confer with Sherman did not succeed in restoring power into the hands of the proper authorities. Casey was seized, tried and hanged by the Vigilantes.

During these events, Cump was tireless in his efforts to support the forces of law and order, and requested, but did not obtain, the help of the U.S. Arsenal in Benicia. Feeling that nothing could be done, he resigned his command of the militia. Even after Casey's execution, the Vigilantes would not give up their power; there was violence and disorder in the city, and Cump sent his family to San Mateo until the trouble subsided. Since Ellen was expecting another baby in October, he felt it was better for her to be away from excitement and possible danger.

When Ellen's family in Ohio heard of all this, Mr. Ewing wrote Cump urging him to send the family home for a while out of such an anarchical state of government. He added — and when Ellen read the letter she smiled at the craftiness of the suggestion — that Cump would then have a chance to lay up some cash after they were gone.

But the trouble subsided, and the fears passed. Ellen came home again and, when she saw how happy Cump was to see her, she decided she would never leave him again. He was working very hard now, and he had little help; sometimes before the arrival of a steamer he spent the whole night in his office working on the outgoing mail. He could not ask for a larger salary, however, for the profits of the business did not justify it; but the fact was that they were not living within their income. Everything Cump earned, and it was a good salary, was spent immediately. Ellen tried to economize. She let one servant go; she sold the cow and sent the horse to pasture and dismissed the man who drove her carriage. Food was the great item in their expenses, but she managed to cut down here and there. "One thing I don't buy," she wrote her mother, "and that is strawberries, for they are five dollars a quart."

Despite the coming baby and the two others to care for, the Shermans entertained a great deal that summer and autumn. They gave several dinners each week, the guests being people from Cump's office, the military who lived in the city, occasionally the Archbishop or his assistant, Father Hugh Gallagher.

"Sixteen years ago," said the Archbishop as he sat at their table one evening, "your mother entertained me in your home. I wish she were with us this evening. I could thank her then in person for the fine things she sent for our cathedral, especially that exquisite stole the ladies embroidered for me."

The Archbishop, as an old Ohio man, was interested to hear that the cars now went right to Lancaster. "It is the greatest imaginable convenience," Ellen told him. "To go to Cincinnati takes but five hours now including the omnibus."

Cump and Ellen were receiving a great deal of family news those days. Tom had married Ellen Cox of Philadelphia, and now there was another Ellen Ewing in the family. Charley was going to Kansas to carry out some work for his father there. The coming presidential elections were causing great excitement, for Lancaster was very much divided between Buchanan and Fremont.

"Well," said Ellen, "if I had twenty votes, Cump, I'd cast them all for Buchanan and against Fremont. I'm like you; I'm in favor of the Union."

News of Minnie was a part of every letter from home. She weighed forty-nine pounds on the scales at Miller's store, and Mrs. Ewing sent Ellen a paper strip showing the child's exact height. She had lost two front teeth. She knew her letters, and Uncle Charley had bought her an alphabet in big letters, each on a separate card. Mrs. Ewing had taken her to Somerset to see an ordination at St. Joseph's, and they had gone to see the Sisters afterwards. They invited Minnie to come to school there as her mother had done years ago. "Maybe I'll come some other time," Minnie had answered politely.

At Somerset the cornerstone had been laid for another church, the walls of which were to be built around the little old one. It was St. Dominic's day and the Sisters had prepared a fine dinner to which Archbishop Purcell invited Mrs. Ewing and several other ladies, but they refused. "We knew the men could have a better time alone," she wrote. Minnie, a favorite of the Archbishop, had given him material for a story which he repeated often. He asked her why she always wore blue and Minnie told him, "Because I am addicted to the Blessed Virgin."

They had gone on a trip to Cincinnati and there met Mrs. Sarah Peter, whom Mrs. Ewing liked very much. Mrs. Peter in her turn was much taken with Minnie, who had solemnly assured her when introduced that "there are three generations of us." She invited them to call and showed them her wonderful collection of fine paintings and sculpture, collected during her numerous travels.

Mr. Ewing was now much better. He sent word to Ellen that he planned to stay for a long time right in Lancaster — "my favorite watering place."

Ellen hoped that her baby would be born on her own thirty-second birthday, but he did not arrive until a week later, on October 12th. He was a fine boy — "ten and a half pounds with only one petticoat, a night slip and a light flannel shawl on," reported Cump, after he and the doctor had weighed him. He was born with a caul over his face. "That means he will have second sight," said his nurse. Ellen, looking at the fuzz on top of his head, was certain it was not going to be red, but even so he looked exactly like Cump.

The Archbishop was out of town and Father Gallagher officiated at the baptism. There was no doubt about the baby's name: Thomas Ewing Sherman.

The children loved him. Lizzie called him her "small baby," and wanted to hold him. But meantime she constituted herself chief nurse for Willy. "Come, it's your bedtime," she would say to him sternly, and when he was undressing she kept up a stream of remarks. "Take out your little hands. Pick up your foot. Now over your head." The fact that he was much bigger than she did not seem to bother either of them.

One day Ellen took them both to town and bought Willy his first suit. "I'll go home in it," he announced. "I won't take it off." He was so proud that he insisted on riding in front with the man and not with the ladies in the carriage. When he strutted before his father that evening in the new suit, Cump laughed and said, "Ellen, he looks just like his grandfather Boyle." And Ellen agreed.

Each night when Ellen went upstairs to see if the three of them were well covered, she had a picture in her heart of Minnie asleep in her little bed in her grandmother's room. The holy angels were guarding her, she reminded herself, when she grew rebellious — could any watch be better? But when Lizzie sometimes asked, "When can we go to Minnie?" Ellen's heart echoed the question.

Christmas 1856 was a gay day and the nursery was deep in presents. During the week that followed Ellen was very busy, for Cump had made plans for a New Year's reception, and she had all the arrangements to make. She set the tables the night before, loading them with two turkeys, large cakes, nuts and candies and olives. There was to be coffee, brandy and champagne. Almost a hundred callers came, and Lizzie was brought to the parlor in a little blue and white embroidered dress which her grandmother had sent her for Christmas.

When the Archbishop came, Ellen took him to see the baby asleep in his crib, and tried to tell him of her feeling that this child would do some special work in the world. "Perhaps," she said, "he'll even become a famous priest and some day preach in this very diocese." The Archbishop said he would pray that this might come to pass.

Early in 1857 Cump came home evenings with talk of business troubles in the city, still disturbed from the Vigilante riots. One night he said it might be a good idea if he sent Ellen and the children home to Ohio, and so saved the heavy expenses — growing heavier almost daily — and also the continuous uncertainty as to what might happen. There he would have them all in safety. But even though Ellen wanted to be at home again, she opposed his plan: if she went Cump might get sick again, and besides she did not want him to be alone.

"Why can't we all go?" she asked desperately, but Cump shook his head with finality. He had made a contract and he must stay. But when there was a question of the firm of Lucas, Turner and Company closing their San Francisco office, Ellen began to make actual preparations to go: Cump would follow soon, she was certain.

And then one evening he brought home wonderful news: he was coming with them to Lancaster, and see them settled there. Then he would take care of business for his firm in the East, and perhaps even be able to arrange for a transfer to the New York branch.

Ellen wrote to her mother that they were leaving. "Pray we may have a safe voyage," she ended. "The Star that guides me will I know rest over the home I love."

On a bright day in June the five Shermans drove from Columbus to Lancaster and on the same day reached the house on the Hill. This reunion was a wonderful one. For the grandparents there were two new grandchildren to be admired. For the parents there was Minnie, a big girl of more than five years, very shy with her mother and father. It made Ellen's heart sink to see how she still turned to her grandparents as if they were her parents. She knew Cump saw it too, though he never mentioned the matter.

Of the Ewing children, Sissie was away at school, Tom and Hugh were in Leavenworth practicing law and engaging in a land agency business which they hoped would prove highly profitable. Philemon and Mary still lived in Lancaster with their children.

Gas had been installed in the Ewing house since Ellen's last visit. It seemed odd to be writing and sewing by gas light, and Ellen thought privately that it was not so agreeable for ordinary use as was a lamp or candles — and downright dangerous in bedrooms. "But what an improvement when you have company evenings," she said.

Maria had exciting news to tell her about Mrs. Judge Whitman, who had come out in a new costume: pantaloons, coat and hat. "A ribbon on the hat was her only adornment," said Maria, who had not herself seen the amazing sight as yet. But those who had, said Mrs. Whitman's coat was only an inch below her knees and when she sat down her limbs were exposed from the knee down. A troop of children followed her when she walked on the street.

Cump could stay only a few days, and then went on to New York. Ellen persuaded her parents to take Sissie and go for a trip to Canada while she took charge of the housekeeping.

She and the children went often to the farm where Charley was now in charge. There were strawberries, as many as the children could eat, and they could run about all day watching the ducks and chickens and the dairy-maid milking the cows and making butter, and they hunted eggs to take home for their dinner.

Ellen felt a deep content during those summer days for she was sure Cump would not have to return to the West for some time, and she sang like a lark at her work. Minnie and Lizzie and the canary sang too, and Willy joined in his deep voice which, said Ellen, was more like the croaking of a seventeen-year-old than the tender wail of a child. There was only one minor tragedy: one of the dogs ate Willy's best hat.

Of them all Minnie was the only one who was ever unhappy. She was gay and satisfied during the day, but at night she wanted her grandmother, and she often wished Grandpa would come home so he would play cards with her, for he and Minnie were accomplished Old Maid players. Minnie was growing more and more affectionate with her mother and the rest of her family, but she made it very clear that she did not want to go with them if it meant leaving the Ewings.

In the fall unhappy news came from Cump. Matters in New York had gone well until, in late August, a series of bank failures threw Wall Street into a panic, and western stocks also tumbled. Cump's firm again weathered the storm, but the St. Louis branch came close to failure and Cump was ordered to take funds banked by them in New York back to St. Louis with him. Then he was to go to San Francisco and wind up the firm's business there.

This time Ellen's buoyant spirits sank very low, for it meant nearly another year of separation — a dark prospect indeed. The one ray of light was Cump's promise to stop in Lancaster before he went West. But where were they to go next? What would happen? She had wandered enough with her children, she said to herself, and when one letter from Cump suggested he might go back into the army, she wept in dismay, for that meant only more wandering.

When he came in December, she found him so low in mind that it was she who had to pretend to be cheerful. "Am I to be only a vagabond?" he asked bitterly. "I'm beginning to lose what little self-respect I ever had. And how can I cut myself off so completely from you and the children? I really envy those businessmen who just nonchalantly wipe out old accounts and begin again and feel no regret."

Ellen put her arms around him as he sat hunched up on the old sofa. "You did your part and your motives were of the best. And you have fine assets left — among them a strong will and a good intellect."

Cump managed a small smile. "Well, there is nothing to do but to see how this works out. Surely by next spring we will know where we are going."

Ellen nodded. "And God has already given us so many blessings. Surely our future will be one of quiet peace and joy. I do feel that, Cump."

The year 1858 went by slowly and sadly for Ellen Sherman. There was plenty to occupy her hands with work in the house and with the children. But Lancaster, the beloved city, was no longer her place of delight since Cump was not there.

In the late summer word came from the West: Cump would be home in September and Ellen counted the days and waited impatiently. She even figured out the exact time of his arrival on the omnibus. When the vehicle actually appeared, she was waiting at the gate, like a young girl come to meet her lover, and the first news she gave him was that she had that very day put up twenty glasses of currant jelly for his exclusive use!

This time the two had seriously to consider their future, for Cump was thirty-eight years old, with only his army experience and his unhappy business years behind him. Thomas Ewing had several suggestions to offer, but they were merely that. "You could be my agent for my salt works in Chauncey," he said. "I am badly in need of a good man there, or even better you could handle the investments in Indian Creek near Leavenworth for me, and then you would be near Tom and Hugh. Leavenworth is full of Lancaster people and you two would feel at home there."

This latter plan appealed to Cump, and he decided to take the offer and go out immediately. This time Ellen was glad to have him leave, for it meant they would soon be together. She tried to impress on him that he was not to worry because they would have so little money. "When you get there if your means won't permit anything else, rent a log cabin, get a rag carpet and a stove and if we have fuel and bread, meat and coffee and sugar we can get along."

Cump laughed at her earnestness, but she meant it. She would wear cheap clothes, she told herself, and dress the children inexpensively; she would live far away from her church if necessary. She would do all her own work. No matter how small or mean the house, she would make the best of it if only they could cheer each other with their undivided love.

From Leavenworth he wrote that prospects were brighter than he had anticipated. He had met army friends and had been offered a position as bridge superintendent by Major Van Vliet, and he could devote time in addition to the Indian Creek real estate business. Tom and Hugh also wanted him to come into their law firm for as long as he wished. He had already been admitted to the bar, he wrote, without examination — "on the ground of general intelligence."

The Ewings went to Washington to attend Hugh's wedding, and Sissie was one of the bridesmaids. The bride was Henrietta Young, daughter of the house where Ellen had spent such happy days when she was a homesick girl at Georgetown. Father Dominic Young performed the ceremony in the private chapel at Gisboro.

Mrs. Ewing came home a week after the wedding and insisted that Ellen take her place with Mr. Ewing in Washington, "you have had so much housekeeping," she said. "Now you shall play the fashionable lady and I will stay home and attend the house." And because she thought Ellen looked white and tired she sent with her a jug of currant shrub, specially made by the Ewing cook. "It is of course best to put a little brandy in it," she advised.

Hugh's wedding had been wonderful, she said, with great numbers of guests — Youngs and Fenwicks and Ewings, Blaines and Walkers among them. There had been frozen Roman punch and cakes of every description, and the champagne and punch made everyone very happy.

Ellen only half agreed to stay until her father was ready to come home, even though she loved Washington — "so much better than that stiff-starched Philadelphia." But it turned out just as she had said it would: before long, Ellen was homesick, longing for her children. "I cannot live out of the sound of their voices," she told her father.

On October 12th, Ellen had an urgent letter from Cump: could she come to Leavenworth right away and bring the children? He supposed she would have trouble getting Minnie and the Ewings away from each other, but his letter took it for granted that Minnie would come with the rest.

This time Mr. Ewing said nothing about leaving any of the children, even when Minnie showed signs of distress at the idea of going away from her grandparents. "So look out for all of us," wrote Ellen to Cump, "and make up your mind to keep us the rest of our lives, for we will never be shaken off again even for a season."

But, on November 4th, when the little group left Lancaster, one was missing. Mrs. Ewing and Minnie had wept so bitterly that Ellen had to agree to leave the child again in Lancaster. How to face Cump she did not know, for he had written in his last letter, "I suppose you had a hard time tearing Minnie away from her grandma."

This time even Mrs. Ewing was uneasy. "Tell Cump with my love he must not feel too disappointed that our little pet, the first of his flock, is not with the rest," she told Ellen. And she promised that he would see a great improvement in Minnie's studies when he saw her again.

They reached St. Louis on November first, and, after eight long tiresome days on the Missouri River, landed at Leavenworth. They had not been able to travel during the nights which were so dark that they had to tie up at the dock when it grew dusk. But Ellen dreaded more than any danger in the dark, Cump's disappointment when he found Minnie was not with them.

Willy was very homesick for Lancaster all the way. "I can't go to Tommy Ewing's yard today," he said, when his mother asked why he looked so glum.

At the wharf in Leavenworth were Cump and Hugh and Tom, their faces beaming as they greeted the travelers and hurried them to the house which Hugh had built for his bride, and Henrietta made them very welcome. Cump had glanced in a general way at his family as they came off the ship, and then had looked questioningly at his wife whose eyes filled with tears as she shook her head. Cump's face grew dark, but the shadow lifted when he saw Willy. Ellen hoped fervently the older son would make him at least partly forget his disappointment that his daughter was not there.

Tom's wife Ellen was away on a visit with her family in the East, and Tom had suggested that the Shermans live in his house until they found what they wanted. Would Ellen stay there until Tom's Ellen came back, and would she board her brother too? And Ellen gladly agreed.

Cump was looking well and he said the climate agreed with him. "Not a trace of asthma since I came here," he declared.

Ellen liked Tom's pleasant roomy house and only wished it were her own. The Leavenworth markets were very good: the food was not too expensive. Even Willy gave the town a grudging approval, perhaps chiefly because in one of its shops his father had bought him a bear hunter's cap.

Lizzie was becoming a great help to her mother. She dried dishes and dusted and made herself so useful that busy Ellen sometimes wondered what she would do without her little services. She was planning to send Lizzie to the Sisters' school in the spring and Minnie with her, for the Ewings had promised to visit Leavenworth and bring Minnie. When, in discussing this visit, a letter from Lancaster hinted that Minnie thought she was coming only for a visit too, and expected to go back with her grandparents, Ellen was so shocked that she wrote in return that she and Cump had definitely expected Minnie to stay with them this time — "for the rest of our lives, and not merely for a visit." She even wrote a letter to seven-year-old Minnie to explain why she had been away from her parents for so much of her short life. "Because I have given you up," it ended, "you must not think I love you less, but rather let your heart yearn towards me as one enduring a trial through you and for your sake. I know that you are happier and that Grandpa and Grandma are happier or I would not be separated from you now."

Christmas was a bad day for Ellen, remembering last year's gay holiday in Lancaster. There was no money for presents this year either, but the children were happy with stockings full of nuts and candy, cake and apples. Her father sent Ellen a check for a hundred dollars and she put it aside for a time of great need. In her heart she was increasingly afraid that time was near at hand.

The winter in Kansas was almost like an Ohio winter — cold, bright and sunny. But occasionally the weather grew temperamental, very unlike Lancaster weather; once the thermometer stood at eight below zero in the morning and the next day was warm with a thunder shower.

The children were in fine health and played happily in the yard and the house. Once during that season Ellen was saddened by news of the death of a small cousin in the East, and Tommy wanted to know what it meant. "Gone to Heaven," said Ellen, and Tommy wanted to go to visit him immediately. But his mother said he might be afraid to go, for it was a long, hard journey.

Tommy shook his small black head emphatically. "God will hold me tight," he said confidently.

During the evenings the Shermans read aloud to each other, but not, alas, in front of an hospitable open fire. There were only dark closed stoves here, and the coal, which was very scarce in Kansas, was of a poor quality. When they read aloud Irving's Life of Washington, Ellen said that now for the first time she had some real understanding of the science of war. "And what they endured — those brave soldiers who won our independence. I ought to know American history better. My grandfather Ewing was in that war."

Cump nodded. "And so was mine."

Sometimes during the evenings they discussed what they would do when Hugh's wife returned to her home. Cump thought they might build a house on the Leavenworth lots which Mr. Ewing had given Ellen, and make a farm out of the place, with a garden, ducks and chickens. "We could build on that spot where the ground slopes, and have the house ready by May. Four rooms on each floor would be enough."

Ellen agreed — that would give plenty of space, with Minnie and Lizzie in one room, the boys in another, a room for her and Cump, and a fourth for the visiting Ewings. For this time Minnie must stay with her parents, that they were both agreed. Mrs. Ewing had written that Minnie was in colors now, for she was past seven. She had, said her proud grandmother, a bright red silk dress, with a new necklace of gold and coral ear-rings. Ellen read this description with mixed feelings, for she did not want her mother to get an elaborate wardrobe for the child. She was planning to dress the two little girls very plainly in ninepenny calicos and stout shoes.

In February a check came from California. The furniture which had been stored there had been sold for four hundred and fifty dollars. The money was badly needed, and Cump had to take a hundred of it for office expenses, for since Hugh and Tom had undertaken other business outside town he had been left with the Leavenworth law office to handle. Lots were not selling either, and he was unhappy because he was not earning enough to keep his family.

Since Cump did not know much about legal details and was a stranger in the city there were few clients for the law office. The Shermans had a house to live in until Tom and Ellen came back; she had a little money saved, but that was all.

When Ellen realized beyond any doubt that the move to Leavenworth had been a failure, she sat down to write a letter home. She hated to write it, but she felt there must be some certainty in case things went too badly, and she knew that she and her children were always welcome on the Hill. "Would you faint," she wrote her father, "if a tribe of small Shermans should invade your premises this summer?" and she added that there would be another small Sherman in September.

Her letter crossed one from her father, inviting the whole family to come to Lancaster for the summer. "I have made full provision," wrote Mr. Ewing. "I will have a fine supply of everything, the earliest and the best a farm and garden can provide. It would be a pity to suffer it all to waste unused."

Cump agreed that to accept would be best for the immediate future. Tom wrote that he was returning to Leavenworth and bringing several important law cases; there was a small revival in the real estate market, and by fall everything would be better.

So in early spring of 1859 the Shermans went home to Lancaster which even at the end of winter was lovely in Ellen's eyes, and everyone was happy to welcome the travelers.

In April a letter came from Cump, a thoroughly unhappy letter: to Ellen's dismay he had decided to give up the office in Leavenworth entirely. He came to Lancaster in the middle of July, with an offer from a banker who wished him to open a business for him in London. Ellen was aghast. In the face of that, even California looked like a welcome choice. But Cump had also applied to his friend General Buell for a vacancy existing in the paymaster's department of the army. "Ellen, I know you don't want me in the army again even in a civilian capacity, but the precariousness of civil life seems to me to be worse just now than being in the army." And Ellen had to agree that he was right.

A quick response came from General Buell. There was a good opening for Cump as superintendent of a new military institute and college in Alexandria, Louisiana, patterned after the one in Virginia. There were fifty students from fifteen to twenty years old, ready to begin their studies. More buildings would be erected as soon as possible to accommodate more students. The State was supporting the Institute, so there was no difficulty regarding funds.

Cump accepted the appointment, which carried a salary of thirty-five hundred dollars and provision for living quarters. There was no immediate space for his family, but a house would be built for them as soon as possible.

Ellen was delighted at the prospect. Cump tried to warn her against too much optimism, for he knew that part of the South well: "There are no markets at all, for everything has to come from New Orleans. You can buy chickens and a few vegetables from the Negroes but otherwise it will be much like living at sea." Ellen hardly listened to such warnings, for this would be a permanent home and they would be together and at peace; nothing else mattered.

There was a month of gaiety and happiness in the house on the Hill. There were trips to the farm, where Charley was still in charge and getting rather bored with all the advice his father, now in Washington, was sending him. He showed them a few paragraphs from one of the letters: "In rolling you will have the horses go astride the row. That rolls the space between the two rows. Skip one row and then go astride of the next one and so on, and so you will go over the ground just twice as fast in marking."

Charley groaned and handed them another one: "Have the wheat put in large stocks, at least sixteen rows apart, twenty is better, and let the sowing and harrowing follow the cutting as close as practicable."

"It sounds like good advice," said Ellen.

"Oh, it is," admitted Charley, "very good, but there is so much of it."

To Ellen it was the greatest of earthly joys to have Cump and all the children and Lancaster at the same time. Sometimes she tried to hide from him her deep love of the town where she was born and her love of her family; he could not understand it. He loved his family and his birthplace too, but not in the way Ellen did. After a few days, Lancaster bored Cump. He wanted to go about to see people and a few days in Lancaster exhausted the number of these.

Minnie seemed much happier with her family this time, especially with her father, and he was with her and Lizzie a great deal during these days at home. Once when Ellen told them that their father had in earlier years painted pictures, they asked him to do some for them. He took two pieces of wrapping paper and went to work with Minnie's watercolors, the girls watching with absorbed attention. The first drawing was a bright-eyed woodpecker with a red topknot, and he gave it to Minnie. "This is you," he told her. He turned to make another sketch, this time a dove, dark-eyed and gentle, and gave it to Lizzie. The delighted girls ran to their mother with the pictures, and Ellen promised to have them framed and hung in their room.

# 10. The Civil War Begins

[1859-1862]

CUMP did not have to leave for his new position until the fall term began at the "Louisiana Seminary of Learning and Military Academy," and so he was still in Lancaster in September 1859, when their fifth child was born. It was a girl who looked exactly like Cump, more so than any of the other children. Ellen wanted to have her named for one of the Shermans, but Cump overruled her and the baby was baptized in St. Mary's Church and given the name of Eleanor Maria Sherman.

In October, Cump left for Alexandria. Ellen admitted she was still a "little weak in the knees," but the doctor said Cump was not to worry; she and the baby were in good condition. Cump promised to hurry the building of the new home. "And this time we will, I hope, never be separated again."

"Oh, we can't be," said Ellen fervently. "It is time now to begin building a home of our own and devoting ourselves to the improvement and advancement of our children."

Ellen knew this winter must be spent in Lancaster, and so she decided on a drastic step. There were so many in her own family now that she no longer felt comfortable in her father's home. Her mother was far from well and the children were often a disturbance. So she decided to find a house of her own for her "orphan asylum," but near enough her mother so that she could run in at any time during the day. Mr. Ewing, of course, thought this a lot of nonsense, but Ellen knew she was right and went ahead with her plans. She found exactly the house she wanted, a comfortable one opposite Philemon's.

She had the fence white-washed, the yard put in condition and a new gas lamp hung on the porch. There was no need of buying much furniture: the big house had far more than it needed. Cump had Ellen's personal effects sent from Leavenworth, and she bought a few cheap rugs and stoves. "We will have a winter of comfort even if a lonely one," she wrote Cump. "The house is fine, but, of course, there is one sad want: it is a poor home with the father gone."

This time neither of them minded greatly, for soon they would be together in Alexandria. Cump wanted to know all sorts of details of the children's lives. In one letter he said he hoped they were getting enough exercise, and Ellen smiled as she read it. For at that very moment the four older Shermans were playing pussy-wants-a-corner in the dining-room: if Cump could hear them he would certainly be satisfied at least with the exercise they were giving their lungs.

There was only one cloud on the horizon; the excitement regarding slavery was rising. Ellen knew just what she for one thought about that: there would be no end to the problem until there was an end to slavery. What troubled Ellen most was the fact that Cump was a Northerner in Louisiana. Would this cause trouble in his new position, she asked her father, and he said he could not tell, but one could always hope that the whole problem would be settled short of disunion.

"Cump wrote that I would have a lot of trouble hiring a servant down there," said Ellen. "Most of the people in the town simply buy slaves, he says. Well, I shall certainly change a lot before I do that. I won't invest my money that way."

Cump had sent her sketches of the house that he was building at Alexandria and Ellen pored over them joyously. "The grass is green here now," wrote Cump. "The flowers are budding. The children will have a fine time even if they can't use a sled. Perhaps this is the place where we will spend all our lives."

It looked wonderful, it sounded wonderful, thought Ellen. And if the town had no markets, then they would have to do that much less entertaining, and could be by themselves and have a quiet time with their books and their children and their garden. They had been so tossed about that she knew they would both hail a resting place.

Spring came to Lancaster with hyacinths blooming and blue-bells nodding in the Sherman yard. In one corner a quince tree blazed with bloom. Humming-birds and bold robins were everywhere. The children each planted a little garden and promised to supply the family with corn and beans.

On May first, Ellen Sherman had been married ten years, and as she thought over the anniversaries, she realized that on only four of them had she and Cump been together. But separations would soon be over now, and she sang as she began putting up the first jams and jellies to take South with her. She was waiting only for the opening of the river to send her furniture to Louisiana.

By summer political troubles were growing. Many people felt the whole course of the future would hinge on the coming presidential election, and there was great dispute regarding the candidates. Some of the family were Douglas men, but her father, after long consideration, came out definitely for Lincoln. Ellen knew where she herself stood: now that the Know-Nothing element had left the Republican party, she was all for Lincoln too. She told Willy and Tommy to hurrah for him during any political meetings, and she wrote Cump, "Do you think they will hang me for an abolitionist when I come South?" and then, more seriously, "Cump, do you think there is any prospect of serious difficulty between North and South?"

August and September were holiday months at the military school, and Cump came home to be with his family. Little Elly, who cried every time a man came near her, wanting only feminine attention, went straight to her father with no fuss at all. "As if she loves you at sight," said Ellen. They tested her out again on Charley and Mr. Ewing and Philemon, but she still cried bitterly when they tried to pick her up. Cump was the only man who pleased her, and he was proud of her preference.

On the last day of his vacation there was an encampment of the

Ohio Militia, and Charley, who was acting quartermaster, persuaded Cump to put on his uniform and review the company, to the delight of the children. Next day he was gone, and Ellen was glad she had plenty of work to do so that she had no time to be lonely.

His next letter reported that the house was completely ready. There was only a little painting left to do, and she might as well bring the family down at once — "*all* of them this time." And then within the week came a second letter: the political situation had suddenly grown so much worse in his neighborhood that she was not to make any further preparations until she again heard from him.

When Philemon came to the house to bring her a cake made by Mary, he found Ellen in tears, a rare thing for her. When she told him what was the matter, he said, "Ellen, it is the only thing to do. South Carolina is going to secede and the rest of the South will be very sympathetic. It might be actually unsafe for you to go there now."

"But Father thinks there will be no disunion," insisted Ellen.

Philemon smiled. "You know Father. He always persists in believing what he hopes for." He told her that Hugh, who was almost as surrounded by sons of the South as was Cump, had written from St. Louis that many people were wearing secession cockades, and business was dead. There were no boats in port, and idle men were begging for work, while the city looked like the Sahara desert.

Before long even Mr. Ewing was not so certain of his earlier opinion. Ellen herself thought northern Democrats were partly to blame for stirring up bad feelings. "But I am for Lincoln, and if I did go down there now they'd put me off at Mason and Dixon's Line if someone asked me how I stood," she said to her mother.

The one thing that was clear was that there would be no permanent home in Louisiana. "Ellen," wrote Cump, "what I have been planning so long and patiently, and thought we were on the point of realizing, the dream and hope of my life, that we could all be together in a home of our own, with peace and quiet and plenty around us — all I fear is about to vanish. Must I be a wanderer all my life, leaving all my children to grow up at Lancaster without me?"

In mid-December of 1860, South Carolina seceded. On December 23rd the Louisiana Convention met. Ellen was sure that by the beginning of the year Cump would be at home again — so sure in fact that she rented Dr. White's house for the coming summer, her lease beginning in April. It was a much more retired and pleasant place than the one she had, and she wrote Cump what she had done: "And don't worry yourself by fears for the future. We can come down to linsey-woolsey and coarse shoes, to hominy and corn bread if necessary, and we will do it long before we encourage treason by word or look."

Cump, still in Louisiana, wrote Ellen that personal friendship, had that been all that mattered, would have kept him in the South. But when in January, the governor of the State seized the United States Arsenal in Louisiana and forced the departure of the garrison, Sherman promptly sent in his resignation. It was accepted, but with the acceptance came a note from the governor, expressing regret at the loss of so able a superintendent. It ended, "you will bear with you the respect, confidence and admiration of all who have been associated with you."

Sherman promised to wait until a man could be found to take his place, but when, in February, Louisiana also seceded, he left for the North. If he stayed, he wrote Ellen, he might have to fight for Louisiana — "and that I could hardly do."

Mr. Ewing had been called to Washington to act as one of the commissioners for the North who were to meet commissioners from the Southern States to discuss peace.

"But what are they negotiating about?" asked Ellen as her father prepared for his journey.

"Trying to avert war, Elly."

"But the North has done nothing wrong. Why should there be any compromising or concessions to the South?" she asked.

"To keep us at peace, Elly."

She shook her head sadly. "I used to dislike the Abolitionists but their folly sinks to insignificance when compared with the treason of the South."

Cump reached Lancaster early in March, thoroughly disheartened. For one thing this was his fourth change of position in as many years. But this time his discouragement was also fear: his fear for his country.

"Ellen, over the main door of the Academy is the motto: 'By the liberality of the General Government of the United States. The Union — *esto perpetua.*' I heard just before I left that they were cutting out those words. And some day, Ellen, I'm going to put them back."

He returned again and again to the same topic. "You see, Ellen, I had to leave. If it were just a plain college I could have stayed and waited, but it was an arsenal with guns and powder. I prefer to keep my allegiance to the Union. I wrote in my letter to the Board just how I felt, that on no account would I do any act or think any thought hostile to or in defiance of the old government of the U.S. After all my family helped frame the Constitution and it is sacred to me."

"Of course," said Ellen warmly, "and I feel just as you do. But why do these States continue such illogical thinking?"

"It is a delusion they have, of course," he said, "but when people believe a delusion they believe it harder than a real fact, and under the delusion that we are trying to steal their slaves and incite them to rise up and kill their masters, they are going to break up their government."

That was the larger issue and it made them sad. But the small personal issue was a saddening thing too: that they must give up all thought of a pleasant home for their children and themselves, and the promise of security and peace that went with it.

In March, Cump received word from his brother, Senator John Sherman of Ohio, saying that he was seeking a political post for him, and advising him to come to Washington. "I'm going to see Lincoln while I'm there and tell him what I saw in the South," he said to Ellen. "Up here no one seems aware that there is a crisis or cares. But down there they are preparing for war and at a fast rate."

When Cump reached Washington he told John his reasons for

resigning the Louisiana post, and added emphatically, "There is going to be the biggest civil war of modern times. I've come here to offer my services to the government. I was educated at its expense and my sword belongs to it."

He came back disgusted and bitter. The Secretary of War had been very cool. He thought Sherman unduly excited: the feeling in the South would subside. And Mr. Lincoln, when Cump and his brother John went to the White House, was not much more worried. "He can't see it," said Sherman almost disbelievingly as they left. "He's so deep in political problems that he can't see the danger." He had spoken to the President about an emergency army, but Mr. Lincoln shook his head. "Oh, well, I guess we'll manage to keep house," he said.

"Lincoln thinks the whole thing will be over in three months," he told Ellen, on his return to Lancaster, and there was despair in his eyes as he spoke. "You might as well try to put out a fire with a squirt gun as put down this rebellion in three months' time."

When an offer came from St. Louis, the superintendency of a street railway in that city, Cump decided to forget about an appointment from Washington and accepted. There would not be much salary at first — only two thousand dollars — but it was an assured position, and Major Turner had already promised to find them a furnished house in St. Louis.

The Ewings were sad at having them go, especially because this time Minnie was going with them. She had been their own child for so long, that it was much more than having a dearly loved grandchild leave them. But there was a general conviction on the part of all — with the possible exception of Minnie herself — that the family must be together from now on.

In Minnie's "Album of the Heart" Mr. Ewing wrote, "As your Mama is about to send you from home, I write this as a remembrance. You have lived almost all your short life with your grandmother and myself, and have been a dutiful and affectionate little girl. We are sorry to part with you but hope you will be restored to us soon, improved by education and cultivated in manners, and still as good and kind as ever. God bless you, my daughter. T. Ewing."

When Ellen read this she sorrowed over it, partly because her parents were this time really losing Minnie, and partly because she knew that Minnie herself still felt them her real parents. Those years of separation had made Minnie more at home with them than with her parents, and the name "daughter" which Mr. Ewing had called her pointed the fact.

A very tired family reached St. Louis late in March and settled into their rented house. There was need of additional furniture, but Ellen had to shop with great care and economy; there was little ready money, and the salary of two thousand dollars was very small for their needs. "We'll have to be close-fisted for a while," said Cump, and Ellen, the ever generous, had to agree.

The older girls started for school at the Academy of the Sisters of Charity, only a square from the house, where the principal, Sister Lucina, remembered Sissie at the school in Washington and also knew Mrs. Ewing. Cump wanted to send Willy to the public school, but after he looked it over he did not like it, so Willy went to a small Catholic school instead.

It was a busy life they led in St. Louis. Cump got up at six and so everyone else was roused. He did the marketing while Ellen got the children ready for school. Then he spent a long day at his office, sometimes even the evenings. There was so much work for Ellen, with so many children and so little help, that for the first time in her life that year she could not find the time to go to church on Good Friday.

On April 12th, Fort Sumter was fired on. Missouri was a divided State now, with the legislature wishing to secede; but when a convention met to consider the matter, the vote was against doing so. President Lincoln called for a three months' enlistment. When he heard that, Sherman sighed. "It will last many years," he said soberly. And by May the President had made a new call for three years' service.

Ellen, busy as a woman might be with five small children to take care of, was not so busy as to be unaware of the secession sentiment. However, she had thought it only talk until one day shopping in downtown St. Louis she heard a report that the Union sympathizers, composed mainly of Germans in the city, were planning to get together and sack St. Louis. The people actually believed it, and men, women and children were rushing into the country for safety. Although carriages cost thirty dollars for a short trip, some of her own friends had hired them and were already gone.

When Cump came home that evening he was disposed to ignore the whole story. "I've been to see General Lyon just to make sure, and he says there is not the slightest reason for rushing away in a panic."

From then on it seemed to Ellen that all she heard was "sesesh talk." She could hardly believe that people she knew well were for the Southern cause — Major Turner, for instance. The pleasure of chatting with friends was gone, for one had to be very careful not to express jarring sentiments. She could not agree and she did not want to offend them. She could not even go to see the Archbishop any more, for she knew his sympathies lay with the South.

Rumors of war filled the city. There was a headquarters now of Southern sympathizers called Camp Jackson, where men were being instructed in the art of soldiery. There were several companies of United States troops in St. Louis as well as the Home Guards, composed mostly of Germans. People were barricading their homes.

One day when Cump and Charley Ewing, now practicing law in St. Louis, were walking with Willy toward their home, a man came running up the street, shouting "They've surrendered." They went with the hurrying crowd toward Camp Jackson and learned that the men there had been made prisoners by the Union troops.

Suddenly someone fired a pistol. Others followed and in the general stampede for safety some in the crowd were hit. Charley threw Willy to the ground and himself on top of the boy, and Cump fell flat next to them. Later it was learned that several had been killed, among them little children. Cump went home to assure a distracted Ellen that Willy was not hurt.

But now he could no longer defer action. Officials from Washington came to see him and asked, if he were offered a colonel's commission in the regular Army, would he accept? Cump said he would, and a few days later came a dispatch: W. T. Sherman had been appointed Colonel of the Thirteenth Regular Infantry, and he was wanted immediately in Washington.

On Sunday morning Ellen went to church with a troubled heart. She prayed that her husband's life might be spared in the coming conflict. She told herself that she wanted him to have an honorable and distinguished position at a time when his country was in peril, but she could not help praying for a life of peace for them as well as for the whole country.

From Washington, Cump wired that he would not be returning to St. Louis, and that Ellen was to store the furniture and go to Lancaster with the children. And again the Ewings welcomed the family, happy to have them back, sad at the necessity which brought them.

Because she was expecting a baby within a very short time, the Ewings moved Ellen upstairs, giving her and the children the entire second floor of the house. It was well filled now, for Henrietta was there too with her children and nurses.

On July 5th, another daughter was born to the Shermans, another little redhead like Minnie and Willy. It was no wonder that people in Lancaster said that if Ellen Sherman put her children along a fence the woodpeckers would feed them. The newcomer was named Rachel, in memory of her great-grandmother Ewing — "a woman of great fortitude and character," Thomas Ewing said of her, happy to have a grandchild bear her name.

Lancaster was full of excitement during those days. On a single morning a hundred men left, with drums beating and fifes shrieking, while their families stood watching, tears rolling down their cheeks as their loved ones marched away.

The children in the Ewing house shared the excitement of the war preparations. Willy and his cousin Tommy Ewing brought down from the attic a little brass bound drum and drilled the neighboring children. Even peaceful Lizzie was heard to say stoutly that she did not believe they could take Washington, no matter how hard they tried. As for Elly, she broke into patriotic song all through the day, usually a single line from her favorite: "Our flag is still there."

Recruiting was brisk in Lancaster. Nine full companies were drilled and equipped by September and more were forming. Hugh Ewing joined in August as Colonel of the 30th Ohio Volunteers. Tom was joining and so was Charley.

Letters had come from Cump, now in charge of five brigades across the river from Georgetown, letters that told of the plans for campaigns, letters in which he discussed matters with someone he trusted in order to clarify his own mind. When he learned the baby had arrived safely, and that she and Ellen were well, he wrote that now he could set out with a lighter heart, that he would acquit himself as best he could, and she was not to worry about him. It would be well for a while to mail her letters to John Sherman in Washington, who would know his movements fairly well and who would see that mail reached him.

Soon news came of the repulse of his forces at Manassas Junction and the papers headlined: "Sherman's battery is taken." Denial followed. There were stories of Sherman in Washington, consulting with senators and military men, and of his appointment as Brigadier General of Volunteers. At last came personal word to Ellen: he was on his way West and would stop in Cincinnati. Could Ellen manage to be there?

Willy and Minnie and Lizzie went with Ellen and the week they spent at the Barret House in Cincinnati was a wonderful one despite the fears ahead for them all. But it was soon past, and Sherman was on his way West to get all possible aid in the way of troops and arms to meet the threatened invasion of Kentucky. "I tell you, Ellen," he had said to her, "if the Confederates take St. Louis and get Kentucky this winter, it will be worse than if they take Washington. Whichever nation gets control of the Ohio, the Mississippi and the Missouri Rivers will control the Continent."

In late October he wrote her of his worry about getting arms for his soldiers. The West had none. If he did form the Kentuckians into regiments — of what use would it be if they were not given arms? Secretary of War Cameron came through his camp and Sherman explained to him that he needed sixty thousand men at once, but the Secretary, so Cump wrote Ellen, had listened indifferently. Next day through newspapers Ellen learned that Cameron had given a memorandum of his visit with Sherman to the War Department, and had said the whole idea was unwarranted — in fact, he said, "It is insane."

The word insane, so carelessly used, gave the reporters their chance. They felt a cordial dislike for Sherman because he would not allow any news to be published from his camp, and now they used this one word over and over; again and again they wrote about the "mad General."

Ellen decided it was time someone went to see Cump; taking Tommy with her and escorted by Philemon, they went unannounced to the camp at Louisville. As she had expected, she found Cump very despondent, and she set about bolstering his spirits. She went on to Memphis with him, and there shopped and mended for him. When she left him he was in a better frame of mind. But in a few weeks the flood of abuse rose again, and again she went to him, this time to St. Louis, to find him in so despairing a state that General Halleck thought he ought to go home to rest for a while. "Take him home, Mrs. Sherman, and don't let him talk politics or read a newspaper for at least two weeks," he suggested.

General Sherman was willing to go. It was the middle of winter and he knew there would be no immediate action. Even if the circumstances were not happy, the family reunion was. The children and he and Ellen went for drives or read aloud together. War was never mentioned.

On the evening before his return to his army, he sat watching Ellen affectionately as she put away a volume of Scott from which she had been reading to him. "Ellen," he said, "I'm sorry I haven't the Catholic faith to console and strengthen me as you have."

A prayer welled in her heart, but she said nothing aloud. "If you hadn't been so calm and self-possessed during these two weeks," he went on, "I don't think I could have borne what I have, or face what is coming."

But he could not have dreamed what was coming. Next morning the *Cincinnati Commercial* arrived — three days late — and the headline on the first page read: "General William T. Sherman Insane."

When Ellen saw Cump's expression she leaned over to see what he was reading. "Painful intelligence reaches us . . . General is insane . . . stark mad . . . has of course been relieved altogether from his command . . . deepest sympathy in his great calamity." So much she read in a hurry. Then she looked up to see him staring at her, and at the misery in his eyes she dropped the paper and ran to him and threw her arms about his shoulders. It was only when she realized that he was weeping that she managed to control herself.

From Mr. Ewing in Washington came a letter, full of sympathy and of anger at "the scoundrels who have libelled you." But even before the letter came, the quiet and usually gentle Philemon had acted, calling on the *Commercial* to retract its remarks at once.

The final decision of the family was that Sherman go back and report for duty as if nothing had been written about him at all. Soon after a letter came to Ellen from General Halleck: she was to pay no attention to such stories, and the newspapers which had printed them ought to be treated with contempt.

That Christmas was a cheerless day, but the children had their presents as usual. Cump, despite all his troubles, had sent some too, and Minnie was highly delighted because her father had sent her water-color paints instead of a toy. He wrote often to his eldest daughter, letters that were not really letters to a child. It was as if he felt he must make her understand what he was doing and why this war was necessary. "Don't get into the habit of calling people by hard names like traitor or rebel, Minnie," ran one letter. "Just remember how easy it is for people to be deceived and drawn on, step by step, until war and death are on them."

"This is a strange war," he wrote. "We are fighting our own people, many of whom I knew well in earlier years."

When Ellen wrote to ask him if it were true that soldiers were destroying property, he answered that she must remember that wherever an army went there must be destruction of property. From Alexandria, Virginia, he had written earlier, "We have not disturbed a single slave; even the slaves of Colonel Lee are at Arlington cultivating the farm for their master who is with the Virginians." And now he cautioned her not to believe all newspaper reports, especially those criticizing General Grant: "He is a brave good gentleman; don't let news accounts mislead you."

Again and again he said he wished he could be at home with them all — "but the war will have to go on until peace is restored to our country, and until no men will dare again insult our flag and national honor."

Ellen answered his letters with long, loving, encouraging letters of her own. But Cump only wrote back bitterly that he had brought disgrace on them all. He apologized for his blue letters, "but this unnatural war does weigh heavy on my mind and heart." And his men were so cold in the bitter winds, so many were sick that he always left the hospital sad at heart.

Suddenly a plan came to Ellen: she would write a letter to Mr. Lincoln. She sat down and stated to him exactly what had happened, a full account of the story which was everywhere quoted, that her husband was insane. She wrote that she realized many took no stock in the statement that General Sherman was mad, but no official contradiction had come and her husband was in a subordinate place in General Halleck's army, which lent color to the story. "As malice cannot prevail where justice rules," she wrote, "I look for speedy relief from the sorrow that has afflicted me in this trial of my husband. That your name may be handed down with undiminished honor to pos-

terity and that eternal joy may be your portion hereafter is the wish
of your most respectful, Ellen Ewing Sherman."

She mailed it and waited, a bit worried at her action. When her
father came home from Washington, she learned that the letter had
been received, and that Mr. Lincoln had been very sympathetic. As
for Cump, when he learned what she had done, he was not only not
angry: he asked her to do still more. He wanted her to go to Washington with her father and make a personal appeal for him.

In mid-January of 1862, when Mr. Ewing was returning to Washington on an important case, she went back with him, taking Lizzie
with her. It took some days to make, through the new Secretary of
War, Stanton, an appointment with the President.

Ellen had feared that at this interview she would be very nervous
and make a bad impression, but when she sat with her father in the
office facing Mr. Lincoln, all her nervousness vanished. His face was
so kindly, his voice so warmly sympathetic, that she told the whole
story with no hesitation.

"Mr. Lincoln, do you think my husband was insane when he commanded Fort Corcoran?" asked Ellen.

"Certainly not," the President said promptly.

"Well, he is no more so now," she said. "I've known him since he
was ten years old and he is just the same now as he was then. He
has enemies among his fellow generals and of course among the press
people, who have several times let out military secrets for which he
castigated them, to their deep resentment. But I am not," she said
hastily, "telling you such things because I have come here to ask anything of you, Mr. Lincoln, except to see that his good name is vindicated."

The President spoke in high praise of her husband. "Mr. Seward
and I were strongly impressed in his favor when he was in command
at Fort Corcoran, and I nominated him for brigadier general before
the Ohio delegation sent in his name. I was sorry when he was sent
to Kentucky." And he told her that General Sherman's recognized
abilities would soon bring him further promotion.

Mr. Ewing was very pleased with the interview and the way in which Ellen had handled it. She wrote a full account of it to Cump, and sent him the next week a letter from Tom: he had been to see the President and the latter had wished to send his compliments to Mrs. Sherman to whom, he said, he had "taken a great liking."

# 11. The Dark Years
## [1862–1863]

IN EARLY spring 1862, it was evident from Cump's letters that a great conflict was near. "May the Lord of Mercy protect him," Ellen prayed. On April 9th came word of a terrible battle at Shiloh, followed by the news that General Sherman had been wounded, that a cannon-ball had shot off his right hand. But that night came a direct dispatch: "A great battle has been fought. General Sherman is alive and well."

A letter told the story. Cump had received a wound in his right hand and had an injured shoulder from a spent ball; a bullet had that day gone through his hat; three horses had been shot under him. But most of the letter dealt with the sad news that Holliday, his orderly, was dead, killed as he stood beside the General by a shot meant for Sherman. "A handsome, faithful young soldier," Cump wrote, "who carried his carbine ready always to defend me." He had had the boy brought back to his own camp and had buried him under a tree seared by cannon fire.

National Gallery, Washington, D. C.                                                    G.P.A. Healy

ELLEN EWING SHERMAN
Wife of General William Tecumseh Sherman

The papers were filled with blame now for General Grant because of this temporary setback of the Northern forces; Sherman, on the other hand, was being praised for his work. Ellen sighed at the unfairness of all such quick judgments.

At this time Mrs. Ewing was far from well and Ellen spent much of her spare time with her mother, comforting the ailing woman who had so many sons in the army to worry about. When Ellen was not there, Mr. Ewing worked in his wife's room, busy with a sketch of the life of General Sherman which he was writing as one of a series of short biographies Charles Dana was publishing. Tom and Cump and Hugh and Charley — Maria Ewing worried about them all, and Ellen brought all her letters from them as soon as they arrived. Like all the women of the North, they waited for news, waited to hear whether their loved ones were still living or, if they were alive, whether they had escaped injury in the hazards of battle.

There was another fear in the hearts of the women of central Ohio during those months: the dread that Morgan's raiders might reach their cities as he had the southern cities of the State. General Morgan and his cavalry had all southern Ohio in a panic. He would appear suddenly by night, destroy property, and kill defenders before help could be brought. In Kentucky and southern Ohio he had destroyed millions of dollars worth of military stores, captured railroad trains, burned bridges, destroyed culverts. He had with him a telegraph operator with whose aid he misled his foes, and at the same time was able to learn the whereabouts of enemy supplies and destroy them in his rapid moves.

Grant had succeeded Halleck in the West and had immediately put Sherman in command of Memphis. In October came a dispatch from Captain Charley Ewing: he was going to Memphis and could take Ellen to visit Cump. On the next day she left with Tommy for Cincinnati and took the packet *Manora* bound for Memphis.

It had been just one month less than a year since she had seen her husband, and his delight was no greater than hers.

"How are the children?" was his first question.

"I'm very fortunate in my regiment of light infantry," said Ellen. "They are in fine order and thriving. But I am so glad that at last I see my commanding officer again."

He had taken rooms for her and Tommy at the hotel, and since there were other staff wives visiting, Ellen's time was well filled.

A few evenings after her arrival, she and Cump were in the hotel parlor when a group of officers arrived, General Taylor and Colonel Kilby Smith heading them. Major Sanger whispered to her, "There is to be a sword presentation."

By this time Cump realized what was going to take place, and whispered in his turn, "Ellen, please do go away for a little while." So she slipped out to please him, but stayed near the door and heard most of the speech. The sword was beautiful, with a monogram in diamonds. There was a sash too, gold colored. But what pleased Ellen most was the evidence of the affection and confidence of Cump's officers in him.

Tommy had a wonderful time during this visit, usually taking his blankets with him to the camp and sleeping there. The company tailor made him a uniform sewn with corporal's chevrons, and he wore it proudly all the time.

In late November the visit was over, for Grant wanted Sherman to join him in a combined movement against Vicksburg. The latter was glad to be leaving Memphis; it had been a difficult command for the townspeople were Southern sympathizers and there were many problems regarding the Negro slaves and fugitives.

Having seen that Cump's clothes were mended and having made a note of the things to be sent back to him, Ellen went home, glad she had made the trip, for it had given Cump a chance to talk himself out on subjects he could not discuss with his officers. "Ellen," he had told her, "I have lived so much in Louisiana and Carolina, that in every battle I feel I must be fighting some of the very families in whose houses I used to spend happy days. Of course I know I must fight, but — whenever the result can be accomplished without a battle, I prefer it."

Mrs. Ewing had been sent to Columbus for treatment and Ellen went to take her all the news about the children. She told her that Rachel was becoming very pretty, and Elly was the smartest and most interesting child of them all. Her mother smiled at that, for Ellen said exactly the same thing of each of her children in turn.

Ellen had earlier taken Minnie and Willy to Notre Dame, Indiana, Willy to the boys' academy, Minnie to the girls' academy which was in charge of her cousin, Mother Angela, once Eliza Gillespie. "Willy seems very happy at Notre Dame, Mother," she reported. "He has been six times at the table of honor and he enjoys the games. But somehow I can't feel right to have the little fellow so far away. I only comfort myself by saying he is learning his faith, and if my letting him go away from me gives him a firm spiritual training it will be worth the separation."

"And Minnie?" asked Mrs. Ewing eagerly, for this child was still her favorite, this child who was, Ellen sometimes felt, more her mother's than her own.

"Minnie is fine. And so pretty, and with such a sweet temper and such intelligence and with such a lovely faith" — she stopped breathlessly, and the two women smiled at each other. Their pride lay in the same places — in their husbands, in their homes, in their children.

Early in 1863, Ellen saw with dismay that the newspaper persecution was beginning again, and Cump was taking it badly, according to his own letters. He said he would treat reporters as spies. "They publish all dates. They gave away our plan to attack at Haines' Bluff. I am notifying Mr. Lincoln of my intention."

He had, in fact, threatened to resign his commission if the newspaper men were not withdrawn, but such talk Ellen could not bear to hear. "As long as you keep on as you have been doing, Cump," she wrote, "I can only feel more and more proud of you when the ignorant and malicious assail you. But if you abandon your country when so few are competent and willing to serve, then I shall be distracted. It is not Lincoln but the country you are serving. Whatever you do, Cump, do hold to your commission."

She could not blame him for his earlier anger when they said he was insane, or when statements were made that his troops were mutinying and he was unfit to command. But if he would only realize that people at home were eager for news, that the reporters did not want to tell secrets; if only Cump would be pleasant to them, all would be well.

"They cannot injure your good name, Cump," she wrote. "On the contrary, it only shines the brighter for the rubs it gets . . . don't let the snapping turtles get you down."

This letter had good results. Cump wrote her from St. Louis that he was heeding her counsel about the correspondents, and that he would no longer "exclude the spies," but allow them to come freely and go freely and "collect their budgets."

It was hard for him to be in St. Louis and not to be able to see his old associates — Turner, Lucas and the others, friends of old days. "I am cut off from the only class of friends left me here save relations. All the old families here, even Campbell, are now secessionists and nothing will change them."

Ellen herself was facing a similar difficult situation in Lancaster. The Ewing women had always been loyal to each other and still were. But Henrietta had decided she wanted to go home with her children: she was a Southerner, and found it difficult to conceal her feelings in this household of Northerners. But the women cried in each others' arms when they said goodbye. "What troubles and separations this cruel war is causing," said Mrs. Ewing to her weeping daughter-in-law. "May the God of all consolations bless and comfort you."

Mrs. Ewing had improved greatly during her stay at the cure in Columbus, looking about her domain again with the eyes of a housewife and not with the weary gaze of an invalid. She was a little less worried now about Charles and Hugh, for both her sons were with Cump, and that was a great comfort to her. "Charley and Hugh are earning their honors," Ellen had read her from one of Cump's letters.

Several times that spring Ellen had felt a sudden desire to go to see Willy, being, for some reason, worried about the child, but Minnie's reports showed her how foolish was the fear. Besides, Mrs. Ewing had a relapse and the doctor ordered an immediate operation, which proved successful, insofar as an operation for a disease malignant in its nature could be considered so. She rallied and was so much her old self that Ellen made new plans to go to Notre Dame for the commencement exercises, and to bring the children home with her.

It seemed impossible, she thought, when she saw Minnie in the parlor of the Academy, that this girl with her mature look and manner was her little Minnie, and she glowed with pride when "Miss Maria Sherman of Lancaster, Ohio" was awarded first premium in the seminary classes. At the school exhibition for the boys she watched with other parents her son in pantaloons and jacket and his first shirt with a standing collar, as he received four first premiums in one class and two in another. All she needed now was Cump beside her, to rejoice with her over these wonderful children of theirs.

As soon as they reached home, she sent Willy and Minnie up to their grandmother's room. Minnie hugged and kissed her and Mrs. Ewing examined carefully the apple of her eye. "How tall she is, Elly — head and shoulders taller than you," she said. When it came Willy's turn she looked at him and then at Ellen. "Now that he is taller and thinner, he looks exactly like Cump, doesn't he?" And the resemblance was indeed a striking one.

Her father was full of plans and most of them, as usual, involved keeping the Sherman family as close as possible to the Ewings. "I thought I might tear down my office and use the materials to build a new house at the farm. You could go there with the children if you are so insistent on a place of your own."

Ellen's eyes shone. "That would be wonderful, Father. What fun

to meet Cump with an array of ducks and lambs and colts when
he gets home." They went to see the location he had chosen — a
little valley with a brook running through it, and a good water supply
from the spring at the top of the hill. And it was close enough to the
Ewings, so that Ellen could see her mother every day.

In July 1863, the city of Vicksburg finally capitulated after a long
and arduous siege. "The first gleam of daylight," Sherman wrote to
his wife. The news reached Lancaster in time for the Fourth, and
there was a big celebration, with shooting of cannon and fireworks,
with speeches and songs in the streets.

But the General also wrote that he could not feel too happy about
the victory, save that it presaged the war's end — "Pray for the end,"
he wrote home, "but pray too that it may end before our people
become robbers and murderers . . . Hundreds of children are being taught to hate my name, but that is war . . ."

"Your mama and grandpa think it is a great thing to be a high
general," he wrote Minnie. "I would in any war but this, but I cannot
look on these people but as my old friends, and every day I meet
old friends who would shoot me dead if I went outside camp, and
who look on me as a brutal wretch."

Maria Ewing's health was much worse; she had had a second
operation, and was very weak. "I think she is better today," Mr.
Ewing would say hopefully, but even his optimism was beginning
to break. Cump had arranged that her sons come home to see her
for a brief leave, but he himself could not get away. However, since
all would be quiet for a time and he was now in a finely located
camp, he suggested that Ellen come to visit him and bring the children, or at any rate the older ones. When the doctor said Mrs.
Ewing's condition would probably not change for some months
and it was safe to leave her, Ellen decided on the trip.

"I'll take Minnie and Willy and Lizzie with me," she said, excited as a girl. "Oh, Mother, the thought of going down there where
Cump is, has spread sunshine over everything. Oh, God grant that

nothing may happen to mar the happiness we look forward to."

Even while they talked they heard the firing of cannon, and when Mr. Ewing came in he told them it was to celebrate the capture of Morgan and the last of his men. Relief came into their hearts to know that at last the fears of a raid were over, that the people of Ohio could again sleep peacefully at night and not fear possible massacre before morning.

When, late in August, the five Shermans reached Vicksburg, Colonel Rawlins met them with news that Cump had been made a brigadier general in the regular Army, and that Charley, who had been reported killed, was safe and a hero besides. Two standard-bearers had fallen, and Captain Ewing had seized the flag. A moment later a bullet hit the staff, and another had cut through his hat, but he managed to lift the flag and keep it flying. It was agreed he had saved Grant's life, for when the latter was going down a road where the noise of firing was so loud he could not hear voices shouting to him that there was an ambush ahead, Charley had galloped up, seized the bit of Grant's horse and backed him down a steep bank to safety.

Next morning, the Feast of the Assumption, all the family went to Mass. The church was a sad place, its walls bullet-pierced in many places. Most of Vicksburg was in ruins; they saw its desolation as they went to the camp by carriage through the chilly morning; the driver pointed out the deep caves where women and children had hidden during the days of siege.

The camp was set in a beautiful spot, a grove of oak trees facing an open field where parades were held. There was a happy reunion and it was almost like being home again to see so many Shermans and Ewings together. Everyone lived in tents; a small one next to the General's was set aside for Lizzie and Minnie and their nurse. Tommy and Willy had a place in their Uncle Charley's tent. Hugh's was not far away. And Ellen found an old friend, the chaplain — Father Carrier of the Congregation of Holy Cross, who said he had just received orders from France to go to Notre Dame immediately. But the General would not release him; there was no substitute —

"and there are so many Catholics in my army I don't want them to be without a priest," Cump told Ellen.

When they went about, Minnie and Willy and Tom rode horseback, and Lizzie traveled in the carriage with her mother. Sometimes in the mornings the ladies of the party walked over to see Willy proudly riding to review with his father. The Thirteenth was very fond of the General's boy and made him a sergeant in the company; Willy was studying the manual of arms and going seriously through the drill. Whenever the General allowed it, his son rode at his side, at any gait and for any distance.

The brief time together ended all too soon. Word came of the defeat of the army of the Cumberland in the Chickamauga Valley, and Grant ordered Sherman to take his entire corps and relieve Rosencrans. The morning after the orders came, Ellen and the girls and Tom went by carriage to take the boat for home, while Willy rode with his father.

The heat and the haste gave Ellen a blinding headache. Minnie, who had had a touch of fever, was still ill, so when they reached the boat Ellen put her to bed in the cabin, and lay down for a while herself. Tommy was taking a nap and Willy was sitting quietly by the window. She hoped he was not too disappointed about the wonderful little double-barrelled gun which had been promised him, and which a soldier was to have brought him as a parting gift from the company. Willy had lagged behind as they rode, and the General, supposing it was because the gun had not come, told the child not to worry: he would send it later. Ellen had brushed Willy's hair that morning until it was silky and said to him, "Aren't you well satisfied, Willy, to have hair just like Papa's?" and he had said "Yes," with a proud smile.

"I love red hair best," she said, "and your hair I think is the prettiest of all." He had gone out of the room with his head high.

In the late afternoon the steamer came to Young Point, and the General called his family to the upper deck to show them the site of his old camp. Everyone felt refreshed and came at his call, but Willy, to his father's surprise, arrived last. He looked at him sharply. "Are you sick, Willy?" he asked.

Willy looked almost shamefaced at having to admit such a weakness, but he nodded. Ellen thought his cheeks unusually flushed and took him back in the cabin. She removed his sergeant's uniform and put him to bed, remembering now how a while before he had come to lie down in the cabin, that he had eaten little for breakfast and could eat no dinner. She had thought it the excitement.

The General called his physician who said that Willy was a very sick child; he was afraid he had camp fever. Ellen looked at Cump with fear in her eyes and saw it mirrored in his: camp fever was so often fatal.

As the boat crawled along, Ellen kept cold compresses on Willy's head. At the other side of the bed Lizzie fanned him steadily. There was no chance to get the proper medicines until they reached Memphis.

When the boat docked, Willy was too sick to lift his head. The General carried him to the hotel, and another doctor was summoned. All possible help was at hand now, but it was clear to all there that Willy was steadily growing worse.

Father Carrier came with them off the ship and, in the early morning hours when he was alone with the little boy for a few moments, he began to talk to him of Heaven, trying to prepare the child for the death which was now almost inevitable. Willy's face showed no fear, but he looked very troubled. "But I don't want to leave my father and mother," he said pleadingly.

Father Carrier could hardly hold back his tears, as he tried to find words to soothe him. "Willy, just trust in God and the Blessed Virgin and all will be well with you. If it is God's will to call you to Heaven, you will meet your good mother and father there again surely."

Willy looked at him as if accepting this. "Well," he said slowly.

When his mother came back he smiled at her faintly. "Uncle

Charley sends word he has the gun and is taking care of it for you," she said. "And when we go to the country you can shoot all the game you want to for me."

"Yes, Mama," he said, and then her control slipped and she sank down beside his bed and began to cry. "Are you willing to die if it is God's will, darling?" she asked. She felt his little hand on her cheek, and heard him say, "yes." Then he added in a whisper, "But I'll pray for you to follow me."

She lifted her head. "Willy, you know how we love you, don't you?"

Again the faint smile and the little nod. An hour later, with all who loved him around him helpless to aid, Willy died.

For all his grief there was little time that General Sherman could give to this private agony. He could not even go to Willy's burial which was to take place in Lancaster.

"Oh, Cump," Ellen wept, "I wish he hadn't been away from me all last winter. And I wanted him back so much. I never once went to sleep without wondering if he were covered up and warm."

"Mother, he loved it there," Minnie, still ill with the fever, tried to comfort her. "He was happy and cheerful; I saw him many times and he was always happy."

"If he had only complained those last few days," said Ellen, "but he wanted to appear soldierly and brave in your eyes, Cump."

"He never complained," said the General sadly. "You remember when we moved from California and he was so seasick, he tried to fight it off until I told him it was all right to give in."

"And last summer when he fell from the cherry tree and broke his arm, he never once cried," said Ellen.

But even for loving reminiscences there was little time. A coffin was procured, and the little sergeant given a military funeral by the grieving soldiers. Then the others continued on their way home, and Charley went with them. But Cump and Hugh had to go back to their military duties.

Willy was buried in the Lancaster cemetery next to Grandfather

Boyle, after Father Lange had sung the Mass of the Angels in St. Mary's Church. Sherman, far away with his army, wrote that day in his diary, "They brought Willy's body to rest in the only place we can now call home."

The loss was almost as shattering for the Ewings as for the Shermans. For once Mr. Ewing was bent with grief and Maria, so ill herself, wept, "If only I had been taken instead." As for Ellen, she could not write about the burial to Cump at all, only one broken note in which she said Charley would give him all the details. "He will tell you all. My heart is nearly broken. I cannot write about it."

Only her Faith helped Ellen now, and she sorrowed that Cump could not have that comfort. She prayed that he would find consolation, and would feel that Willy was close to him as she felt he was always near her. And then Cump wrote as if in answer to her thoughts: "If it be so that Willy can see our hearts from above, he will read in mine a love for him such as would not taint the purest Heaven that you ever dreamed of. God spare us the children that are left."

In the big trunk that held so much of the happy past, Ellen put away Willy's things. The little sergeant's uniform, so lovingly given, so proudly worn, his beloved shirt with the standing collar, his school cap, his sergeant's commission, his card of admission to the Holy Angels' Society at school, the wreath that had covered his coffin in the church.

Then she took up again the care of her family, and especially of her mother, who was so broken with grief that Ellen had to lay aside her own. The tragedy, said the doctor, had put Mrs. Ewing in a really dangerous condition.

It still troubled Ellen that Willy had been so long away from home the year before. "But I thought it best for him, Mother. And there wasn't a night he was away that I didn't pray he was sleeping well, nor a day that I didn't want him with me. But I never wrote that to him for I didn't want to make him homesick. But he knows I loved him, doesn't he, Mother?"

And her mother would assure her that he did. And then it was Ellen's turn to comfort her mother.

"I realize now that what you have always taught me is so true, Mother," she said to her one day, "that our life is only a probation and we really live only in our home above. If I couldn't feel that and I couldn't feel He hears my prayers and is near me, I couldn't bear it."

"Don't make any plans to have us go to the farm this fall," she said to her father, "I couldn't bear it. It was for Willy I wanted it most. I know I ought to go for the others, but somehow I can't. Sometimes, Father, I can hardly keep from praying that I may die. I know that is selfish for it is my own sorrow and loss I am grieving over."

When a soldiers' magazine asked her to write a short article about Willy, she complied with the request and ended the little article: "The angel of morning brought him to earth. The angel of night bore him to the living Source of all life and light and love." Just writing it made her feel better and she thought her grief had spent its force. And then, going to her box of patterns for one to use in making waists for the girls, she drew out first the pattern of a jacket for Willy, one she had used only three months before. And again the full measure of her loss swept over her.

But there were the other children left to her who needed her. "May God help me to do my duty to them and to you," she wrote to Cump, and told him that every day they all prayed together for Willy.

She treasured and put away the little note his father had written to Tommy, dated midnight, October 4. "You are now our only boy, and must take poor Willy's place to take care of your sisters and to fill my place too when I am gone. I have promised that when you meet a soldier who knew Willy that you will give him half you have. Give him all if in want, and work hard to gain knowledge and health which will, when you are a man, insure you all you need in this world. Your loving father, W. T. Sherman."

## 12. The War's End

[1863–1865]

As the autumn of 1863 turned to winter, Mrs. Ewing's condition grew even worse. During one brief period when she was better, on Lizzie's eleventh birthday, the Shermans had a family party in her room. Two weeks later Maria Theresa Ewing was married in her mother's room to Colonel Clement F. Steele, who had been sent home wounded. It would have been a sober ceremony had it not been for the Sherman children who helped give it an air of gaiety. Even small Rachel did her part. She came in leading her nursemaid. "Here's Nora," she said to the bridegroom, and then, "And here's Uncle Steele," she introduced him to Nora.

In October, General Sherman had been placed in command of the Department and Army of Tennessee; soon after came the victory at Chattanooga and the raising of the siege at Knoxville. Now winter had closed down and as most operations must cease, he sent word he was taking advantage of that fact to come for a brief visit to Lancaster. The visit was quiet, because their recent loss was so near. They often spoke of Willy, and once Ellen said sadly, "Oh, Cump, why does my miserable heart keep mourning so for Willy, when I know God loves him with a tenderness no earthly father could feel."

"Ellen, only God Himself can tell the deep secret springs of human woe," Cump told her comfortingly.

On New Year's Day Cump's furlough ended and, since they had decided that Minnie was to go to the Academy of the Sisters of Notre Dame at Reading, he took her there on his way back to camp. A few days later, he wrote to Ellen that he had seen her safely in the school.

"I confess I am amazed at the calm and easy manner of Minnie — at all times unabashed, almost too much so for her years, and yet she is loving and kind. To me she acts like Willy with that simple confidence that is very captivating." He said that he was glad Ellen was at home now, since the next June, the month of Willy's birth, she was expecting another child.

At the end of January the doctor told the family that Mrs. Ewing could live at most a week longer. All through the nights Ellen sat dozing by her mother's side, waking if she but stirred; beside her sat Thomas Ewing, at last convinced that his wife would not get better. Philemon, now in Pittsburgh, and the three sons at war were telegraphed for. Messages began to come in answer: the sons were coming home. Only Cump, dear as a son, could not come: he was about to march into eastern Mississippi. Mrs. Ewing had sent him a message only a few days before by Ellen: "Tell him he has my prayers, and that I hope he will pray himself that God will bless his arms and restore him to his family."

Philemon came, and then Tom and his wife. Hugh and Charley arrived from their posts. At the insistence of Mr. Ewing, Minnie was summoned from school, and Maria Ewing's eyes brightened as one after the other they leaned over her bed. She recognized them all and called them by name, and a smile came to her lips when she saw Minnie. There was little life left in the wasted body; she could scarcely move her hand or speak above a whisper. Archbishop Purcell came to his old parishioner to give her the last rites and to bring her the special blessing of the Holy Father.

On the night of February 19th, the family was summoned to her room to recite the prayers for the dying led by Hugh. Thomas Ewing did not join in, but he knelt reverently with the others.

With her children and her best loved grandchild, who had been like a child of her own, gathered about her, Maria Ewing passed away early on the following morning. She was sixty-two years old. She had had a full and happy life, and as she lay there she looked young and lovely, with all suffering gone from her face. "She looks just the way she did when we were children," Ellen wrote to Cump. And Thomas Ewing, looking at her peaceful face, thought what a wonderful woman she had been — loving her husband, her children, her home, her friends, the poor and the distressed, and loving God all her life.

At St. Mary's Church the Archbishop sang a pontifical High Mass for her, and at the altar before which her body lay her sons and daughters received Holy Communion. Then they went their separate ways.

It was so lonely after her mother's death that Ellen felt rootless for the first time in her life and could hardly bear to stay in the house. With her father planning to spend much time in Washington, with Sissie and her husband in charge of the house, with so many children of her own and another coming in June — Ellen knew that she must find a place of her own, if only a temporary one. She was wishing she had Cump to advise her when word came he was on his way home, after having been given supreme command of the armies in the West.

He reached Lancaster at three of a very cold morning. They built up a fire for him, and even Tommy woke and came down to see his father. In the days that followed, the General devoted much time to his only son. It was evident that it gave him comfort to find Tommy so well and strong, since all his hopes of carrying on his name were in this boy. "You'll have to take care of the family," he told the little boy solemnly. "The girls will marry, but you will always be a Sherman and you must represent the family. Whatever happens to me you are old enough to remember what I am saying to you, and to take my place. And I want you to know, even if you can't understand the things now going on, that whatever I do is for you and our country. We must have peace but we can have it now only by war."

They were walking in the yard and the General shortened his steps to the little boy's, sighing as he looked at the house and thought of the love it held. "Tommy, I am now a great general and if I were to come home with victory they would gather around in crowds and play music and all such things. That is what people call fame and glory, but I tell you, Tommy, I would rather come down quietly and have you and Willy meet me at that door than have the shouts of the people."

After only two days General Sherman left for Chattanooga where plans were to be discussed to begin a march on Georgia. "It will be a hard task," he told Ellen. "The country is hostile. There is only one railroad, and we will have to repair it and use it and guard it too." But Ellen saw with relief that he was sure of himself now, and was borne up by the good opinion behind him. His health was better too. "Just be prudent and unconcerned like Grant and Halleck and your health will keep up," Ellen had told him.

On June 11th, 1864, Ellen's baby was born, a strong and lovely boy, and soon afterward he was baptized Charles. She herself was very ill and had to remain in bed for a longer time than usual. She found it a pleasure during those days of enforced idleness that the new church was so near that she could hear the music and the priest's voice preaching. As soon as she could be propped up on pillows and hold a pen she wrote Cump to relieve his worries about her.

By that time General Sherman's armies were over a hundred miles past Chattanooga, and had defeated Johnston at various points, until at last he was retiring toward Atlanta. When Cump wrote complaining that he was getting no mail from home, Ellen sent him one long epistle with full statements about everyone: Minnie was home from school, all but grown up. Charley, the new baby, was well and had a good disposition, although he showed a bit of Sherman temper now and then. His hazel eyes saw more at six weeks than the others had at three months and she thought he looked even more like Cump than any of the others. Tommy loved the baby and wanted to walk around holding him all the time; he was so delighted that this was not one more girl; there were enough in the family now. Rachel and Elly were growing fast; Lizzie was in better health than she had ever been.

She also wrote that she hoped he would like the present Lancaster was preparing for him. Over seventeen thousand dollars had been collected, and the town was hesitating between a silver service and a fine horse. She knew well which was her choice, but she was not surprised when they decided on the horse. Ellen asked Cump's advice in regard to taking a house at Notre Dame, putting the girls and Tommy in school there and keeping the smallest with her either in a house or at the hotel. Cump wrote back that he approved of this idea and urged her to go ahead. They both knew it would not hurt her father's feelings if she did this, as it inevitably would if she took another house in Lancaster.

Mr. Ewing was opposed to having baby Charles taken away, but Ellen thought the clear air in Indiana would be good for him, as he was suffering from a cough.

"But I'll never stay away from Lancaster very long," she assured Mr. Ewing. "I'll fit up a temporary lodging in the old Ewing homestead and live camp style every time I come here," she promised. She arranged her affairs in Lancaster and in the late summer went to South Bend with the children.

On September 1st, General Sherman sent a laconic wire to Washington: "Atlanta is ours and fairly won." The North was filled with rejoicing at the defeat of the army of General Hood, who had replaced Johnston, and at South Bend Ellen found herself quite the heroine of the celebration in the reflected light of Cump's glory. People she did not know called on her at the hotel. One evening there was a serenade outside her window, and Dr. Kenrick pulled her to the window and introduced her to the crowd.

It was a deep satisfaction to her that Cump was now being lauded to the skies. But Ellen Sherman no longer spoke as boldly as she had in other years about the war or about the people who opposed the efforts of the Union. The hard years had given her patience and understanding, and now she was only waiting for the end, praying it would come out well for the country after these tedious, heart-breaking years. She felt exactly as her husband did when he wrote Minnie: "Tell the Sisters who teach you that you are the child of one who is fighting that they may have a country and peace."

The Mayor and the Councilmen of Atlanta had made numerous petitions to General Sherman against the evacuation of the population of the city, but the General had written them that he could not do less than what he had to do, that war was cruelty and it was difficult to refine it: "You cannot have peace and a division of our country. I want peace and believe it can only be reached through union and war, and I will ever conduct war with a view to perfect and early success. But, my dear sirs, when peace does come, you may call on me for anything. Then will I share with you my last cracker and watch with you to shield your homes and families against danger from every quarter."

Ellen was especially glad to have baby Charles at South Bend, for in that clear air the cough which had troubled him grew better. But he was no longer the gay laughing baby who crowed so joyously that mother and nurse both ran to be the first to pick him up. In Lancaster when Ellen bathed him there had always been an admiring crowd around, one holding the pin cushion, one the starch bag; everyone wanted to give just one pat to the fat little body, and the baby enjoyed it all as much as they did. Now, when the girls came from school to visit, they were amazed at the change in Charley, and Minnie wrote to her grandfather they could not believe this was the fat and healthy baby they saw at home only three months ago.

Ellen tried to tell herself that the child's illness was temporary, and that good nursing would make him well, but when the illness suddenly turned into pneumonia she admitted to herself what she had known for some weeks: Charley was not going to recover.

Mother Angela came to help nurse him and Ellen hung over his bed day and night. On December 4th, the doctor said his life was a matter of hours. Ellen held him on her lap, his tiny hands in hers; she was still holding him, his wide open eyes looking straight at her, when he died.

Heartbroken, Ellen dressed the baby in his best white dress, and she and Mother Angela took the little body to the Academy parlor, where students who were Children of Mary kept watch about his coffin; flowers were placed about his small head, a tiny palm leaf in his hand. Father Sorin, the superior of Notre Dame, performed the funeral rites for the small citizen of Heaven. Four children carried the casket with its embroidered white pall and the mourners followed.

Only Cump was not there. In fact he did not even know the baby was dead. Charley was ten months old when he died and his father had never seen him. For several months Ellen had heard nothing from him. The prognosticators said it was Charleston or Augusta for which General Sherman was aiming, and that there General Lee would meet him in surrender negotiations. Peace rumors had flown about ever since Lincoln and Seward had met with Southern peace commissioners, and there were reports that rebels and sympathizers were already escaping to Mexico.

All Ellen knew was that the General was engaged in some hazardous maneuvers through enemy country, and that he was in the midst of daily skirmishes and battles. Never at any time during those weeks did she know where he was, whether he was wounded, or if he was still alive. He was reported on the march; she knew no more.

Mother Angela, knowing Ellen's grief must have some other occupation than care of the children, filled her vacant hours by enlisting her aid in preparing supplies for the army. Ellen helped fill the boxes and barrels of clothing and hospital supplies sent to the Holy Cross Sisters who were engaged in nursing the sick and wounded of both sides.

It was New Year's Eve before Cump had learned of the death of his little son. Only on Christmas Day he had written Ellen that he hoped she and the little one were enjoying it. He knew then the baby had been ill but hoped he would weather it.

He learned of Charley's death from an allusion in one of Mr.
Ewing's letters and later he saw the obituary in the *New York
Herald*. He wrote Ellen a comforting letter about the loss of the
"little baby I never saw," saying he had hoped so much that this son
would fill the great void left by Willy's death. "But it is otherwise
decreed and we must submit to it." And Ellen knew that was what
her own faith bade her to do.

Cump had made no mention of what he was doing, and this letter
had come to her without a postmark. She knew vaguely the great
objective of his campaign: to cut off Georgia and the Carolinas as
sources of supply for the Confederacy, and the defeat of General
Johnston, who was again in command against him. But one rumor
was strongest of all: peace was in the air and the war was almost over.

Ellen had received an invitation to be one of a committee which
was planning to hold a great fair in Chicago in the early summer of
1865. At the time it came she was too sorrowful over Charley's death
to think of accepting, but when in March Bishop Duggan of Chicago
wrote urging her to aid, she decided she would do so and agreed to
take charge of the Catholic exhibit.

The fairs then being held in many parts of the country for the relief
of soldiers and their families were a part of the work carried out since
the first year of the war by a group of churchwomen who had raised
funds for evangelical work among the soldiers and who called themselves "The Christian Commission." Before long it had become ap-
parent that it would be better to give badly needed material aid first
and to follow with the spiritual. So the Sanitary Commission as it was
now named, had ever since labored in many cities. The great Chicago
Fair was to be one of their activities.

Ellen took Tommy with her as escort and left the other children
with Mother Angela. In Chicago, she attended the committee meetings, and found herself so enthusiastic that she wrote to ask Cump
if he could possibly send something for her table. "We have ten thousand dollars to start with and expect to realize a million," she said.
He answered saying he had nothing to send her — "my saddlebags,

a few old traps, etc." — but that he would try to find something.

It was Ellen's first visit to Chicago and she liked the city immediately. It was prettier than Cincinnati, she thought, and she wrote Cump that the people were "very clever and social and compare well with the best people anywhere."

When Ellen returned to Notre Dame she found a distressed and unhappy Minnie: Mother Angela was being transferred. "We have a fine lady in her place," Minnie admitted, but she wept over Mother Angela's loss. She was much distressed too about the attitude of some of the Southern students toward Mr. Lincoln. "But most of the girls are for him, and I told the Southern girls that the Fathers all voted for him at the college," she said.

Soon afterward Mr. Ewing wrote Ellen that he was very lonely, and he was ill. Wouldn't she manage to come home for the summer? If she insisted on a house of her own, he would find one for her and her brood. She found his letter disturbing and decided to pay a quick visit to Lancaster to see how he was. She reached home on April 10, a happy day, for news had come of the surrender of General Lee to General Grant on the previous day.

"Oh, Father, can it really be true?" she said, tears of joy running down her cheeks. "No more fighting and killing and at last the people of our whole country North and South may hope to live together in peace and amity once more."

Mr. Ewing was as happy as his daughter. "But there are still obstacles, Elly. Will Johnston surrender at Raleigh? Or will he let his army simply disperse and bring a prolonged occupation on the country?" But such worry was brief, for less than a week later word came that General Johnston would surrender to General Sherman at a point midway between the two lines.

True to his promise, Mr. Ewing had found a house, and Ellen, with the war's end a fact, prepared it for occupancy and then went back to get the younger children. The others were to stay at school until the term was over, much to the annoyance of Minnie who wrote sadly to her grandfather that she was not coming home, as he no doubt had thought she would, but must stay "until I have reached the summit of the hill of science and surmounted all the difficulties attendant."

On April 16th, came news that made everyone forget the end of the war. Abraham Lincoln had been shot as he sat in his box at the theater, and no hope was offered for his life. When word of his death reached Lancaster, they shared the grief of the nation, and Ellen remembered what Cump had once said to her after one of his meetings with Lincoln: "Of all the men I ever met, he seemed to possess more of the elements of greatness combined with goodness than any other."

At St. Mary's President Lincoln's death was announced while the academy students were in the recreation room. A Southern girl had jumped on a desk and waved her handkerchief high over her head to show her joy. At this the usually gentle Minnie, who was standing beside her, quietly put her hand under the desk and tipped it over. The girl fell headlong to the floor, and at first it had been thought she was badly injured. But when it was learned she was not, the school authorities decided to consider the incident closed.

The news of Lincoln's death had reached General Sherman as he was leaving his train to join General Johnston, in a meeting which would, as General Johnston phrased it, let bygones be bygones. A day later Cump wrote Ellen the outcome of the meeting, dating it, "In the field, Raleigh, North Carolina." Terms had been arranged for the disbandment of all the Confederate armies as far as the Rio Grande, and submission by all to national authority. He said that when this had been ratified at Washington, "this cruel war will be over. I can hardly realize it, but I see no slip." He spoke again of the death of the President: "The South has lost its best friend. It may rue the day when these fanatics murdered the President, for they killed their best friend too. Did you know that two soldiers from Lancaster had been there in the theatre and helped carry him out? And Captain Sears said he would always keep the coat that was stained with Lincoln's blood."

He added that he had not forgotten the trophies for the fair; he was sending Ellen the Columbia flag and a Revolutionary seal, and giving her circulars to others who would collect trophies for her. "It will take all May and June to muster out," he ended, "so that the Fourth of July may witness a perfect peace."

When the peace terms between General Sherman and General Johnston were announced, Ellen, in common with many other people, thought them too mild. "I should never have agreed to such policies as that to deserters from our Union," she said to her father. But Mr. Ewing told her that this was only partisan speaking and that Cump knew what he was doing. "His only mistake, Ellen, is that he is ahead of his time."

But Ellen was not the only one who shared this feeling. There were indignant meetings of citizens throughout the North. In Lancaster an effigy of Sherman was burned in front of the Ewing house.

The objection became official. Secretary of War Stanton published in the papers of the North two war bulletins which officially rejected the terms agreed on, and General Halleck, then Chief of Staff, sent a telegram to Sherman's generals, telling them to pay no regard to truce orders from him. He called Sherman disloyal to the Union and partial to the South because of old friendships there.

A letter from Cump showed his anger at the accusation. "If Mr. Lincoln were alive, I should never have been insulted like this. We neither of us are the kind to kick an enemy after he is conquered. They almost dub me a traitor because I tried to bring peace to the country. What do they know in Washington? How can I tell them, shut up in their offices and rooms? The people here want peace, and for Heaven's sake let them have it. Do they want to keep on forgetting there in Washington that the war is over?"

Even Minnie wrote from school that everybody said the Johnston terms were too mild, but Ellen told her not to be disturbed by a little clamorous abuse. Her father had been in advance of his time and people had caught up with him before, though at the time they called his wisdom folly and supposed his end was to be without honor: "He is breasting a storm similar to others which he has ridden through in triumph and there is no doubt of the results. Be perfectly serene and *know* your father is not only brave and pure and good, but that he is *right.*" And she urged her to keep her mind off politics, and pray for him.

"I know Cump's motive is pure," she said passionately to her father. "How can they help but honor him and respect the heart that prompts such terms? I shall write and tell him that he is far dearer to me when people blame him than when they praise him."

Before long the entire attack against General Sherman backfired. President Johnson was angry that the matter had been so badly handled, and hastened to invite Sherman to call on him as soon as he reached Washington. Ellen was not to worry, wrote Cump, no matter what she heard: the President said neither he nor the rest of the Cabinet had seen the bulletins until they were in print, and he expressed his regret, as did all the Cabinet members except Stanton, who remained silent.

It was as Ellen had known it would be. Even bitter calumny would never hurt Cump. He had been through storms before and this was not the first time he had known abuse. General Sherman would always be sustained by the sober second thought of the people. As he had written to General Johnston: "The cause which made you and me enemies in 1861 is as dead as the rule of King George in 1776, and, like Humpty Dumpty, all the king's horses and men cannot bring it to life again."

The Grand Review of the Armies was set for May 24. Ellen and Mr. Ewing were invited, and Cump suggested that of the children she bring only Tommy since seating-space was limited. But it was not the review that interested Ellen; it was the wonderful fact that after eighteen months of absence, of suspense and fear, she would see Cump again.

She reached Washington the afternoon before the review. General Grant's review had taken place that same day, and General Sherman

had been on the stand with him. John Sherman met her at the depot
and drove her through crowded streets to his home; Cump had promised to be there as soon as he could get away from the reviewing stand.
She was waiting for him close to the living room window and she
waved as he looked up. When next he saw her the door had been
thrown open and she was running into his arms. She stepped back
to take a long look at him and saw that though he looked well, he
was very thin and his face carried deep lines of weariness.

The next day was warm and sunny. Washington was filled with
flags and bunting; the streets were crowded with men and women
and children, who carried flowers and bouquets to toss to their pet
regiments. At nine came the signal gun, and General Sherman, attended by his staff, rode slowly up Pennsylvania Avenue, his brigades
behind him, the streets lined with cheering crowds.

On the center platform of the stands erected on both sides of the
avenue were President Johnson and the guests of honor. General
Sherman rode past the President, saluting with his sword, and the
President and those with him returned the salute. Tommy, standing
beside his grandfather, gave a fine soldierly salute befitting a corporal
in his father's brigade; Ellen's may have lacked the military touch but
lacked nothing in fervor.

When he reached the gate the General left his horse and came to
the stand. He smiled at his wife, at Mr. Ewing and Tommy. He
shook hands with the President and the various Cabinet members.
But when he saw Stanton's hand extended he ignored it and went on
to the next man. Ellen applauded to herself the quiet way in which he
handled this situation, which had been unnoticed even by those near
him. Then he turned to stand beside General Grant, and took the
salutes of his men as they marched past.

For over six hours the lines marched by, the torn old banners carried as carefully as if they were cloth of gold. Mr. Ewing sat very
straight when Charles Ewing, slim and erect, came by, a brigadier
general at less than thirty years. Charley was looking straight ahead

as befitted a soldier, but when he was in front of the President's stand
he turned a bit, as if conscious of his father's eyes on him, and gave
him a light salute.

A gay week followed. There were evenings when Cump and Ellen
simply talked to each other, these two who had been parted so long,
who had suffered so much and who had the good fortune to be still
among the living at the war's end. There were receptions and ban-
quets, and a visit to West Point, which Tommy especially enjoyed.

When the week was over, the Shermans went to the Sanitary Fair
at Chicago. Ellen had hoped to have Cump's trophies to take with
her; to her delight she was to have not only the trophies but the General himself at the Fair.

On their way they stopped at Notre Dame where they paid a visit
to the girls at St. Mary's and together visited Charley's grave. Then
Ellen went to see the Sisters, and the General attended a dinner given
in his honor by the University.

He was met there by Father Sorin, President of Notre Dame, and
Father Carrier. At the dinner Thomas Ewing, Philemon's son, welcomed him in the name of the students, and Thomas Corcoran spoke
in behalf of the faculty, referring to the Sherman family's various
connections with Notre Dame; during the years of war it was there
that the General's children had been sheltered — Tommy and Willy
and the baby who died while their father was leading his armies.

When General Sherman rose to answer, it was evident that he was
deeply affected. In his speech he spoke of his children: "Who was a
playmate of Willy's is dear to me. I look upon Notre Dame with more
than ordinary interest, to it I am warmly attached," and he added that
the scenes of Notre Dame were made sacred to him by the associations of his son which it held. A scholarship was then presented to
him, and he said he would give it to the son of his old friend, Kit
Carson, the Indian scout, who was a Catholic.

That evening the Shermans boarded the train for Chicago. Ellen
had good news for the committee: General Sherman had agreed to
open the Fair and to act as its honorary president.

A fine gift to the Fair was made by General Grant, who sent his horse Jack, well known to the western armies. In a letter to Ellen he said the gift was a slight testimonial of his interest in the Fair. He wrote of the horse: "I left Illinois on him in July 1861 . . . I rode the horse more than all others put together . . . until called east in March 1864. . . . If I was not deceived in the purchase of Jack, he is now near eleven years old. He is a very fine saddle horse and very gentle in harness." This letter, said Mrs. Sherman, would be presented to the purchaser of the horse.

On the last day of their stay, Bishop Duggan gave a dinner in honor of the Shermans, and thanked them both for their help in making the Fair such a success — "especially our table."

## 13. The Shermans Return to St. Louis

### [1865–1869]

THE summer holiday in Lancaster was a happy one, and began with a series of festivities in honor of the return of Lancaster's famous son. The Shermans' arrival on a June day fragrant with early summer found a big crowd streaming behind them as the Ewing carriage went slowly up to the Hill. That evening everyone sat on their lawns to see the fireworks and listened to the songs in honor of the occasion.

Cump and Hugh, Charles and Thomas — they were all at home now, the four soldiers of the Ewing family, home at last from the dangers and trials of the past four years, years that had been full of anxious waiting for those at home. There was only one missing in the circle of the family, and that was Maria Ewing. But she lived on in the hearts of her children and grandchildren.

There had to be a parting, of course, of Ewings and Shermans, but it was not like the sad ones of earlier days. According to orders, the United States was now divided into five military divisions with General Sherman in charge of the Mississippi section — all the states north of the Ohio River as far west as the Rocky Mountains and as far south as New Mexico. His headquarters would be in his old home — St. Louis.

"We are going to have a home, Cump," Ellen said contentedly as they sat in their rooms at the Planter's Hotel in St. Louis in September, "and I hope we are going to live there for a long time." Cump had not wanted to settle on a house until Ellen saw it too. In the fine carriage he had bought, they drove to the house he thought the best of all he had looked at, a large red brick mansion, its front door opening into a hospitable entrance hall, with big parlors on one side and a library and dining-room on the other. It had four large bed-rooms, good servants' quarters and a finished attic. There was plenty of cellar space and an enclosed porch at the back. The front porch would be a pleasant place to sit on warm evenings.

Within five days they were in possession of the house, and the Shermans were settled at last. Though the General would have to be away often, even now, there was a home for him to return to; there was a home to stay in for Ellen — not someone else's house, even though it was the beloved home of her childhood. This was her own and Cump's.

There was plenty of company. There were card-parties, skating in winter, theater parties on Friday nights and minstrel shows on Saturdays. The neighbors often came over evenings and joined in community singing; officers from the General's staff came to call. Sometimes the family spent happy evenings alone.

On New Year's Day, 1866, Ellen was ill and Minnie was deputed to receive the guests. She felt very grown up in a new silk dress with lace trimming and flowers at her waist, a gold ornament in her hair. Heart beating fast, she welcomed the first caller, but after the first few arrived it grew easier. Many of the gentlemen did not know Ellen and they marvelled to find the General's wife so young. "I'm his daughter," Minnie had to explain blushingly again and again. It was the General who pointed out after the party that young men had come back to the Sherman house after paying calls elsewhere.

They had been for some months in the new house when the General broached a plan: he wanted to acquire a family lot in Calvary Cemetery at St. Louis so that Willy and Charley could be buried there. He and Ellen selected a plot, and on a trip to Washington the General stopped at Lancaster to get Willy's coffin, and again in Cincinnati for the monument which the Thirteenth had given as a memorial for the little sergeant. He had already written to Father Sorin at Notre Dame asking him to help with the removal of Charley's coffin. His friend Colonel McCoy was to bring the body to St. Louis.

The little boxes, brought from so far away, rested for a night in the Sherman parlor, with a blessed candle burning between them. Next day the family went with them to the cemetery where Father Walsh blessed the graves. Then the coffins were placed side by side in the ground; later the monuments would be placed over them.

It was a cold cheerless day and Ellen felt as if she were living over again those terrible days when her little boys were dying. At first she had been sorry about the removals and wished she had had both children buried in Lancaster and monuments erected there, but she could not oppose Cump's wishes. Now she was glad it had been done: she could visit the graves and see that they were well taken care of, and she had all her children in one city with her.

The end of the war had not meant any lessening of work for General Sherman. Railroads were being built across the West and trouble with the Indians had become very serious. The land had to be care-

fully reconnoitered before the work began to make certain the tribes
would not be hostile.

St. Louis was the gateway to the Indian country. The fur-traders
and steamboat men had their headquarters there, as did the great
scouts like Kit Carson and Jim Bridges. But there was one St. Louis
resident who dealt with the Indians for whom General Sherman held
greater respect than any of the scouts: the Jesuit missionary De Smet.
This priest's past history was one of great adventure among the red
men and of remarkable work, not only among peaceful Indians but
among even the warlike Sioux, whom most white men dared not
approach.

In late May of 1866 a letter came from Mr. Ewing. "Come and see
me soon," he wrote Ellen. "The country is very pleasant and the roads
good and it will soon be very hot in St. Louis." He had no exception-
ally fine carriage to offer her, he said, but the horses were of the best.
Would she come for a while and bring her five children; especially
since Cump was to be away for part of the time? As an extra lure,
he mentioned that the early cherries were ripening and it was going
to be a wonderful strawberry year; she would be able to do a great
deal of preserving to take home with her.

Ellen yielded as she always did when her father called, especially
since Cump said the family ought to get used to St. Louis summers
gradually and it might be a good idea for them to cool off in the Ohio
breezes. So she and the children left in mid-June, all excepting Minnie
who would join them later. She was going, with her cousin Kate
Willock, on an inspection trip with General Sherman — a wonderful
trip in a private car all the way to New York, with the president of
the road to see them off, and exciting stops in various cities. General
Sherman was still a hero, and crowds gathered at the stations to greet
him. The girls giggled with glee when, at a town on the western
frontier, an old-timer took a good look at the General, and said disap-
pointedly, "Well, now, I thought you was kind of a old cuss."

They were at West Point for Class Day, arriving in a carriage decorated with flags, and for Class Day at New Haven. They stayed in New York at the Astor House, in what Minnie thought were gorgeous rooms. Kate, a young lady of twenty-five years who had had seasons in society in Washington, was not too impressed, at least not outwardly, but Minnie was. She felt tall and awkward beside Kate, and though she tried to pose as a young lady she felt painfully young.

Philadelphia was visited, and then Boston where there were great ovations, and where they drove along streets decorated with flags, and later in the morning attended a great reception in the General's honor. In Boston a young man named Michel, one of a party of students escorting the visitors about the city, was very attentive to Minnie who at first did not realize that the attention was actually meant for her.

The afternoon she spent with her father, but Mr. Michel appeared at the hotel that evening. "Did you have a pleasant afternoon?" she asked him.

"As pleasant as one may be expected to have who sees everyone else enjoying what he would wish," he said gloomily.

"Why are you so dissatisfied?" asked Minnie innocently.

"Because you are so satisfied," he retorted. "I wonder how long such a state of affairs will last."

"As long as my father is my hero," she answered, "and I hope that will be always."

He laughed. "Sometime you'll fall in love and be sorry you spoke so lightly of love."

That made Minnie feel badly, for she hadn't exactly meant to do that.

Next day she went with her father to the Jesuit church and in the evening to a party where there was fine music, and where Mr. Michel soon appeared and took her to the conservatory to show her the lovely roses; he liked the red ones best but Minnie said she preferred the pale flowers. Next morning Miss Minnie Sherman received a big bouquet of pale pink roses, and the next day another. When one arrived on the third day the worldly-wise Kate began to regard her cousin with new respect.

When they went to Harvard for Class Day, Mr. Michel was unable to be in her carriage, but he was in it on the return trip. His face lighted when he saw she was wearing pale pink roses. But too many Harvard boys had been buzzing about Minnie, and this had evidently annoyed Mr. Michel. "Why didn't you give your flowers to those doting youths?" he asked.

"I never give away presents," said Minnie primly.

"I should think you would throw those away," said Mr. Michel eyeing the roses.

"Why?"

"Because of your feeling about the party who gave them to you."

"Would that show indifference?"

"Well, it would give him an answer to a question he wants to ask, and it might save him and you some trouble."

They were just crossing the Charles River bridge, and on impulse Minnie threw her flowers into the river. It was his answer and it startled not only him but Minnie too. She looked at the others in the carriage, but evidently they merely thought that she was throwing her bouquet away because it was faded.

In the evening an elderly gentleman took her for a stroll through the grounds of the house where she had dined. He told her tales of the old Boston he knew well, and that evening she confided to Kate, "I think I like old people best."

For the girls the trip ended at Cleveland, while General Sherman went on to Washington to receive his commission as lieutenant general. Minnie was glad it was over; she could go back now to being a little girl again in her grandfather's house. There was something a bit wearing, a little hard to live up to, in this grownup social life.

Mr. Ewing was happy that summer with all the Shermans under his roof, for even the General was able to spend some time there. Tommy took swimming lessons and became an expert. Lizzie and her grandfather had many quiet talks under the trees in the side yard. The little girls ran about them happily all day long. And of course Mr. Ewing was always supremely happy when his Minnie was with him.

Ellen had found her father looking older, but his brain was as agile, his wit as lively as ever. When she asked how he felt, he smiled a little wistfully: "Well, daughter, not the way I did the year I threw an axe over the courthouse steeple." But he pushed aside inquiries about his health. The doctor had tried to cure him. "He resorts to heroic measures sometimes, but he talks me almost dead."

In late July Mr. Ewing had a return of his illness, with hemorrhages that left him pale and thin. When he was again able to be out of bed it made Ellen sad to see how bent he was and how old he looked.

When she came to Lancaster she had found him reading a great deal of Church history and many books on theology. One day he said to her, "Ellen, I have been praying earnestly this year that I may have the joy of sharing your mother's religion."

"Then I shall add my prayers to yours, Father," said Ellen eagerly.

"You see I have done a lot of thinking lately. We have seized and controlled nature, I said to myself, that is true. But I begin to think that all our increased knowledge is of matter. Of soul and spirit, of man's being here and his final destiny, we are being taught nothing. It is all beyond the reach of human research and experimental philosophy." He drew from under his pillow a worn little book, a copy of à Kempis. "Do you remember when Archbishop Purcell gave me this book, Ellen? Well, I've taken it with me everywhere and if I didn't have it along I'd feel lost."

"Perhaps some priest could tell you more than you could puzzle out for yourself," Ellen suggested.

"I've had him already," he assured her. "Father Stonestreet at the Jesuit Church of St. Aloysius in the capital — I went to talk with him when I was down there."

"I'll send you something you will like when I go home," Ellen promised, "some of Brownson's articles. He has a brain like yours and he had to think his way into the Church just the way you will have to."

When she went back to St. Louis she urged the family repeatedly to pray for Grandfather Ewing, and she asked her brother Hugh to do so when he came to see them on his way to Holland, where he had just been appointed Minister to the Hague.

Two old friends arrived and stayed for several weeks that winter — Mother Angela, with whom Ellen reminisced about Notre Dame and the Gillespies, and Mrs. Bowman with whom she renewed old days in San Francisco. Ellen had news to give them: she was expecting another child early in the new year.

Cump was in Mexico on a delicate errand of diplomacy for the President. He would be home in time to greet the new arrival, he had assured Ellen, and he was. In fact, he came home in time to plan an open house for the New Year, with Minnie to preside in her mother's place.

If Minnie felt any qualms on this first formal occasion of being hostess she did not show them outwardly. During the day, from eleven in the morning until late at night, she received her father's guests, almost a hundred of them, in the parlor. The General was complimented over and over on her aplomb, and he watched with pride the nice manners of the young girl in her simple silk frock. As for Ellen, she was delighted to have a daughter old enough to relieve her of some of her social duties, and planned that after a while they would alternate in performing them.

On January 9, 1867, their last child was born to the Shermans, a boy who looked like a tiny edition of Cump. He was to be named for his father and his uncle — Philemon Tecumseh Sherman, and because he was frail at birth his sister Minnie baptized him the day he was born.

When Tom heard the choice of names for the newcomer he gasped.

"Philemon Tecumseh! That certainly mixes Greek and Indian in a great confusion, Mama."

Ellen laughed. "Well, we'll call him Pancratius Sebastian if you and the rest don't like my choice — after the two characters in *Fabiola*." And Tom subsided.

When the baby was six weeks old, General Sherman took him to the little church of St. Bridget to be formally baptized. His godfather, by special permission of the Jesuit authorities, was Father De Smet, and he and the General came to the church together in the latter's carriage. All the family was present and Minnie, standing proxy for Mother Angela, the baby's godmother, held him in her arms the entire time.

Little Cumpy was not a very strong baby, and his delicacy worried his parents. Elly and Rachel loved him wholeheartedly and were a little uneasy when he cried, fearing the family might send him back. "You'll keep him anyhow, won't you, Mama?" Elly would ask earnestly.

The whole house circulated about this new baby and even the General tried his best to use a tender and persuasive tone when he spoke to his small namesake. The intention had been to call him Philemon, but somehow that was forgotten and he became Cumpy to everyone.

The Sherman household at Garrison Avenue was a happy, busy place that winter, with Minnie the only one of the family absent. She was in New York, finishing her education at Mme. Chegary's school. She enjoyed New York with the limited freedom the French school allowed its pupils. There were the Hoyt cousins to visit and Uncle Charley Ewing called at the school whenever he came to New York, and always managed to get permission to entertain his niece. She was beginning Latin, she wrote home, "But I suppose Tom will get ahead of me since he started first. And I hear he is studying Greek too," she added enviously.

Her letters were well written and Thomas Ewing was very proud of those she wrote him, and complimented her highly: "Your letters are good and written in a bold handsome hand — good letters, well composed and would do no discredit to your mother who writes as good a letter as any Lady I ever knew."

The house on Garrison Avenue in St. Louis ran smoothly and well. The nurse was still the Emily who had come to them when Elly was born, a young German girl, now married to Pat Quinn, the General's orderly. The cook was a very efficient person who formally called Cump "the Master" and Tom "the Young Master." "How absurd," said Ellen, "when in every well regulated family the woman is master," but that did not move the cook who saw no humor in the remark. This cook was a stingy soul on occasion, not with the family but with other servants, and Ellen had to see to it that the colored man who worked for them got enough to eat.

Living was cheap in St. Louis. There was venison, quail and grouse in abundance; there was wild turkey, its meat to the children's surprise, all dark. A whole deer cost five dollars and good beef was only twenty cents a pound. Ellen often drove to the markets and filled her carriage with enough meats to last a week, for they kept well in one of the cellar rooms which Cump filled with river ice.

The General had gone South that fall and returned home very happy at his reception there. All classes, all sorts of people, had flocked to see him and offered him hospitality and marks of friendship. "Bragg came to see me and he was friendly like the rest," he said. "If there is resentment it is not against me." He had made the entire trip by rail, over the very country through which he and his army had marched long weary weeks three years before.

He made a western trip also, for the Indian situation was worse. In 1867, an Indian Peace Commission was organized to effect agreement with the friendly Indians, but the Sioux refused to be present. They said, in fact, they would kill any white man who approached them. In this crisis the Commission turned to Father De Smet, and he agreed to go and talk to the Sioux. He left on his mission with a few interpreters and a small escort of friendly Indians, and pushed

over three hundred miles into the Sioux encampment on the Yellow-
stone River. He was well received, and held long talks with the chiefs
— the much feared Sitting Bull among them — persuading them to
send delegates to meet the Commission. Then he went quietly back to
St. Louis with his report. The General could hardly credit it. "It is
one of the sublimest feats ever ventured on among hostile Indians,"
he said to Ellen.

He knew that anyone but Father De Smet would have taken a
troop of soldiers to cross the plains. As it was, he had found out the
chief reason for the Sioux' hostility: buffalo would not cross a railroad
track, or come near them a second time, and this meant scarcity of
hides and robes and meat, the necessities of life itself for the Indian.

To add to the General's difficulties, the Treasury was refusing to
give him the money which Congress had voted for disbursement
among the Indians, and which was to be paid them for the land taken
by the railroads. He decided to see the President about this, and that
opportunity came sooner than he expected. In October President
Johnson called General Sherman to the White House for a confer-
ence on another matter. He was engaged in a bitter fight with Congress on the method of reconstituting the Southern governments, and
himself a Southerner, he could not agree with the harsh tactics of
Sumner and Stevens or Stanton, his Secretary of War. Eventually he
asked the latter to resign and put Grant in his place as temporary
Secretary.

The situation grew worse and Ellen wished with all her heart that
Cump were not involved. Even though the mildness of the surrender
terms had not been to her liking, she did not for a moment want to
see the South put under military government, for which there seemed
absolutely no need unless to serve tyranny and selfishness. While she
cared for the baby and sewed for the family and read the papers, she
was forming her own opinions on political matters. "I have made my
ticket," she wrote her father. "It is for Andrew Johnson and Tom
Ewing. With that ticket we can sweep the country."

The family was divided that Christmas, for the General was still

in Washington. For Minnie it proved a wonderful holiday, for her
father came to New York for her and took her to the capital with
him. She stayed with her Uncle John's family and had a gay time,
even dining at the White House with her father and her grandfather.

At home little Cumpy enjoyed his first Christmas stocking. While
the rest watched, he ate the candy dog he found in it, calling it bow-
wow between bites, took out all the small toys and broke them rapidly, tore up the book placed in the toe — and his holiday was over.
Later in the day something, perhaps the candy, made him ill and
Ellen called a doctor. After he had diagnosed the illness as not serious, she asked him to have a glass of wine and offered him one of
the General's best Havana cigars. The aroma in the room as he
smoked was delightful, and it reminded her vividly of her absent
husband. "I hope you will soon be smoking by your own fireside
with no politicians to molest you," she wrote to him that evening.

In February the General came home. "Good," said Ellen. "I'm
tired of being both wife and widow."

The winter had been very cold but when Ellen went to Mass on
St. Joseph's Day the air was mild, the spring sun warm. She had
always had a deep devotion to this saint and it grew as years went
by. He had been the earthly guardian of the boy Saviour, and he
was the patron of little boys and young men. She prayed that he
would unite his prayers with hers for the two sons who were no
longer with her and for the two who were still in their home, and
for all the little wayfaring brothers in the world.

As soon as the weather made it possible she saw that the little
graves in Calvary cemetery were bright with flowers. She still went
there often but she did not need the sight of the graves to keep her
memory green. Every year she made a note in her diary when their
birthdays came. "Willy would be thirteen today," she wrote this
year in her diary on his birthday, and a few days later she wrote,
"Little Charley would be five years old today."

As usual, Mr. Ewing had been urging the family to come to Lancaster for the summer, and when June came, with a temperature of 105° in the shade, Ellen was glad they had decided to go. Minnie, home from Madame Chegary's in New York, was already on her way to Ohio, openly rejoicing that her trip would end in Lancaster. She was going with her father to Cleveland to be bridesmaid for her cousin Mary Sherman at her wedding to General Nelson Miles. Minnie had not been well when she came back from New York, but now she was quite herself again. It was being with her family that had made her so much better, she declared — "and a few weeks in Lancaster will complete it."

When Minnie reached Lancaster the rest of the family was already well settled in the house on the Hill. The General had gone on to Washington after the wedding — "but I won't stay," he promised. "I want to keep away from there if I possibly can," he told Ellen, who was already worried as to whether not only he but all of them might have to go to Washington that coming winter. For Grant had been nominated for the presidency and if he were elected, it would mean that General Sherman would be General of the Army, with headquarters in the Capital. She was afraid that he might not reach Lancaster at all that summer, but he did. He came just in time to spend the Fourth with his "Sherman bummers."

The General had brought with him a gift presented to him during his journey: Roger Sherman's watch, which he had carried when he signed the Declaration of Independence. It was a curious instrument, very different from any watch the Shermans had ever seen, with its silver hands for the months, weeks, hours, days, minutes and even seconds. They all agreed it was "quite a curiosity" as Tom said.

"I will give it to you when you are a man," the General promised him.

General Sherman received in Lancaster a long letter from Father De Smet at St. Louis University, thanking him for a book of maps sent him. He said he had recently made a trip to Holland, and at the Hague he had delivered messages and packages entrusted to him for Hugh Ewing. He was old now and tired, he said — "but I would gladly devote the remaining of my days among the Indians." He expected to go West again soon and hoped he might consult the General on the subject of new difficulties which had lately arisen, and to solve which he hoped he might have his "assistance, counsel and advice."

Father De Smet had brought gifts for the Shermans from Rome, and would present them when they returned home — a painting from life of Pius IX which he was anxious to give to Ellen, and a relic of the True Cross, for which he had had made a silver locket with her name engraved on it. For his young friend, Thomas, a relic of Saint Stanislaus and another relic for his dear little godson.

In August Tom, who was now twelve, and Minnie, who was seventeen, left Lancaster with the General, who was going on a tour of inspection of the West. The building of the Union Pacific railroad had caused new uprisings among the Indian tribes, especially the Sioux, and it had become necessary to send soldiers to guard the workers.

The train stopped at various forts along the way — Fort Leavenworth, Fort Laramie, Fort Sanders, and at each place it was welcomed with flags and bands and salutes. There were parties too, for the army posts in the west were staffed with young officers just out of West Point, and Minnie had a gay time. At Fort Sanders they were to make a stop of several days, and General Sherman planned to make short side trips while Minnie and Tom stayed at the post. He knew his daughter would have a good time, for there was dancing and much gaiety and, what Minnie loved even better than dancing, fine horseback riding over the flat countryside.

Letters arrived in Lancaster from Minnie chronicling the wonderful time she was having. But late in August came bad news from the General: Minnie had been thrown from her horse and badly hurt. With no delay Ellen hurried to her, going to Omaha by train, then the rest of the way by army ambulance, a heavy wagon drawn by mules, a very slow method of transport to Ellen who was anxious about her daughter.

She hoped she would find her already on the way to recovery. Instead she found Minnie lying in bed, unable to speak, badly bruised and with injured eyes, her head entirely covered with bandages. There were no broken bones, but evidently the shock to the nervous system had been severe. The horse had run away and thrown her on a pile of rocks placed there for building the railroad bed. Her heavy hair had undoubtedly saved her life.

As soon as the doctor permitted her to be moved, Ellen took her to St. Louis. They traveled in a private car courteously supplied by the president of the railroad. It had been built for President Lincoln before his death, and was now sent because it would be more comfortable for the injured girl.

Then Ellen went to Lancaster to bring home the rest of the family. Mr. Ewing had enjoyed his Shermans longer this summer than he had expected. And he was happy when Cumpy, his youngest grandson, did not want to leave Lancaster at all and made a big fuss about going. Then Elly and Rachel joined in his laments, and Lizzie was almost as bad. Grandfather Ewing was greatly pleased with all this woe, and reminded them that he expected them all back next summer.

Not long after their return home came news that General Grant had been elected President. Ellen had herself favored Chase, and openly, but the General begged her to modify her views of Grant, and she did, at least to the extent of modifying her expression of them. But the chief reason she regretted the election of Grant was because she was afraid that the Shermans would have to leave their pleasant home in St. Louis and go to live in Washington.

## 14. *Social Washington*

### [1869–1872]

IN the spring of 1869 what Ellen Sherman had feared came to pass. With the election of Grant to the presidency, General Sherman became General of the Army, and Washington his official home. The house in St. Louis was closed and the Sherman family went to the capital to live.

The home in Washington to which they came was the gift of a group of admiring New York and Boston friends and had been formerly the home of General Grant. It was at 205 I Street and was a three-story brick house, with stables and gardens. It was some distance from the War Department and General Sherman usually went to his office on the one-horse streetcar which ran down the next street. The Sherman ladies found it too far away from the center of things, although Mrs. Grant had bemoaned the fact that she had had to leave it. More than once she told Ellen she wished they were back in the old place; they weren't half as comfortable at the White House as they had been in the house on I Street.

It soon became evident to General Sherman that the house was too large and too expensive for him, and he had it converted into two homes, renting one side to General Giles Smith, the postmaster general. Even so it held quite a household — Minnie, Lizzie, Elly, Rachel, Tom and the baby as well as their parents. Some of the children were away at school for months at a time, but two were permanently there — Lizzie and Cumpy.

The ménage ran like clockwork. Breakfast was at seven-thirty: fruit, steak, potatoes and hot cakes. Luncheon was at twelve. Dinner at five. On Sundays the Shermans often went to the White House for a family dinner with the Grants. Cumpy usually went along and ate sitting on top of the White House's unabridged dictionary.

For the first time in her busy life Ellen Sherman was called on to act as hostess on a large scale. It was not a role she cared for and she often sighed for the quieter life of St. Louis. The Shermans had frequently to give dinners and receptions for diplomats, both foreign and American, and for men in military and social life. When Mr. Ewing was in Washington and attended a party at the Shermans' house, he liked to watch his daughter rather than the company, to see her "queening it," delighted to see how well she knew what was needed for social success.

During the summer months, Ellen took some of the children with her to Berkeley Springs, a rather unfashionable resort, where the guests were quiet people who wanted to rest, as she did. There was a good band, croquet and bathing for the children, while Ellen sat in the shady groves, listening to the stream ripple over its pebbles, reading and soaking in the sunshine.

All too soon the busy life began again. The younger girls were at the Visitation Convent now, and Lizzie went as day pupil to the same school, while Tom was at the Jesuit college in Georgetown. Minnie, her education finished, made her debut, and assisted her mother at parties and receptions and the days at home.

Ellen often urged her father to come to live with them. Even with the Shermans occupying only half the house there would be plenty of room, she told him. She would close the doors between the parlors — "and you can have the back parlor and rest all you like," she wrote coaxingly.

But, although he paid them several visits during the winters, he insisted each time on going back to his own home to live. Mr. Ewing was an old man now and could not take part in social events as he had in other years. What he loved best of all was to gather his grandchildren around him and tell them stories of old Ohio days. Minnie often read to him and they talked politics; during the afternoons he and Ellen took pleasant drives together about the city. But after a few weeks he grew lonely for Lancaster.

If the gaiety of the capital did not appeal to Ellen Sherman it did to her eldest daughter. Ellen liked best those dinners with only the family present, with herself at one end of the table, the tureen before her, Cump at the other end carving the meats. But Minnie, like her father, loved parties, and she had her fill of them in Washington. Not only did she aid her mother at social functions, but as time went on carried out many of these duties alone.

Washington was a delight to Minnie Sherman. She loved it all — Pennsylvania Avenue, lively with the hum of passing crowds and children trundling their hoops on the broad walks, people promenading up and down past the White House, the War Department, the Treasury Building.

Washington was gay that year, for the bitter war, in which so many had suffered, lay in the past. In December the social life was well under way. Days at home and evening receptions were divided among the official set, so that friends would not invite the same guests on the same dates. Supreme Court justices had Mondays; Cabinet officers, Wednesdays; Senators, Thursdays; the others arranged the times between.

Mrs. Grant gave receptions twice a month at which the Marine Band played in the East Room of the White House and the conservatories were the place for trysts. Mrs. Hamilton Fish, wife of the Secretary of State, entertained charmingly, as did Lady Thornton, wife of the English Minister, at whose table the clever people gathered and where the talk was enthralling. At Mrs. Blaine's house, where Miss Dodge, who wrote under the pen name of Gail Hamilton, was often a guest, all was quiet dignity. One evening Minnie confided to her that she had a hard time keeping her calling lists straight and managing the invitations, and Miss Dodge patted her shoulder sympathetically. "Do you know what I do when things get all tangled up and in a snarl? I just get out my stocking basket and darn them all off."

Minnie was often at the White House, for Nellie Grant was one of her best friends. That winter the two girls had the idea of collecting military buttons, begged from their various owners, and they proudly displayed trophies given them by the President and General Sherman, by General Thomas, who nobly cut buttons from a suit worn in the battle of Nashville, by General Slocum, who gave them several from the coat he wore on the march to the sea, by Generals Sheridan, Meade and Schofield, Admiral Porter and others.

The President had seemed surprised at their request, but he called to his wife, "Julia, please go and cut some buttons off one of my coats for the girls — a coat that has been through the war."

Mrs. Grant thought it rather forward of them. "Ulysses, I don't think —"

"Never mind, my dear, just go cut them."

Admiral Porter's house was the rendezvous of the naval people, just as at General Sherman's home there were always many army uniforms to be seen. Minnie loved the glittering apparel, though she was sometimes amused by the young officers' pride in their regalia; they could hardly pass a mirror without a glance at the splendid image it reflected.

At the Admiral's there were many dances, to the delight of the young people, but few at the General's. Ellen permitted lanciers and other square dances, but she would have none of her daughters dancing the obnoxious waltz.

The wife of Admiral Dahlgren, who was in command of the Navy Yard, was an author, and the shining lights of the literary world came to the Dahlgren receptions, where the diplomatic corps and the Catholic clergy were also represented. Admiral and Mrs. Ramsey made the Arsenal a delightful post. There was always a band there, and though the roads leading to it were bad the pleasure that lay beyond was worth the trouble.

Another favorite drive was the grounds of the Soldiers' Home, where the roads were good and on bright days crowded with carriages. Long roads led through groves of tall trees, across bridges overgrown with luxurious vines; beautiful vistas opened at every turn. The Home itself was filled with veterans of the War of 1812 and the Mexican War who loved to talk about their own long-ago days of strife.

Minnie was often invited to dinner with the Grant family at the White House, in the private dining-room upstairs where there were no other guests and little ceremony. Mr. Dent, Mrs. Grant's father, who lived with them, was always present. Unless the weather was cold he spent his days sitting on the front porch of the White House, his hat on his head, his hands clasped on the top of his cane, his chin on his hands, red bandana in evidence. Ellen always enjoyed hearing him assure the President's guests that he was a Democrat, had always been a Democrat — "and I will always be a Democrat," and his Republican son-in-law seemed to enjoy this too.

At parties the talkative Mrs. Grant was always the center of a chattering group. She took a deep interest in accounts of parties, of dresses and hats, and even in harmless gossip. But the President was a silent man; at all parties, large or small, he sat perfectly silent and listened.

Once Minnie and a group of girls wondered if they could entice him into a real conversation. General Sheridan overheard them and said he would give a pair of gloves to the girl who could do it. Some of them tried, but a smile and a monosyllable were their only reward. Suddenly they were amazed to see the President talking animatedly to Minnie Sherman. Later she claimed the gloves, and General Sheridan asked how she had ever brought about such a burst of conversation. "I remembered Jack — the horse he gave mama for the Chicago Fair — and we talked about him," Minnie said.

The most unusual callers at the Sherman house that winter were a group of Indians, calling on Walk-a-Heap, as they had named General Sherman. They were tall, coarse-looking men, with stern forbidding faces, who refused to sit down. Ellen offered them ice cream which they had never tasted and which they ate with no sign of enjoyment.

The General gave them cigars to smoke, and these they did enjoy. When they were departing he gave the Chief a whole box of them which was acknowledged by grunts. Just as they were leaving, the Chief turned and handed the box to the interpreter who explained to the General that the Chief wanted to know if he might return the cigars and have Walk-a-Heap's daughter instead. The exchange was not made, and they filed out, leaving a somewhat alarmed Minnie who thought the "hgh, hgh," of their farewells almost as threatening as their suggestion regarding her.

There had been another Indian admirer of Minnie's at the Sherman house that year, but of a very different sort. Colonel Boudinot was a tall handsome Cherokee Indian, who had been an officer in the Confederate Army. He wore his hair long, to his shoulders, and had so beautiful a voice that when he began to sing, with Minnie playing his accompaniment, everyone came trooping into the parlor to listen. He had one song which he sang especially to her, his dark eyes on her red hair as he sang in melting tones, "You have tangled my life in your hair, Jeanette." He was always a welcome visitor in the Sherman home and the whole household called him by Minnie's name for him: Indian Sweet Singer.

In the winter of 1870, Prince Arthur, Duke of Connaught, son of Queen Victoria, toured the United States and Canada. On reaching Washington he was lavishly entertained, and among others the Shermans gave a reception for the distinguished visitor and Sir Edward and Lady Thornton. The pleasant parlors of the house on I Street were filled with guests in uniforms and in gay dresses. After the Prince had chatted with his hostess and her daughter, the General took him into the gun-room and from his treasured collection offered the young man his choice of two fine rifles.

Next day a ball was given at the British Legation and the Shermans attended. Ellen thought Minnie had never looked prettier, in her frock of white tulle over blue, her cheeks pink, her eyes bright. During the evening the Prince's equerry came up to tell her the Prince was claiming the next dance. When Minnie learned it was a waltz she excused herself. "I am not allowed to waltz," she explained.

"But His Highness desires it," said the equerry a bit helplessly.

"I cannot help it," said Minnie simply, and the equerry went back to the Prince. In a few minutes he returned. "The Prince asks if he may have the first square dance instead," and Minnie accepted.

At the end of the dance the Prince said he wanted to send Miss Sherman a little gift. What would she like? His picture, said Minnie.

Next day arrived a miniature enclosed in a gold locket, with a five-pointed star of diamonds and a pearl in the center. Later that week, the Shermans heard that when someone had asked the Prince which of the young women he had met in the States he thought the most engaging, he did not even hesitate in his answer: "Miss Sherman, without question."

With Minnie taking her mother's place at many social functions, Ellen could give more time to her charities. She was president of several societies and organized an Aid Society in the Jesuit parish of St. Aloysius. She became deeply interested in a Charity Fair to raise funds for building an Industrial Home for Girls in Washington, asking donations from her friends and from business firms, who contributed what one of the priests called "ponderous and costly presents." President Grant and the entire Cabinet promised to be patrons of the event and Mrs. Grant asked Ellen to come to the White House to tell her what she might do to help.

The General went every evening to the Fair, which was opened by the Mayor of Baltimore and where the Secretary of the Treasury made an address. He was always accompanied by a friend who could be counted on to spend generously. The affair proved a remarkable success and netted a hundred thousand dollars for the projected home. When it was completed, it was put in the charge of the Sisters of Notre Dame whom Ellen had been instrumental in bringing to Washington, and who already had a parochial school and an academy in the capital.

But perhaps those for whom Ellen reserved her deepest interest were the Little Sisters of the Poor who cared for old people. Early in 1871 she made them welcome, when they came from France to begin their work in the new world, and procured and furnished for them a small house on H Street. She took them small comforts, wrote letters for them, and read and translated their English ones. The Sisters soon became a familiar sight on the streets of Washington, as they went about their daily begging.

"But their place is much too small for them," said Ellen one day to Cump. "They can't take in more than six old women at a time." So Washington was asked to contribute funds to build the Sisters a home. Money came easily — perhaps because Washingtonians could not quite bear the sight of those small women lugging immense baskets and even carrying wood home on their shoulders.

This was work Ellen really loved, aiding the nuns in their good work and answering appeals for aid. She drove around Washington for hours from one department or bureau to another in the interests of a priest or brother who needed help. Sometimes in cases that touched federal jurisdiction she was a great aid to bishops and priests and sisters pleading for some poor unfortunate.

"You do Mrs. Sherman a favor when you ask a good work of her," said one priest.

In that year Bishop Vaughan of London came to Washington in the interests of his plan for an order of mission priests for Africa and the colored people of the United States. Mrs. Sherman invited him to luncheon to meet others who could help him. He told her he thought Americans an extremely kindly people, but the one thing he could not understand was their attitude toward the Negro.

Ellen having had no chance to talk to him herself, invited him after the luncheon to drive with her in her carriage anywhere he wished to go, hoping for a little conversation with her guest. However, as soon as the carriage door closed and they drove off, the Bishop took out his beads and said, "Now we can say the Rosary for the success of my mission." He led the prayers, Ellen made the responses, and when they had finished, the Bishop had reached his destination. At

dinner she told her amused family that all the private conversation
she had with the great prelate from overseas had been a greeting and
a farewell.

"Perhaps," suggested her husband, "he thought you might be ready
to say something about the Irish question. The *Times* carried some
excerpts on the subject from his *London Tablet* and they were very
controversial."

There was a twinkle in his eye, for he knew that Ellen lost no opportunity to show her pride in her Irish ancestry. On one March 17th
she had decorated her house in honor of the day by putting an Irish
flag above her front door. It happened also to be her regular reception
day, and when Mr. Hamilton Fish called he said, on greeting his
hostess, that he had hesitated to walk under that flag.

"You should feel honored," said Ellen.

When in the autumn of 1870 news came that Rome had been captured by the Italian government and that Pope Pius was a prisoner in
his own Vatican palace, Ellen at first read the news with unbelieving
eyes. When she realized it was a fact, she hung from the upper window of her home a yellow and white papal flag with crepe fastened
to it.

An hour later General Sherman was informed by the Italian minister that the home of the ranking General of the United States ought
not show its sympathy in such a way.

"What did you tell him, Cump?" asked Ellen, when her husband
told her of the incident.

"Well, I sent word back that I lived there and maintained the
house, but that it was Mrs. Sherman's house and I could not inter-
fere."

For a month the flag with its black rosette hung from the Sherman
house on I Street.

Late in the fall of 1871 Ellen learned that her father was very ill.
Tom, who was visiting at Lancaster with his family, sent a message

asking her to come immediately, and Ellen's heart sank, for she knew the end must be near.

Hugh was already there when she and Cump arrived. When she stooped over her father's bed there were tears in Ellen's eyes, but he smiled faintly and told her not to grieve. "I have outlived my span of life, Ellen, and I hope I will soon join your mother."

The next day he asked her to read to him Chateaubriand's meditation on faith, love and charity. When she finished she looked up and saw that her father's eyes were glowing. He told her that he had decided to enter the Catholic Church.

"It is no sudden thing I am doing, Elly," he said, and talked of incidents in his life which had moved him toward the Church. "Once in Boston I went into a Unitarian church and there were only a few worshippers in the fine pews. On my way back to my hotel I passed a Catholic church, evidently too small to hold the congregation for there were many kneeling outside on the damp ground. Such a picture had its effect on me. And there have been others."

Very unexpectedly Father Dominic Young passed through Lancaster during the next few days and stopped at the Ewing house. He too thought that Mr. Ewing was very ill, and on learning that he was ready to become a Catholic he gave the sick man absolution and extreme unction and said prayers in which the family joined. Two days later Archbishop Purcell came with the Blessed Sacrament, heard Mr. Ewing's confession and gave him Holy Communion.

Four days later he passed away very peacefully, and with his children about him. His last words were to Ellen, when he saw she was crying. "I have lived a long, useful and eventful life," he whispered, smiling faintly to comfort her, "and I am ready to go." Had he lived two months longer he would have been eighty-two years old.

St. Mary's Church was so crowded it could not hold all the people who wanted to attend Thomas Ewing's funeral services. Many came from a distance to the little town to offer their last respects to the old statesman. With Archbishop Purcell on the throne, Father Young sang the requiem Mass. Then Thomas Ewing was laid beside his Maria.

Thanksgiving of 1871 found Ellen Sherman once more without her husband who had decided to make a tour of Europe. He sailed on the U.S. Frigate *Wabash* as guest of Admiral Alden who was himself on his way to take command of the European squadron. Two young men were to accompany him — Colonel Audenried, his aide, who promised Ellen he would keep a faithful account of the trip, and Lieutenant Fred Grant, the President's son. The Grants and Shermans went together to New York in the President's private car to see the travelers sail.

But the *Wabash,* whose maiden trip this would be, did not arrive from Boston on time, so the President and Mrs. Grant had to return to Washington before the frigate departed. A few days later they came to I Street to hear about the details of the sailing from the Sherman ladies.

Mrs. Grant was much worried about Fred's shirts, fearing he had not taken enough with him. "Don't worry," the President comforted her, "they wear one for a while and then throw it overboard." This being no reassurance to Mrs. Grant, he added, "Of course with a string attached to wash it." Mrs. Grant was annoyed but Ellen laughed as heartily as did Grant at his own joke.

The day after Cump sailed was Thanksgiving, and Ellen, resting in her own room after the big dinner, thought that even with Cump gone one could not feel too lonely when there were so many young Shermans about. Ellen and Rachel were reading at one end of the room. Minnie would at any moment return from riding, and so would Lizzie who had gone to call on her Aunt Cecilia Sherman. Tom was down in the basement playing billiards with a boy who was spending the holidays with him. Young Cumpy was running up and down the hall shouting.

Ellen planned to spend much of Cump's absence in compiling a memoir of Thomas Ewing. Especially she wanted to preserve and hand down the story of his conversion, for to Ellen the greatest thing in his long useful life was its end — those years when he had studied the Faith so carefully, his final submission. To her his greatness lay there, despite all his other fine achievements.

The voyager in far places kept his family well informed as to his whereabouts. In December he had reached Madeira. "Odd foods," he reported, "custard apples and alligator pears". He had gone about in a strange carriage drawn by oxen. From Gibraltar the party had made a tour of Spain to Bordeaux, through the south of France and thence to Italy.

Rome had made him very welcome. He had attended a musical at the home of Mme. Jenny Lind Goldsmith, a luncheon at the home of Anthony Trollope's brother, and a ball given in his honor by his American friends, the James Lorimer Grahams. Prince Humbert had received him and his aide. He had visited Mr. Healy the artist, and Mr. Simmons the sculptor, both Americans, and at dinners at their homes met many members of Rome's artist colony.

Dr. Francis Chatard, rector of the American College, had arranged an audience with Pope Pius IX and taken the American party there. On the way Colonel Audenried asked nervously what General Sherman was going to do about "this kneeling business." The General replied he always acted according to regulations, and Audenried said sharply that he would not get down on his knees to any man.

General Sherman and his aide went through several rooms, through corridors, past people waiting their turn to see the Pope. The General reported to Ellen that when Audenried saw others kneeling he knelt too — "ahead of me."

The Holy Father and the General talked together in French. The Pope looked at the buttons on Colonel Audenried's uniform while he was talking and asked the name of the bird on them.

"The great American eagle," said Colonel Audenried with pride, and the Pope smiled at his emphasis.

In January the General had reached Naples, where he called on the King of Italy. He described him to Ellen: "He was dressed simply, his hair combed back, his face flushed and his large rolling eyes gave him a wild look." He liked much better the looks of the Prince Royal.

Writing from Cairo, the General spoke of the terrible mud huts in which the majority of the people lived, and of the great pyramids built for the dead: "My thinking is, it would have been much better for them to have taken more pains with the living. Our Negro slaves had better homes." He had seen boys and girls no older than Elly and Rachel carrying in their hands loads of stone and mortar that he could not himself have lifted from the ground.

From Egypt the party went to Constantinople, Sebastopol and Tiflis in the Caucasus. They were persuaded by the Grand Duke Michael to take a six-hundred-mile trip by carriage to Taganrog, on the Sea of Azov, where the new Russian railway system began.

From Moscow the General wrote that he had decided it had not been a bad idea for the small nations of the Caucasus to be swallowed up by Russia. Since Russia had ruled them their quarrels with each other had ceased; they lived in peace instead of eternal war. The Russians drove fast, he observed — "like Jehus." In Moscow he had met the Czar and Czarina. But what impressed him above all in Russia were the feats of horsemanship which the Cossacks had performed for him.

He promised to carry out Ellen's commissions when he reached Paris — "the region of shops and fashions." She wanted some braids of hair for herself and the older girls and she sent him samples to match the colors. Cump wrote he had sent the girls red and blue velvet jackets, embroidered in gold, from Egypt, and a lady's formal dress from Turkey, as well as jewelry from Italy: "then in Paris I shall balance accounts and see what else I can afford."

General Sherman had suggested that late in June, when Fred Grant had to return home, Tom come over to meet him in Paris and that they go together to the British Isles. This had caused a flurry in the Sherman house in Washington. Ellen and the girls had rushed about getting the boy outfitted and he sailed on the Cunarder *Russia*. He was only fifteen, very young to be going so far alone, but the captain of the ship promised to look out for him and his mother knew he was a very self-reliant boy.

Tom's letters began to come and they were very enthusiastic. Paris was wonderful. The Pinchot family from New York had offered to share their quarters near the Arc de Triomphe with the General and Tom. "It is easy for us to circulate and see everything," he wrote his mother.

In England he visited the fleet with his father and was presented to the Prince of Wales and Princess Alexandra, who was, he said, very pretty. Archbishop Manning was out of London, but General Sherman sent Tom to call at his residence and leave their cards. The Archbishop returned before they left and called upon the General, bringing Tom a book and a rosary.

In mid-August the General and Tom were on the way home: "and I'll come home prepared to stay quite a long time — unless Greeley is elected," wrote the General. "Then we will have a prompt hint that the pen is the mighty instrument and that Uncle Sam has no need of professional soldiers. I think General Grant must now be convinced that we of the old Army had better stick to the profession, however, than venture to cope in politics with those who are trained to it."

In September, Ellen Sherman with Minnie and Lizzie was on her way to New York to meet her husband and son. There was a grand reunion at the Astor House.

When his bags came, the General showed them the gifts he had brought — lovely laces, the gloves Ellen had asked for, gifts for the younger girls and Cumpy, and an oddly shaped package which held three long switches of hair. "I matched them myself," he said proudly, and Ellen and the girls laughed until they cried at the story of their father carefully shopping for switches in Paris.

Lastly, he laid in Ellen's lap a velvet case containing a gold brooch which framed a beautifully painted miniature Madonna by Raphael. "I bought it in Rome," he told her.

"I shall wear it always," she said, pinning it to her collar, and there was a world of thanks in her voice.

They reached home to find Cumpy waiting to ask his father a question after he had impatiently submitted to a kiss. It turned out to have nothing to do with his father's trip at all. He stood squarely in front of him and asked, "Papa, when you marched through Georgia did the Johnny Rebs run?"

The General looked at his youngest in surprise. "Run, Cumpy? What do you mean?"

"Did they really and truly run?" insisted Cumpy.

The General chuckled, his eyes merry. "No, Cumpy, they didn't. They walked and they walked all-fired slow."

# 15. *Minnie's Trip to Europe*
## [1872–1873]

AFTER his return to the United States, General Sherman began planning a grand tour for his eldest daughter, a tour inspired by his own. He arranged for Mr. Byers, once a colonel in his army and now Consul General to Switzerland, who was returning to his post, to take care of Minnie on the voyage. In Europe the Grahams and the Pinchots, American friends of the Shermans, would look after her.

The General prepared a long list of those whom Minnie must call upon and many letters of introduction. With the aid of Ellen and Minnie herself he mapped out an itinerary for her. Each of the three had a "must city." The General spoke of Paris; Minnie wanted especially to go to Rome; and Ellen was insistent that she go also to Donegal in Ireland to the town from which the Gillespies and Boyles had come.

All preparations completed, a very excited girl waved farewell to her parents from the deck of the *Celtic* on December 12, 1872.

Though the weather was stormy, Minnie was not seasick. Sometimes, she reported to her father, she was the only lady at the Captain's table. "And even the gentlemen were not there in crowds. The Captain is offering me a certificate of good behavior."

There were agreeable people on board, and the pretty red-haired girl with the gay wit and nice manners was a favorite. She was half sorry, when, early on Christmas Day, they landed at Liverpool. Mr. Byers escorted her to Mass in the city, and, since he was very anxious to get to his post, he hurried her through London without pausing and in Paris consigned her to the care of Mrs. Pinchot, in whose home she was to stay. To Mrs. Pinchot's salon came many distinguished Americans living abroad to pay their respects to General Sherman's daughter. Mr. Washburn, the United States minister to France, gave a dinner in her honor. Mrs. Pinchot's handsome brother, Johnny Eno, escorted her about the city and showed her the sights, and Mrs. Pinchot's young son, just Cumpy's age, made her feel at home.

Paris still bore many scars of the stormy time through which it had passed in 1870. They were visible in the charred walls of the Palais des Tuileries, and Minnie, looking at them, thought of the story of Empress Eugenie's flight from the palace through her garden and across the Channel to an alien land.

The Paris shops were full of looted belongings. In one of them Minnie bought a china tea-set, white banded with gold, each piece bearing a large N and a crown above the letter. She bought for her mother a pillow-case embroidered with the same N. Mrs. Pinchot helped her select a black veil of rosepoint, a black silk dress with long sleeves, a high neck and a train to wear in Rome at her audience with the Holy Father.

Her final Paris purchase was a little diary, leather covered, not two inches wide. "I shall keep a day-by-day record. I promised Papa," she told Mrs. Pinchot. And that evening she made her first entry, a mention of her visit during the afternoon to the cemetery of Père la Chaise and to the Louvre.

On the 28th of January, her twenty-second birthday, she engaged the maid who was to go with her on her travels. Mrs. Pinchot had suggested her own maid, Teresa, but she thought that Constance, whom Minnie had chosen, was the better choice. Teresa was pert and pretty and very young; Constance was a sober thirty-seven, intelligent and very good humored. "She will know the things necessary for a lady's comfort when traveling here," said Mrs. Pinchot, but the reason Minnie preferred her was because she looked so pleasant and motherly.

On February 6th she and Constance reached Florence, where she was to spend some time with the Grahams. On reaching the old palace on the Lugarno where the Grahams lived, Minnie learned that they were to be out of town for a few days but had made arrangements for her until their return. Her room was large and very cold; the one small grate fire gave out very little comfort, and for the first time Minnie began to feel homesick. She took Constance on a shopping trip and they returned with a few books — *Aurora Leigh* and *Rienzi* — and some photographs of the great art works of Florence.

"I am going to buy them wherever we go," she told Constance. "When I get home I'll have them put in a big scrapbook, and when I have children I'll show them the pictures and tell them about the places I saw. If I don't get married and have children then I'll look at them myself when I am an old lady."

Three days later the Grahams returned and everything was changed. Minnie found herself caught up in all sorts of gaiety, some of which were not to her taste. The Mardi Gras she did not like, with its hideous masked figures, its clouds of confetti, its roughness — "It was ridiculous," she wrote home. But the Fête des Fleurs was very much to her liking. She rode with Mrs. Graham in the latter's open carriage which was pelted with flowers and bonbons as they drove on the Corso.

There were churches to visit too; she and Constance went most often to Santa Trinità. Mr. Graham took her to the Pitti Gallery, where she bought more photographs, and for walks through the charming Boboli Gardens.

Late in February the Grahams took her to Rome with them to stay at their hotel. There were days of sightseeing and visiting friends in the American and English colony.

The Rome of 1873 seemed puzzling to the eyes of an American Catholic visitor. Less than three years before a triumphant army had invaded the city and taken it from the Holy Father. Rome now had two crowned heads and two courts. The King occupied the Quirinal Palace which had been the home of Pius IX, and the latter was a voluntary prisoner in the Vatican palace.

This divided allegiance had entirely changed the social life of Rome; anyone received at the court of the King was a "white," and the Pope's doors were closed to him. The great entrances to the palaces of the nobles were closed and locked, a symbol of their loyalty to the Holy Father; the owners lived in retirement and were popularly known as the "blacks."

Minnie went to call on Dr. Chatard, rector of the North American College, and one day Dr. Vaughan, the recently appointed Bishop of Salford, called on her. In her diary that evening she wrote, "He is charming."

When Dr. Chatard came to tell her that he had arranged a semi-private audience with the Holy Father for the following day, Minnie was so impressed by the news that she hurried to the church of the Capuchins to make her confession and in the morning received Communion there. Then, in the black dress and lace veil she had bought in Paris, she set off in a carriage for the Vatican, with Constance in attendance.

When she stepped from her carriage at the great bronze doors of the Vatican, Dr. Chatard came forward to meet her, and he escorted her past the Swiss Guards in their colorful uniforms up the wide marble steps of the Scala Regia, through several rooms, until they came to a small throne room where they were joined by a member of the diplomatic corps and his family. Minnie's cheeks were bright with excitement and her heart beat fast when Pope Pius, with the monsignori of his household, came from his private apartments. With the others she dropped to her knees; he passed from one to the other, and when he stood before Minnie she kissed his ring and he blessed her.

Dr. Chatard told the Holy Father that this was the daughter of General Sherman who had come to see him the previous year. The Pope smiled, spoke a few words to her in French, and gave her a second blessing after sending a special blessing to her mother and her family at home. He then laid his hand gently on the rosaries hanging on her arm and blessed them.

Later she met Cardinal Antonelli, who spoke with admiration of her father. "The admiration is mutual," she said to Dr. Chatard, as they walked to her carriage. "Papa says he is the most astute diplomat in Europe."

One morning Dr. Vaughan said Mass for Minnie in the crypt at the tomb of St. Peter and she received Communion from him. He told her afterward that St. Peter was his favorite saint. "I like to pray here," he said and touched one of the massive pillars. "St. George has found champions in the Protestant Press — they like his horse and snake so much better than St. Peter. Of course, he remains where he was, one of the three principal patrons of England."

She went to call on the family of Mr. George Healy, the American artist, and in his studio she felt very much at home, for there were many familiar faces on the easels and walls — her father's, those of Grant and Lincoln, and many others of her friends in Washington. Mr. Healy made a sketch of her, but was not satisfied with it and she promised she would sit for him again when she came back to Rome.

For Minnie's visit was drawing to a close; she was to spend the rest of the spring with the Grahams on the Bay of Naples. In mid-March they left.

Holy Week was spent in Castelmare, and often during the services there she wished herself at home. The old cathedral was never well filled and was a cold, desolate place. The palm they gave her on Palm Sunday had been only a bit of boxwood, and she missed the wonderful "Alleluias" of the American choirs.

But there were pleasant things to console her: all-day excursions and drives at the fashionable evening hour, a gay picnic luncheon at Paestum, eaten in the shadow of a Greek temple while strolling musicians sang old Neapolitan songs for them. One day Minnie eagerly watched as the *Brooklyn* of the United States Navy came into the harbor at Naples. It carried two young lieutenants, friends of hers at home, and they were eager to go about with Miss Sherman. The three young people took trips together: a drive to Virgil's tomb; to the Bay of Barae, " 'to which nothing in the world can compare,' says Horace," stated the erudite Lieutenant Buck; to the grove of the Sibyl; to Caserte and its fountains; and along the Via Aurania over which St. Paul had walked to Rome.

On rainy days Constance read aloud to Minnie in French and Mrs. Graham usually dropped in to listen, saying that she was glad of a chance to improve her French. Minnie spent some time during such days in putting her accounts in order, as her father had asked her to do. "Traveling is expensive," she wrote him, "but I can assure you I am as economical as I can possibly be and when I return I can give you an account of every cent I have spent since I left Paris. There I confess I got things a little mixed."

Minnie and the Grahams returned to Rome in the middle of May, and this time she was to stay with the Healys. They had four daughters and a young son, and life with them was much more like that in her own family circle. She wrote her mother that they were a "sociable family, yet truly Catholic and merry."

It was good to begin the day with Mass and to end a day of sightseeing with Benediction at the nearby convent of Marie Réparatrice in the little Via degli Artisti. She loved the hour of sunset — the Ave Maria hour — when the angelus bells rang in all the churches of Rome. At the Trinità dei Monti there were special "Mois de Mai" services which she and the Healy girls often attended in the evening. It was a deep regret to Minnie when her days in Rome drew to an end, and she went for her last drive with the Healys along the Via Nomentana and prayed for the last time in the Réparatrice chapel.

On the evening before they left, Minnie, like every other visitor to Rome, drove to the Fountain of Trevi and threw a penny into its waters with a prayer and a hope that she would come again some day to the wonderful city. In the little diary she wrote, "I will put Rome away as one of the dreams of my life." She knew she would never forget those weeks, praying at the Apostles' tombs, walking the streets they walked, visiting the rooms where great saints had once lived and worked.

The Healys were moving to Paris and planned to stop at various points of interest along the way. They invited Minnie to join them and she accepted, as it would enable her to see many other Italian cities.

On June 16th the party separated, Mr. Healy and Emily going on to Paris where the latter was entering the novitiate of the Madames of the Sacred Heart; the others, including Minnie and Constance, left for the Italian lakes.

Two weeks later they reached Luchon, and again the party divided, Mrs. Healy and two of the girls leaving for Paris while Minnie, Constance and Edith Healy drove over the Pyrenees to Lourdes. It was a three-day trip, much of it difficult mountain travel, and they stopped often to rest the horses and feed them. Finally reaching Lourdes at noon, they went directly to the Grotto and in the morning returned there for Mass.

The basilica being built on the rocks of Massabieille was not yet finished, but shrubs and flowers had been planted and a wide path, almost a road, led from the site of the new church to the Grotto which was enclosed in an iron railing. A gold lamp was suspended from the roof, and under the rocks where Our Lady had stood clusters of tapers burned.

The three followed all the devotions of Lourdes. They went often to the Grotto, to the old church, and to the Soubirous' house, where they bought rosaries and medals, a little bottle of Lourdes water and a statue of Our Lady. Minnie and Edith went to the piscina and were bathed in the pool.

One day Minnie went alone to see the Abbé Peyramale, Bernadette's defender in her time of difficulty. He was still at Lourdes, though Bernadette was now in the Convent at Nevers. Minnie had hoped to see Bernadette and talk with her, and she was greatly disappointed when the Abbé, a tall man with a powerful frame, told her it would be impossible. No one, even of Bernadette's own family, was any longer allowed to see her. "Her life is peaceful and happy now," he said, "and visitors would perhaps grieve her again and make her lose that peace."

But though he could not grant her wish, he was very willing to talk about little Bernadette to Minnie. "She used to go to drink at the spring sometimes," he said. "Few noticed her then. What she was eager to see with her own eyes was the procession of priests go to the Rock, as Our Lady had asked. But in April of 1864, when that came to pass, Bernadette was too sick to come — and so was I!" His voice was filled with regret for that lost day. "I wanted them to lift me to see the grand cortège, but I was too weak. All I had of it was to hear the bells."

"Tell me something more of Bernadette," begged Minnie, "something I can tell my mother when I go home."

"Well, tell her that Sister Marie Bernard is still little Bernadette," he said. "Her face is still that of a sweet child. It is so easy to understand the love of the Virgin for her. She is often ill but always sweet and patient. Sometimes the nuns think she is dying but she tells them, 'I shall not die yet.' She is very busy at the Nevers convent caring for the sick on days when she is not ill herself. And she told me when last I saw her that she loves the peace of her solitude and the joys of charity."

"I think she is a saint," said Minnie warmly.

The Abbé, smiling at her eagerness, gave her his blessing, and she went away with the feeling that she knew Bernadette well, so beautifully had the Abbé Peyramale talked about her.

On July 7th, Edith Healy went on to Paris while Minnie and Constance left for Lyons, and then went by way of Lyons and Montreux to Zürich where Minnie was to spend a month with the Byers. "Miss Minnie," the Consul wrote home to the General, "is resting, rowing on the lake, going on little excursions with us, and seems contented and happy."

The Byers were instrumental in fulfilling a dream Minnie had had ever since she first heard the story of Empress Eugenie's flight from Paris, and her romantic escape to England, aided by one of Minnie's own compatriots. Mr. Byers now asked if the Empress would receive her; and the Duc de Bassano answered that "her Majesty will receive with pleasure Miss Sherman as well as her friends." He offered a choice of days between two and four o'clock.

The Empress was at Baden, a watering place near Zürich, living there incognito as the Comtesse de Pierrefonds. On the appointed day, the Byers, a friend of theirs, Mrs. Cunningham, and Minnie Sherman went to Baden by train. They were greeted at the Empress' home by the Duc de Bassano. "How shall we address her?" Colonel Byers asked him. There was reason in the question, for the Emperor was dead and France now a republic.

"Oh, as Her Majesty, of course — and only as Her Majesty," the Duke said, showing them into the drawing-room, a fascinating place filled with a profusion of lovely things — tiny tables loaded with silver trifles, vases of flowers, photographs in silver frames.

The Empress, in mourning of black and white lace, welcomed them charmingly and placed Minnie beside her on a small sofa, motioning the others to chairs placed in a semi-circle.

"And now what language shall we speak?" she asked in excellent English.

"Your Majesty's perfect accomplishment in our tongue settles that," said Mr. Byers.

She brushed aside the compliment. "I learned it at school, and I lived for a time in London," she said. She asked questions about Washington and those she knew there. Then she observed, "I like the English people, and I like Americans equally well. But one thing that I cannot understand is why in your country you kept slaves and have no respect for black people even now that they are free. Is it true there is a great prejudice against them in your land?" she asked Minnie.

"Not in the part of the country from which I come," said Minnie.

"Then," asked the Empress, "would you marry a colored gentleman?"

"Oh, no," said Minnie.

The Empress smiled. "You see! I have sat many times at the Emperor's tables with colored gentlemen and anyone who sits at the Emperor's table is a fit parti for any lady." Then she turned the conversation and asked about Mrs. Sherman's health. "I have heard often from priests and nuns about your mother," she told Minnie, "and of her many good and charitable works."

When, after an hour of talk, Mr. Byers proposed leaving, the Empress insisted they stay longer. "I have leisure — nothing but leisure and rheumatism. Do stay a while longer and talk with me." The visit lasted a full two hours and later, back at the Byers' home, Minnie wrote home an excited account of it — of the Empress with her eyes blue as the sky and her soft gold hair and her fair skin, of the fascinating drawing-room and the interesting conversation.

On August 8th, Minnie and Constance said good-bye to the Byers and resumed their travels — first to Munich, then to Vienna, where they found the beautiful blue Danube very brown and muddy. To Prague, where she saw the Infant. To Dresden, Berlin, Amsterdam, Antwerp, Brussels. On August 27th they were back in Paris where Edith Healy met them at the train and took them to the Healy apartment. And one of the first things Minnie did was to shop about until she found a large folding fan of black ostrich plumes, exactly like the one the Empress Eugenie had waved so gracefully in the drawing-room at Baden.

Edith took Minnie to see Emily Healy at the novitiate of the Madames of the Sacred Heart at Conflans — a large gray house with gabled windows facing the Seine, lovely gardens and a great farm back of them. They found her happy and content, in fact, Minnie wrote home, "radiantly happy." And she wondered if perhaps her own vocation might, like Emily's, be that of a life in religion.

On September 14th, Mr. Healy helped Minnie with her many trunks, took her to the train, and even loaned her twenty-five dollars, for she had spent so much money in Paris that she had little left and could get no more until she reached England. Despite what Tom had told her of the fogs and mists of the British Isles, the sun shone brightly on her first sight of London and the good weather continued for her day at Oxford. But after a short time spent in sightseeing in and about the British capital, Minnie began to think of going to Ireland and to Donegal — the trip her mother had wanted her to take to the ancestral home of her forebears. In Dublin she and Constance were met by Father Hagerty, who had lectured in the United States and knew Mrs. Sherman. He offered to show them those beautiful spots of Ireland — the lakes of Killarney and Blarney Castle.

In Dublin Minnie also found her beloved teacher, Mother Angela of the Sisters of the Holy Cross, who had come to Europe to get postulants for her Congregation and to see the Holy Father about its Rule. There was much to talk about, but Minnie had little time with her, for Mother Angela was leaving Dublin that same day.

Minnie had used one of her last letters of introduction, written by her mother's friend, Father Butler of Chicago, to Mrs. Hyland, niece of the late Lord Primate of Ireland. Mrs. Hyland welcomed her warmly and Mother Angela wrote to her cousin Ellen, "Minnie is enjoying herself riding about in Mrs. Hyland's elegant carriage which boasts its family arms and outriders."

Mrs. Hyland took her visitor to drive at the fashionable evening hour in Phoenix Park and did all she could to show her about in the short time at their disposal. She paid Minnie a real compliment. "You are like an Irish lady," she said to her, and Minnie knew this was a remark to be treasured.

To reach Donegal, she and Constance found they must take a train to Ballyshannon, and then go by carriage for the remaining ten miles. The trip took far longer than they had planned and they did not reach their destination until six in the evening. The darkness about her contrasted strangely with the sunny, pleasant, lively place Minnie had heard so much about, and she and Constance shivered as they hunted about for a hotel in which to spend the night.

When they awoke the next morning and looked from their windows they could not see for a deep fog, which had scarcely lifted at all when they were ready to make their tour of the town. It was still dark and cold and they could see but little, and although they were told that the weather would clear later in the day they did not have time to wait. Minnie did not realize that they had come too late in the season, at a time when that far northern coast of Ireland was fog-bound and dreary; that in the summer they would have seen its bays and crags, lovely in the soft sunlight.

"Well," she said, as she left, somewhat troubled at thus leaving unexplored the site of her ancestors, "I can tell Mother I've been here anyway."

On reaching London the first time, Minnie had written to Dr. Vaughan, now in his see of Salford, hoping to see him on one of his trips to London. As he was then unable to come down, he wrote to Lady Herbert of Lea that a daughter of his friend Mrs. Sherman was in London. A few days later Minnie received an invitation from Lady Herbert inviting her for the following weekend to her home just outside London.

General Sherman had written of Minnie's visit to Mr. B. L. Stevens, the postal agent at the American Legation, and he and Mrs. Stevens came to call as soon as they heard that she had reached London. With them she went on extensive sight-seeing jaunts — to Hampton

Court, to the Tower, to see the changing of the guard at the palace, to the Cheshire Cheese, to the churches of London. At the end of the week, she left for her visit with Lady Herbert.

She looked forward to meeting Lady Herbert of whom Dr. Vaughan had told her so much in Rome. Born a Protestant, married into the great families of Somerset and Pembroke, she had, under the influence of her close friend, Dr. Newman, become a Catholic. Her husband had died young, leaving her with seven small children, a huge estate, and guardians who would not allow her to bring her children into the Church. Through Dr. Vaughan she had been the source and inspiration of many good works. Especially had she been a moving factor in establishing the Mill Hill Society for the help of missions in Africa and among the colored people of the United States. Dr. Vaughan had been very eager for Minnie to see the convent of the Congregation before she went home, because he was particularly anxious for Mrs. Sherman to become interested in this work.

The first dinner at the great mansion of the Herberts was an unusually formal affair for an American girl; there were many servants in attendance although only the family was at the table. At breakfast the next morning, however, Minnie was surprised to find Lady Herbert herself pouring tea at one end of the long table, and no servants in sight. On a side table were dishes of broiled salmon, chops, and eggs, and each one, plate in hand, helped himself. It was bewildering but pleasant.

As they were eating, one of the sons of the house got up, kissed his mother's cheeks lightly and casually said good-bye. Minnie thought he was going to the city for the day, and not until she saw him get into a dog cart piled high with luggage did she realize she was mistaken, for someone mentioned he was off for an extensive trip to South Africa. She was amused as she thought how the Sherman and Ewing families would act if one of their number were going so far away. The cool manners of the English amazed the American girl.

On Sunday she heard early Mass in the little private chapel of the Herberts, and later attended High Mass at Westminster Cathedral where Archbishop Manning preached. She went afterwards with her hostess to call on him. On Monday she was taken for a visit to Mill Hill by her Ladyship's friend Miss Hanmer, whom the Bishop had suggested as guide. Here she saw Dr. Greene whom she had known in Washington and who was now completing his theological studies. He promised to act as her guide about London on the following day.

After speaking with various members of the Mill Hill Society, Minnie was completely won by the apostolic zeal and spirit she found in this training home for missionary priests. And when Miss Hanmer told her that Bishop Vaughan was planning to establish a society of women to help with the work of the Fathers already laboring there, Minnie suddenly decided to see the Bishop before she sailed for home and speak to him regarding a thing which had been in her mind ever since she had seen Edith Healy at her novitiate in Paris.

After the weekend with Lady Herbert, Minnie and Constance returned to London and made ready to leave for Liverpool, where Minnie would sail for home, while Constance was to return to France. Minnie had written pleading letters asking that Constance be allowed to go home with her, but General Sherman did not think well of the idea, and Constance herself seemed anxious to return to her own country. But she had promised to stay until the boat sailed.

When Minnie went to the Legation to tell Mr. Stevens she was leaving, he asked if there were anything she especially wanted to see before she sailed.

"Yes, there is," said Minnie eagerly. "I want to see the Crystal Palace thoroughly and I can't go by myself or just with Constance."

"That will be a simple thing to arrange," said Mr. Stevens. "There are always nice young American officers in town, and I know one especially who is coming in soon for his mail. I know he would be happy to escort you."

She was standing by the window of Mr. Stevens' office, looking out at the busy London scene below her, when she heard his voice speaking her name. "Miss Sherman, may I present Mr. Fitch."

Lieutenant Fitch was a tall dark-haired young man, who said nothing at all for a moment and merely stared at her. Minnie could not know he was slightly upset because Mr. Stevens had just told him the name of the father of the girl for whom he had agreed to act as guide. The young man had not expected to escort the daughter of General Sherman.

Mr. Stevens broke the silence. "Could you take Miss Sherman to see the Crystal Palace today, Mr. Fitch?" From the young man's expression as he looked at the pretty girl in front of him, her smiling blue eyes, her face framed in curling red hair, it was obvious that he was ready to take Miss Sherman anywhere she wished to go.

Minnie and the Lieutenant spent most of the day at the Crystal Palace, and went for dinner to Simpson's-on-the-Strand. "The Navy always comes here," he told her, "because the beef is so fine."

The Navy was right. The beef was wonderful, and so was everything else — the steaming carts that stopped at their table, the white-capped chef who cut off a big slice and put it on her plate with a yellow slab of Yorkshire pudding. When the flower girl came to their table, the Lieutenant bought Minnie a corsage with a lace paper frill, and she bought him a boutonnière of a red rose with a bit of fern.

The two young people found they had many things in common. Lieutenant Fitch had been in the Navy during the War and told her of his part in it. Minnie told him of her visits to her father's camps. They discovered they had been in Rome at almost the same time. In January, two months before Minnie's audience with the Holy Father, Lieutenant Fitch had been presented to him by Dr. Chatard, who had acted as interpreter. The Lieutenant said the Pope had been very kind and asked him many questions about his ship and about navy life. Then he had given him a blessing for all his family and had said he hoped that God would protect him from the dangers of the sea and those of the land as well.

Dr. Chatard had taken him to see the catacombs, and at parting Lieutenant Fitch had given him a present of a rosary which he had brought from the Holy Land.

"The Holy Land?" echoed Minnie. "Have you been there?"

He nodded. "Just the month before I reached Rome. I had wanted to go there for years — ever since I listened to the Paulists in New York describing it in their sermons. But when I actually arrived it seemed impossible to believe that I was really seeing the land where Christ lived. Some time I'll show you my book of pressed flowers from the holy places. But here is something to prove I was really a pilgrim" — and he drew from his wallet a folded piece of paper.

Minnie examined it curiously. It was a certificate, printed in Latin. "Well," said Lieutenant Fitch, after she gave up trying to read it, "here is one phrase you can understand," and he pointed to the words, "the illustrious Mr. Thomas William Fitch, U.S.N."

After dinner they went to see Ristori in her new play *Renée,* and Minnie told the Lieutenant that she had met the great actress and that she was a friend of her father's. Then the wonderful day was over. The next morning Minnie and Constance went with all their luggage to the station to take the train to Liverpool. Minnie was thinking sadly about Lieutenant Fitch and hoping they would meet in Washington when she heard her name and looked up to see the Lieutenant standing beside her. He was waiting for them, he told her, and was going to Liverpool with them. He had hoped to do even more: he had tried very hard the evening before to get his passage changed so that he might go on her ship, but he had been unsuccessful. He was to sail the very next day while her own ship left some days later, but he assured her they would meet again soon, and he asked for the name of the hotel in New York where she would be staying.

The day before Minnie was to embark she went to Salford, near Liverpool, to keep an appointment made with Dr. Vaughan. In answer to her request for an interview, he had written a pleasant note inviting her to come. "My dear child, you will find a train to Manchester, Salford, on Friday from Liverpool, Lime Street Station, 3:30 p.m. Drive to Marlborough Square. Yours sincerely, Herbert, Bishop of Salford."

With youthful eagerness Minnie at once told the Bishop why she wished his advice. A few months ago, in Paris, after seeing Emily Healy at the novitiate she had felt that she had a vocation to the religious life. And at Mill Hill she had felt it even more strongly. Would he perhaps admit her into his new Society? She knew her mother would agree and she felt certain she could get her father's consent as well.

The Bishop listened quietly, watching her closely as she talked. When she had finished he shook his head. "Your vocation is in the world, child," he told her. "God has not called you to the religious life. I think you should marry the first fine Catholic man who asks you."

Taken aback by his decision, Minnie returned to Liverpool, her feelings a mixture of relief and regret. Lieutenant Fitch, who was speeding across the Atlantic three days ahead of her, was a Catholic! And certainly he was a fine young man. She wondered if the Bishop had sensed something in her own mind as she was talking to him.

On October 18th, after a sad parting with Constance, Minnie sailed from Liverpool. Next day at Queenstown her friend from Dublin, Father Hagerty, came aboard, took her to Mass and to dinner, and then back to her ship in time for the four o'clock sailing.

It was a rough voyage; during the first days the high seas made it impossible for passengers to go on deck. Later the sea died down, but the weather was foggy until they reached New York. Minnie who had been watching all evening for the lights of home to appear, suddenly felt she could not wait another hour to get there.

When she saw her father on the dock all her regret at leaving Europe was gone and only home mattered. In the carriage he answered her series of questions about everyone at home as best he could, and she tried to tell him a little about her adventures. They reached the Astor House in time for breakfast, and one hour later Minnie had a caller — Lieutenant Fitch!

Next day on the train to Washington, Lieutenant Fitch again appeared. His reasons were excellent: he was on his way to Philadelphia for an "examination for promotion." But he rode all the way to Washington, confiding to Minnie at the end of the journey that he had to take the next train back to Philadelphia.

General Sherman took the young man's presence calmly, evidently considering him one more of the youthful crowd that always surrounded his daughters. And when Lieutenant Fitch said that he hoped to see Minnie soon in Washington, the General took no special notice, although Minnie herself looked thoughtful.

To Minnie it was wonderful to be at home again and to compare European recollections with her father. Her mother was especially eager to hear about her audience with the Pope, of her visits to Dr. Vaughan and Dr. Manning. And above all she wanted to know about Donegal.

Minnie tried her best to forget how foggy and dark had been her brief stay there, and to give her mother a fairly pleasant picture of the birthplace of the Gillespies and Boyles. Evidently Mrs. Sherman was satisfied with her explanation that time had been too short to do much sightseeing in Ireland, since Dr. Vaughan had wanted her to come to see him before she left England. But Minnie thought she saw a twinkle in her father's eyes as she was explaining.

Minnie had brought gifts for them all, and her mother had one gift for her in return. She had completed her memorial to Thomas Ewing, and now gave Minnie her copy of the fine cloth volume, with its many pictures. It contained Ellen's own tribute to her father, although much of the book was made up of Thomas Ewing's own account of his earlier days.

Ellen showed Minnie the letters which she had received in appreciation of the work. "Lovingly and elegantly done," wrote Archbishop Purcell, in his shaky old hand, "the last of the grand old statesmen." Archbishop Bayley wrote, "I read it all through, though I am as busy as a man can be with little time for reading. I read it with delight." After his words of praise Monsignor Seton complained that the author had not autographed the volume — "so I pasted on the flyleaf your name from the corner of the envelope wrapper."

# 16. Minnie's Marriage

## [1874–1875]

THE Washington season was now on, and the little pieces of pasteboard which the General so detested were flying about. During Minnie's absence Lizzie had become her mother's social aide, going with her through the interminable calls and other formalities. Now that Minnie was at home these duties could again be divided. The General told Minnie, "The same set perambulates the city in fine carriages, all busy distributing bushels of pasteboard." Nevertheless he admitted that he got just as tired of Washington's "old-men parties."

General Grant's second term had begun during Minnie's absence, and the family gave an account of his second inauguration. One incident concerned a corps of cadets from West Point who had taken part in the inaugural parade. When it was over their officers had marched them to General Sherman's house to be reviewed. They arrived before he had returned from the White House and were made to stand at rest in the street.

The day had begun beautifully, with sunny skies, but by the time the cadets, who had left their overcoats in the train, had reached I

Street a cold sleety rain was falling. The officers had been received by the ladies of the house in the dining-room, but when Ellen had looked out of the window and seen the shivering boys standing there she excused herself and went into the kitchen, where she filled a wash-boiler with hot water, adding sugar and a good allowance of rum. Collecting all the glasses and cups she could find in the cupboard she maneuvered the cadets into the basement through the areaway.

When the officers heard about this there was great consternation, for it was a strict rule that no alcohol be served cadets, and on the General's arrival there were more expostulations, none of which bothered Mrs. Sherman. "The boys were chilled through and needed it," she said firmly. A week later the General told her with a smile that the army doctors had agreed with her and said she had probably saved a goodly number from bad colds and perhaps from pneumonia.

Cumpy told Minnie that he had decided to become a soldier. He had previously intended to go West some day and work among the Indians — an idea which had been promoted by his godfather, Father De Smet. But a recent experience had changed his mind. A delegation of six Sioux had arrived in Washington to see the General, and Cumpy had found them pleasant enough until they noticed his head of flaming red hair. They had insisted on running their hands through it, grunting with what Lizzie assured him was admiration. Now he was glad he had not accepted his godfather's invitation to go among such people.

He told Minnie in confidence that when he became a soldier he was going to wear his uniform all the time, not the plain clothes his father wore. For General Sherman was the despair of his sons, seldom wearing his uniform unless he had to. When full-dress uniform was made regulation — epaulets, gold shoulder sash, jewelled sword and studded belt — he disliked it intensely and was only happy when a later regulation allowed the General of the Army to choose his own uniform. After that he usually wore a simple black suit and black hat, and on his inspection trips a dark blue military cape and officer's soft dark blue hat with no insignia. When he went to the veterans' reunions which he loved he wore a G.A.R. hat like everyone else.

There were many balls in the capital, but in the Sherman family the old ban on waltzes still held. On one occasion late in November, 1873, when a particularly fine German was to take place and Ellen was firmly refusing to let Minnie attend, reinforcements arrived in the person of General Sheridan, who in some way heard that Minnie Sherman would not be present. He called on Mrs. Sherman, and, as she was unable to see him, left for her a card with the pencilled message: "I fear you are in the business of breaking hearts by not allowing Miss Minnie to go to the German. We go off tomorrow and just think of General Forsyth, if not of myself, and many others — do let her go. I will go to church, say my prayers or do anything that's holy and good if you will let her go."

Mrs. Sherman smiled over the message. She knew General Sheridan well, had in fact known him since he was an altar boy at St. Mary's Church in Somerset, when Thomas Ewing had interested himself in young Phil Sheridan and suggested that he take the examinations for West Point. So she sent word that Minnie would attend the German. She did even more: she invited the two generals for dinner before the dance.

Lieutenant Fitch had not delayed very long in making his appearance either. In fact, by January of 1874, he had managed to have himself ordered for duty in Washington.

For some time the family thought him only one of the numerous young men with whom the house seemed always filled, but on Valentine's Day Elly and Rachel, thinking to tease their sister, bought a gorgeous valentine and below the very sentimental verse they printed a large "Franklin S." Franklin Simmons, the sculptor, whom Minnie had met in Rome and who was now in Washington had been a fairly frequent caller since his return; his name seemed a logical one to put on the valentine. Minnie opened it, and looked up puzzled and surprised. "But he didn't sail on the *Franklin,*" she said, and gave away a romance none of them had suspected.

The following month, the engagement of Minnie Ewing Sherman to Lieutenant Thomas William Fitch was announced, and the wedding day set for October 1st, the young man's birthday. Two months after this announcement Nellie Grant was married to Algernon Sartoris, an Englishman and a nephew of Fanny Kemble. Pretty Nellie was just eighteen, brown-haired and blue-eyed, and her parents gave her a splendid wedding in the East Room of the White House. Minnie Sherman was one of the eight bridesmaids, who were all dressed alike in white, four carrying blue and four pink flowers.

During the summer, preparations were made for Minnie's own wedding. The wedding dress made by Worth arrived from Paris in a six-foot wooden box protected by black oilcloth so that salt water in the ship's hold would not harm it. It was of very soft, rich white silk, its long train trimmed with deep flounces, and wax orange blossoms trailed on the skirt at side and back. The veil was of illusion and would entirely envelope the bride. Another important dress arrived at the Sherman house. It was of white with little wreaths of forget-me-nots — Elly Sherman's first long dress.

The General had insisted on one thing when the young man asked for his daughter's hand: he must leave the Navy. For the General, like Thomas Ewing before him, did not want a life of wandering for his daughter.

"If that is the only difficulty," said Lieutenant Fitch, "I shall resign from the Navy."

"But then how can you support her?" asked the General.

"Well, I have a trade, sir. Nine years of active service in the Engineers' Corps and my engineering education. I can easily find some business where I can make a living."

"Can you build an engine?" asked the General rather sceptically.

"Yes, sir, I can — and design one too."

A few days later an offer came to Will, through a friend of General Sherman's in St. Louis — the management of a wire works there whose owner, Mr. Harrison, wanted him to undertake its re-organization. So the first home of the young people would be in a city familiar to Minnie.

When someone said to Will, "I thought men were so wedded to a sailor's life that no inducement could tempt them to forsake it," the young man turned to Minnie with a smile. "There is my induce-ment," he said quietly. "I have promised to forsake all else for her."

Now that her eldest daughter was engaged to a man of her own Faith, Ellen Sherman determined to show Washington what a real Catholic marriage service could be like. She knew that many of the guests had never been in a Catholic church, and now she had an opportunity to show them the ancient and lovely service, the beauty of the ceremonial, the sacredness of the sacrament as set forth in the Nuptial Mass.

The days before the wedding were gay and exciting ones in the Sherman household. Two of the bridesmaids came early — Kit Phillips, an old school friend of Minnie's from Cincinnati, and Bessie Smith from Philadelphia; the latter was not only an old school-mate of Minnie's but the daughter of General Kilby Smith, one of Sherman's own corps in the Civil War.

General Sherman smiled when Bessie came to greet him. "I don't know what I would have done without your father during the march to the sea," he said to her. "He had winning manners and a handsome face, and whenever a crowd of irate Southern ladies came to report some depredation I always said, 'Detach Smith at once and send him here to pacify them.' And he always did."

For two days before the wedding rain poured down, but Thurs-day, October 1st, dawned bright and fair. Archbishop Purcell, who was to officiate, arrived the evening before and was the object of much solicitude, for he was seventy-four years old and broken by years as well as by his labors. He rarely went anywhere now, but he could not refuse to perform the wedding ceremony of Thomas Ewing's grand-daughter.

Will Fitch's party had also come that evening. After Minnie and Will had gone to make their confessions at the Jesuit church, he went to the train to meet his mother and cousins. Will's father was too ill to make the journey, but Father Mooney, who had been the groom's pastor in New York and formerly chaplain of the New York Fighting Sixty-Ninth, was with them.

Next morning St. Aloysius' Church was a blaze of flowers and lights; more than two thousand were in the pews. The President of the United States and his Cabinet were there. Admirals and generals provided a glitter of uniforms, of gold lace and epaulets. Aunt Sissie Steele was there and General Thomas Ewing and Senator John Sherman. The organ loft was reserved for Mother Angela and the Sisters of the Holy Cross, the Little Sisters of the Poor and other religious.

As head of the State, President Grant and his wife were to sit inside the chancel. But Ellen learned that although Mrs. Grant was rather pleased to be asked to occupy so prominent a position the President was too shy to sit there. So a compromise was effected, and the Grants were seated outside the chancel but in front of the pews.

A few moments before eleven, Mrs. Sherman, looking radiant, entered on her brother Philemon's arm and knelt for a moment in prayer. Then came the notes of the wedding march and the wedding party entered, the bridesmaids followed by Minnie, her hand on her father's arm. For this occasion he was wearing his full uniform as General of the Army.

Will and General Hugh Ewing, serving as best man, met them at the altar. Will wore his navy uniform and an unusually dignified air, but for just a moment his brown eyes met Minnie's blue ones in a smile. At the altar, the General bowed and gave her to the young officer just as the procession of clergy came from the sacristy.

In the sanctuary Bishop Wood of Philadelphia was on the throne on the right, Monsignor Seton of Newark on the left. Father Healy, President of Georgetown College, Father Mooney and other priests, and acolytes robed in red and white filled the sanctuary. The celebrant was Archbishop Purcell, in rochet and tunic of rare old lace, a cloth of gold stole over his shoulders, looking like a medieval saint from one of Fra Angelico's paintings.

The Mass proceeded. Archbishop Purcell, leaning heavily on his gold crozier, for it was noon now and he had been fasting since the day before, gave the address. "When I think of the grandfather of the bride, Mr. Ewing," he said at the end, "he who gave such a fine example to his children; when I think of the grandmother of the bride, whom I saw laid out in death, when she looked more like a bride than a corpse; when I remembered how her husband walked into the room and gazed at that lovely form and walked out again — when I think of all this it seems as if I saw those blessed souls looking down from Heaven upon the scene now spread out before us and invoking God's blessing."

During the ceremony Ellen often looked anxiously at the old Archbishop, for it was clear that he was growing increasingly weary; but he carried through to the end, and at the last Gospel he blessed the congregation with a firm hand.

The wedding party left the church for the house and for the wedding breakfast. By one o'clock the bride had cut the wedding cake, healths had been drunk and everyone was ready for the reception which was to begin at three o'clock.

In the front parlor the General and Mrs. Sherman were waiting to receive the guests, while the wedding party was in the back parlor, Minnie and Will in the center under a large wedding bell of lilies, carnations, roses and jasmine, her bridesmaids grouped around her. There they all stood for three long hours while the thousand and more guests came to congratulate the groom and wish the bride happiness. Outside on the grounds the Army band played.

In one room were ranged the mass of wedding presents. A gold necklace from the Grants. From Mr. Stewart, the New York mer-

*Portrait by G.P.A. Healy*

MINNIE SHERMAN FITCH

chant, a wonderful rose-point handkerchief in a lovely case. Gifts from relatives and friends in Lancaster and Cincinnati, from Drexels and Childs and Hoyts, from the Ewings. The Archbishop gave Minnie a painting of the Assumption of the Blessed Virgin. From Cork, Father Hagerty sent her a Belleek salver and tea-set, packed in a japanned tea-box of red and gold lacquer, the packing itself of tea. Mantles and tables were loaded with clocks and music boxes, with silverware and china. There was even a poem, beautifully engraved, called "Epithalamium," the gift of Senator Cox.

From Bishop Vaughan came a picture of the Espousal of the Virgin, and a photograph of the Bishop himself in his episcopal robes, with a written blessing. Among the messages of congratulation was a Papal blessing, sent by Dr. Chatard, now of the Pope's household, who wrote that he was sure this blessing of the Holy Father on their marriage day would be "more acceptable than many a wedding gift." Lady Herbert expressed regret that she could not attend — "but I shall pray very much for you on that day that every blessing may be yours in future life, and I hope if you come to England you will come to see me and introduce your husband."

General Sheridan had come from Chicago for the wedding and his train was late. He had just time to grab a cup of coffee, change to his uniform, and drive at top speed to the church. "Sheridan's second ride," an amused observer remarked as he dashed from his carriage into the church. When the reception was almost over, General Sherman found him looking at the wedding presents. "A lot of things there, Phil," he said.

"Someone just told me there are thirty-six dozen spoons here," said General Sheridan with awe in his voice.

General Sherman nodded. "There are. What do you think of that? And I only hope the poor children will have something to put in them."

For despite all the lavish display of wedding presents, the young couple would have only what income the groom's ability produced.

After a night in Baltimore the Fitches went on to New York, the beginning of their wedding trip, which was to include a visit to Will's relatives in Brooklyn, Niagara Falls, Mansfield and Lancaster.

At the hotel they found a brief letter from Ellen, "Fondest love to my dear children. May Heaven bless you! All pretty well this morning. The Archbishop is better. One bridesmaid is gone. The rest lively and bright. Your little bird has taken a wonderful bath in my room. Your loving Mother."

She enclosed clippings from various papers chronicling the wedding, all of them commenting on its lavishness. But the editorials were kindly and they all contained a note of regret at the fact that the older Shermans as well as their daughters and sons were leaving the capital. For the reception which the Shermans gave their daughter had served another purpose: it was the General's farewell to Washington. At his own request — in fact his insistence — the headquarters of the Army was being transferred to St. Louis.

After lauding the General, one editor said of Mrs. Sherman: "The poor will lose one of their best friends, the young their most thoughtful patroness and society one of its most exemplary members." One and all the papers regretted that the "graceful and cordial hospitality of 207 I Street" would be no more. One writer waxed political, and ended his editorial with the remark that he hoped the General who was now leaving the capital would one day return as President — "we could then see the Executive Mansion restored to its original lustre and the purity of its first President."

"Mother will certainly not like that suggestion," said Minnie. "It is the one thing she is most afraid of."

Another writer praised the General as "the only soldier who distinctly saw the vast proportions the conflict would assume," and who had for his thanks been denounced as a madman. "I remember those days," said Minnie to Will, "for I was at school when it happened, and it almost broke my heart. I knew how good and fine he was and to read such things about him was dreadful."

All in all the clippings constituted a tender farewell to the Shermans. It was evident they were greatly liked, that they were considered unaffected and kind, and that rich and poor felt the same toward them.

While in New York the young couple went to pay a visit to the Fitch family, and Minnie met Will's father whose illness had kept him from the wedding. On Sunday they attended Mass at St. Brigid's Church, where Will had gone to school and served on the altar. Word had spread through the parish that Tom Fitch, once one of their altar boys, would be at High Mass with his bride, the daughter of General Sherman. Long before that hour the church was filled and crowds had gathered on Tompkins Square.

Father Mooney preached a short sermon and welcomed the bride and groom in the name of the parish; when the Mass was over he invited the young couple and their relatives to the rectory where champagne was served and good health and long life drunk to the bridal pair. Then he asked Minnie and Will to step out on the iron balcony which ran across the front of the rectory and greet the crowd gathered below.

That evening Will and Minnie took the boat for Albany and went on to the Falls. Then to Ohio, and after that to their new home in St. Louis.

The winter after Minnie's wedding, Ellen Sherman was once more living in St. Louis in her comfortable home on Garrison Avenue. Elly and Rachel were at school in Cincinnati; Tom was at Yale taking scientific courses at Sheffield College, after having received his degree at Georgetown at nineteen. There were at home in the big house only the older Shermans and Lizzie and Cumpy. But the Fitches' small house on Morgan Street was only a few blocks away.

The quiet of St. Louis was delightful after Washington's excitement. The General admitted that St. Louis was a dirty town compared to Washington and the street paving left much to be desired, but there were things to commend it — for instance, the difference between an honest community and a borrowing one. "There is pretension there and here there is honest substance," he said. The children, however, missed Washington. "St. Louis is the dirtiest city in the country," said seven-year-old Cumpy in disgust.

"But it has the nicest people in it," replied his mother.

Lizzie had chief charge of the household, although Mrs. Sherman retained supervision of the kitchen. The General complained of Lizzie's control only when it extended to the supervision of his own clothing. Her method was simple: she removed his old hats, shoes and suits and ordered new ones. "I don't mind the shoes or suits, Ellen," he said unhappily to his wife, "but I wish she'd let my good old hats alone."

The Shermans still had a great deal of company but there was no occasion for formal entertaining. When the young people were home from school, streams of guests came in and out of the house. There were also visiting relatives, as well as army officers passing through the city, and occasionally a Confederate general came to call.

The General's office was in his home, and to this busy place both Union and Confederate soldiers came for help. Some were completely down and out, others only temporarily out of funds. The only thing the General required was that they show him a certificate of honorable discharge or its equivalent. He would then feed them ham, bread and coffee, which the cook always had ready, and usually they received a little money. Some got clothing, collected by Ellen from her friends, and occasionally they were given an order for new clothing or funds for transportation.

One day during the summer after they returned to St. Louis, Ellen was sitting on the porch, quietly reading the *Louisville Courier,* when she saw on the front page the reprint of an article from the Georgia *Courier Journal,* accusing General Sherman of having burned a cotton factory in Georgia and later of having directed the burning of a convent in Columbia. The writer referred to Mrs. Sherman's great aid to the Catholic Church in the South, and said she had sent contributions to a fair in Atlanta: "Knowing the vindictive tiger she has for a husband, no doubt the burning of Columbia rises like an apparition before the soul of the lady and fills her with a dread of what will be the eternity of her husband."

Ellen read this to Lizzie. "Oh, Lizzie," she said in a voice in which anger and love were mingled, "I can't have them saying things like that about your father. And it is so bitterly untrue. Whenever he could he protected convents in the South and saw the sisters were safe if there was any danger of fire. I know that he sent your Uncle Charley to give help to the Ursuline Sisters in Charleston because he heard their convent was in danger."

She sat up very straight. "I shall write a letter to that paper right away," and she proceeded to pen one of her fervent defenses of Cump, and mailed it to the paper. The General had read the first article too, and, sent an emphatic denial of the story, ending his letter: "Mrs. Sherman is a Catholic, always has been one, and has extended charity to all alike, Catholic and Protestant, with a lavishness that actually impoverishes us. To question the purity of her motives is certainly a most unmanly way to reflect upon me."

He told Ellen not to worry. "Remember the stuff they wrote about General Grant, and later the country made him President. It was a strange war, Ellen, in which we fought our own people. Sometimes I could not sleep for knowing that hundreds of children were being taught to hate my name. And there were old friends in plenty who would have shot me dead if I had gone outside the camp. Of course there was destruction of property. Wherever an army goes there will be destruction. I used to pray for the war to end before our people became robbers and murderers. But that is war."

She nodded. "I know. The clamor never really did you any harm. It never hurt you. You have always been sustained by the sober second thought of the people."

On nearby Morgan Street, Minnie Fitch was not having an easy time on her husband's slender salary. Not that they were in any need, but circumstances had become very different for Minnie. Old

friends had warmly welcomed the young couple to St. Louis. They
had greatly enjoyed arranging their little house, and she had had
the pleasure of selecting and installing her own piano in her parlor.
It was a small, upright Steinway on which she often practiced. But
Minnie found life as the wife of an unimportant young man a very
great change from her rôle as the eldest daughter of General Sherman. There was little money with which to entertain or to return
the hospitality shown her and Will. Besides, her husband was much
too busy for social affairs. He was entirely absorbed in his business
and working hard to regenerate it, although he sometimes feared
it was too far gone for recovery. Mostly he was optimistic, feeling,
as did Mr. Harrison, that it needed only new blood. "I'm sure it will
be the answer to your father's hopes and ours too," he told Minnie on
his optimistic days.

Minnie's chief trouble during her first months of married life was
running a house on a small budget, a matter of which she knew little.
She began by having two maids, but soon reduced her staff to one.
On the first evening off for this general worker, Minnie announced,
when Will came home, that she had dinner ready.

"Good," said Will, "I'm tired and ready to eat."

The table was daintily set with fine wedding china and silver, but
Will looked in amazement at the menu there prepared for him: toast,
tea and cake. He stared at the charming array. Then he laughed long
and loud and hugged an annoyed Minnie. "Wait a minute," he said.
He left the house and returned with a porterhouse steak. "Now
come along," he said and pulled her into the kitchen, "and I'll show
you how to cook a steak."

He blew the fire until the coals were red, then he chanted, "Rub in
salt and pepper, broil on hot coals, rub in plenty of butter and gravy,"
as he worked deftly.

A fine dinner was the result, but Will was not at all sure that the
cooking lesson was as great a success as the steak itself.

In January 1875, Minnie learned of a belated wedding gift. She
received a letter from the Khedive of Egypt, written in French on

fine crested paper. It expressed his pleasure at the invitation sent him, and hope for happiness and prosperity for the bridal pair. He was sending, he wrote, a souvenir and hoped she would honor him by accepting it.

In March the souvenir arrived in the customs and proved to be a diamond necklace, consisting of four strands of diamonds with matching ear drops. Experts placed its value at three hundred thousand dollars, and a demand was made on the Fitches for the payment of a duty of seventy-five thousand dollars before the jewels could be sent to them. The sum overwhelmed the young couple, and it was suggested that the valuable gift be returned. The gift of a reigning monarch, they were told, could not be returned. Eventually Congress passed a bill allowing the necklace to come in free of duty, and in June it was released and sent to General Sherman.

But it did not go to Minnie directly for her mother felt that, since the necklace was really given because of the General's services to the Khedive in reorganizing his armies, it ought to be divided among the four Sherman daughters. Minnie agreed, but reluctantly, since it was, after all, her present. But the General secretly promised that as long as he remained General of the Army, he would send her an allowance of one hundred dollars a month to make up her loss.

The necklace, for months the subject of countless articles and editorials in the press, was sent to Tiffany's and remade into four sets of long pendant earrings and large brooches, and in the summer each of the girls received her share of the Khedive's wedding gift to Minnie Sherman.

In June 1875, the first child was born to the Fitches and named William Sherman. Ellen Sherman held him in her arms while Father Converse baptized him in St. Theresa's Church.

The tiny house was too small now, and the Fitches moved to a somewhat larger one on Eugenia Street. There Will's mother and sister Emmeline came to visit them and to see the new baby. Minnie had seen very little of Mrs. Fitch except at the wedding, and during the brief visit in Brooklyn, but she told Mrs. Sherman she was "gentle and sweet and shy" and a joy as a mother-in-law. She mended and sewed for Minnie during her visit and gave her copies of her best receipts. She began a patchwork quilt for her, but went home before it was finished. "Keep the patches, dear," she told her, "and I'll finish it the next time I come."

By the year's end the Shermans had coaxed the young couple to come to live with them, since there was so much room in the big house on Garrison Street and there were so few to occupy it. Will agreed, but only on condition that he pay his full share of house expenses.

To have a baby in her home again was a joy to Ellen, but she had little time to enjoy her grandson. Before summer news came from Washington that the General's headquarters had again been shifted and that he must return there. Hoping it would be only a temporary arrangement, Ellen decided to stay in St. Louis, while the General went to Washington. But Cump's letters to her were full of worry about income and the expense of keeping up two houses, and he said he hoped she would come to Washington. The move, he was certain, would be a permanent one.

She agreed. "You can trust me," she wrote, "to do the best under changing circumstances for all the children — whom I love better than myself — and for you — whom I love best of all."

She and Lizzie went about the house deciding what furniture to take with them. "I certainly don't want to take that old patched set with me," said Ellen looking scornfully at the living room chairs. "They were shabby when the Grants sold this stuff to your father's friends. Some of the carpets were actually patched — and when I think what was paid for them!"

Minnie and Will were to stay in the Garrison Street house for a time and Tom, who had finished his studies at Yale and was reading law in St. Louis, would board with the Fitches. Tom was to begin his legal career in the office of his father's friend, Henry Hitchcock, who had been on the General's staff during the march to Georgia. "No boy has ever had a better start than you will have," his father wrote Tom from Washington, "and you shall have every possible assistance until you are self-supporting." He sent him bundles of pamphlets and copies of government reports and promised more of them — "as you begin to take interest in public matters."

That summer, before she left St. Louis, Ellen heard rumors that greatly distressed her. The Republican National Convention, meeting in Chicago, wanted to nominate General Sherman. The Democrats were ready to nominate Samuel Tilden, recently a crusading reform governor of New York, and it was necessary for the Republicans to find a strong honest man to run against him. In an editorial the *New York Herald* called on General Sherman to "accept the call."

When Ellen heard of this, she wrote immediately to urge Cump not to be persuaded to do this — "I beg of you to resist all allurements to this terrible step. Let politicians enter the arena. They can bear the brutal combat and you cannot."

The General reassured his worried wife: he had already sent word to various friends who were delegates to the convention to squelch any such movement. And when a wire came from Chicago asking General Sherman to reconsider his decision, he wired in return stating that he would not run if nominated and would not serve if elected.

Ellen laughed with relief when she showed the letter to Minnie. "First your grandfather was done out of the presidency. Now your father does himself out of it."

## 17. Tom Sherman

[1876–1878]

IN MARCH 1876, Ellen turned the Garrison Street house over to Minnie and, with Cumpy and Lizzie, departed for Washington. She had planned to live very quietly but, though she managed to evade most social affairs, she found that before a month had gone she was as busy as ever with church work. The clergy and nuns were very glad to have Mrs. Sherman with them again and to have her help with their problems. And she could not refuse when Archbishop Bayley asked her to undertake a very important work. In the following May, Pius IX was to celebrate his golden jubilee and a circular from Rome had been sent to the hierarchy, asking them that a fitting celebration of the event be made by a united offering to the Holy Father. It would serve, among other things, to show that he was loved and respected and that his people sympathized with him in his imprisoned life in the Vatican.

The Archbishop wrote Ellen that he himself was far from well, certainly not strong enough for so great an undertaking. Would she take charge of the collection? If she agreed, it would be with the understanding that she was to have entire charge of everything.

Ellen agreed and found she had undertaken a gigantic task. She made the Ebbitt House where the Shermans were living headquarters for her appeal; she had a circular printed and sent to the various dioceses of the United States, stating that in this country as elsewhere this collection was to be entirely the work of the laity. She expressed the hope that men and women in every city and town would take on the task of raising contributions and would forward them to her at the Ebbitt House. "Our fellow Catholics through-out the world," read the circular, "have undertaken to celebrate the day and have called upon us to join them. Shall we be cold and in-different or by our offerings give such testimony as shall be worthy of our Pontiff and of us and our country?"

There was no end to this correspondence, for Mrs. Sherman thanked each contributor personally, no matter how small the sum. When the task was completed and the results tallied, the amount her committees had raised ran into the hundred thousands, a fine tribute to a man who was so truly, in his self-made imprisonment, a servant of the servants of God.

When the actual day of jubilee arrived in May, the house of the General of the Army was decorated with the papal colors side by side with the stars and stripes. Ellen Ewing Sherman was rewarded for her hard work in an unexpected and delightful way. In token of his gratitude the Holy Father sent her a gold rosary with a relic of the true cross set into the crucifix, and his portrait with a blessing written in his own hand.

In the early spring of 1878, Ellen took all the children to St. Louis for a visit. She herself was anxious to see not only her grandson but also the young granddaughter who bore the name of Eleanor Sher-man Fitch.

Tom was still living there, looking well, and apparently contented with his work. But occasionally it seemed to Ellen's keen eyes that Tom's interest in the law was not very deep. He himself said noth-ing to give her that idea, and after a while she dismissed the notion.

When St. Louis began to grow uncomfortably warm the Sher-mans made summer plans. Cousin Ellen Cox was ready to rent her house in Lancaster to them, and they all wanted to go, for, more than any fine watering place or summer resort, the Shermans thought that Lancaster was the best vacation spot in the land.

The General begged that at least one child stay with him since he would have to spend much of the summer in Washington and Rachel, now seventeen years old, was chosen. Minnie was to go ahead with her two children and stay in Lancaster until her third baby was born. Tom was to remain in St. Louis and live at Garrison Street with Will Fitch.

Ellen and Lizzie spent their days quietly, reading and paying a few calls, sewing and gradually getting ready for Lancaster. But suddenly the peaceful pattern of their days was broken, and by Tom. He came in to his mother one evening and said he had something important to tell her. Ellen stared at the sight of her usually calm son fumbling for words to express himself. When she caught their import Ellen knew her intuition had been right.

"It is just that I never really intended to be a lawyer, Mama. I tried it out to please Papa. I want to be a priest, a Jesuit. I have wanted that since I was sixteen. I have thought about it and weighed it and I know that is what I want to be."

For one lovely moment Ellen's heart lifted in praise to God. To have her son a priest — no joy could be greater. Then she thought of Cump and her elation died away. What would he say — Cump whose hope was all for a fine career in the world for this beloved son? Willy was gone and Cumpy was only a child. Tom was the son on whom his hopes were set.

Tom read her thought. "What Papa will say I don't know. I wanted to tell you first, and now I am going to write and tell him."

Ellen agreed. "You must tell him fully, Tom, and be sure to write lovingly."

Tom looked at her with worried eyes. "I have not spoken in all these years because I hated to disappoint him. If I had told him four years ago, he would have said it was just Georgetown influence and that it was folly, that I was a mere boy and had seen nothing of the world, that the idea would soon be forgotten. I knew he would tell me to go to New Haven for a while and see if my ideas didn't change. So I did just what I knew he would have told me to do, and lived a regular college life. Although it was certainly not the atmosphere in which priests are made, four years of it only made me the surer."

"If he were a Catholic he would understand," said Ellen. "As it is, I feel almost guilty, for I used to pray for this to come to pass. I even asked Father De Smet to pray for it as well as the Paulists, and Bishop Alemany, when you were a little boy."

"I don't want to get rich," said Tom. "I don't want to have a high place. I want to spend my life teaching the truths of God and helping people to learn them." The eager light went from his face and the boyish look was there again. "But I can't bear to hurt my father. I'll go to England to study if he wishes it. I can just tell people that I'm going for a year of further study there."

They decided not to discuss the matter at all while they waited for the General's reply. They spent quiet evenings reading *Our Mutual Friend* aloud in turn. Suddenly on the third evening Tom broke off reading. "I'm so glad," he said impulsively, "that you will all be together this summer — lots of relatives and friends in Lancaster. Then I won't be so much missed," and he went back to his reading again.

Next day a letter came, an even worse one than they had expected. But the idea which underlay all the General's objections was not that Tom was becoming a priest; it was what he termed "abandoning your family"; it was the blasting of his hope of handing on his name, and that rested with Tom.

He listed all the objections to Tom's decision, and they were just what Tom expected. He himself had thought of them all; he had weighed his duty against his affection, his love of home, his future, against a certain ease and perhaps wealth. And he knew he would do anything in the world for his father — except something against his conscience.

He wrote a second letter: "We start with different premises and we reach different conclusions and arguments are useless." General Sherman had asked him to wait a while longer before he made a final decision. "But how much longer," wrote Tom sadly, "am I to wait? These four years have been a small eternity to me."

Three days later another letter came from his father and this one was much less tempestuous and angry than the others but much harder for Tom to read, for it was full of love and tenderness and this time there was no charge of ingratitude and selfishness. Tom answered it in the same spirit and went more deeply into the details of his decision. He told his father that he had become sure of his vocation during the previous summer when he had gone with him on a trip through the Indian country. He had heard a great deal about the ferocity of the Flat Heads and the Coeur d'Alenes, and he had seen how much more a few Black Robes had accomplished among these Indians than regiments of soldiers. These were priests who had left their homes in Italy, giving up everything in order to teach these savages the simple truths which boasted civilization could not teach them. "Is that selfish, Papa?" he wrote. "I'd rather be Father Joset than Chief Justice of the United States. I don't want you to think that I'm so bigoted either, or that I think a man can't be honest and upright and charitable in the world. It's just that I think God approves all honest callings." Then he outlined what he hoped would be his future work: "I don't want to make money and spend it. I know I'm a selfish person and fond of dress and pleasure, but if you could only understand that the Catholic Church makes great changes in men. As for helping people, it won't be the lawyer who wins large cases and gets big fees from corporations. It will be a man who teaches people and persuades people. To reach them a man must be simple in dress and manners and his head must be stocked with knowledge to guide and improve people."

As he went to mail the letter he stopped by his mother's chair on the porch. There had been no further discussion of what Tom would say to his father, but Ellen knew in her heart what was being written. Tom showed her the envelope. "I'm mailing this to Papa. It is a long letter, and I could fill many more sheets with thanks for all he has done for me. But I think I would thank him most for allowing me to worship God as we think right. That he has done and always."

Ellen's heart went out to Cump in his sorrow; there was no waking hour when she did not send a prayer to Heaven for him. She could honestly say that she had never influenced Tom in his decision and she doubted if anyone else had. Until he told her of it finally, she had not even suspected it. And even now, while he was still with them, she herself felt the terrible loss it would be to have Tom away from the family circle.

She wrote to Cump, reminding him gently that he had always said a man must act according to his convictions. It was not defection, she wrote, but response to a call, even as he himself had answered his country's call, never listening to revilements and abuse but continuing in its service as long as he was needed. He would eventually realize that Tom must act according to his convictions: "I know, dear Cump, that you are stunned by the sudden shock," she wrote, "but after a while you will return to your natural kindness, generosity and justice. We would willingly offer our son's life in battle for his country. It is his belief that he is offering his life in a higher and holier cause, for the country which has no bounds, that he and others may gain entrance therein."

The General had showed Tom's letters to Rachel, and poor Rachel was helpless in the face of the storm they had aroused. She had written to Minnie that she did not know what to do about her father who could talk of nothing else but Tom's wrecking his life. "Why take my splendid boy when they could have brought over thirty priests from Italy to take his place?" he had demanded. Later it was decided that Lizzie would go to her father in Washington, for she was known for her ability to soothe and quiet him. Ellen would go to Lancaster and remain until Lizzie brought the General there, and Tom himself would meantime go to Washington to see him.

Tom had made his final arrangements. He was to go to England as soon as possible, to Manresa, the Jesuit novitiate at Roehampton, and he had already engaged passage on the steamer *Scythia*. "All of you will feel better to have the suspense and doubt over soon," he said.

The visit to Washington turned out better than the rest of the family, and Tom himself, had hoped. The General allowed Tom to say all he wished, let him tell him that Our Lord Himself had showed the way to people like him by Himself living a hard, plain, prosy existence. "There was a Parson John as well as a Captain John among our ancestors," he told him. Finally, when he said, "On some things we can't agree, Papa, but winds of doctrine must not ruffle the smooth sea of the deep affection between us, and the chief thing I want you to know is that I shall always be your devoted son," the General yielded, and gave him a grudging permission to go to England. He asked but one thing of him: that he first see Cardinal McCloskey and ask his advice; they would both abide by his decision. This Tom promised to do.

Perhaps one thing that influenced the General was the answer he had received to his appeal for help in the matter of his son's strange decision. He had written to Mary Anderson, the actress, whom he knew well, and who was herself a Catholic; he was certain that she had friends who could dissuade Tom from his course. Would she herself help to dissuade him? But he had received no help from this quarter. The letter that came in reply was kindly and sympathetic and understanding, but the viewpoint was exactly like Ellen's. Mary Anderson shared his disappointment but she could not share his feeling about Tom's future, and Cardinal McCloskey, when appealed to, gave the same answer. Tom, he thought, must follow his own convictions.

Before Tom sailed for England he wrote to Minnie in Lancaster in answer to a farewell note from her: "Any step seems rash and hasty to all who do not know what it is to watch and wait and hope and pray and long and doubt and despair," he wrote, "until a young heart grows old and can face anything to attain its object — especially if that object is God." There was a postscript: "For Papa's sake ask all to talk little about me." And his last act before he left the country was to turn over to Lizzie his savings, some two thousand dollars in cash.

On June 4, 1878, in the room in which Minnie herself was born, Thomas William Fitch, Junior, came into the world. Ellen did not reach Lancaster until after her grandson's birth for she had been busy in St. Louis getting the Garrison Street house ready for tenants, since the Fitches were planning to move to a smaller home.

Many things had to be stored. All Cump's relics of war days were put away carefully to be kept for the children — his swords, the hat with the bullet hole in it he wore at Shiloh and a few other beloved articles, among them the chest of drawers that was to belong to Eleanor Fitch.

During the summer Ellen had frequent letters from Tom at Manresa. Most of the time he had for letter writing was devoted to his mother, but he told her he had written his father several times. He had not really expected an answer but he planned to keep on writing anyway, since time would surely dim the memory of the sorrow caused by his action.

He regretted now that he had blurted out the news so suddenly. "The plain truth is," he wrote in a letter to Minnie, "that I had no common sense in me at the time. People in love do strange things and having a vocation is like being in love, as there is no love so absorbing, so deep, so lasting, as that of the creature for the Creator. The world sees only the black gown and the penitential aspect and has no idea of the solid peace and true contentment of mind and heart that the black gown brings with it."

The home to which the Fitches now moved was at Côte Brilliante, a farm which General Sherman owned and which his son-in-law rented from him. Minnie named the new home Sherman Place and settled down happily in the red brick house with its big porches. There was an ice-house on the property, a corn crib, a big orchard and garden. There were two horses — one for Minnie to ride, and another which Will drove daily to the wire works, down the little dirt lane that connected the property with the King's Highway to St. Louis. They had a cook, Julia O'Grady, a maid and a nurse. They also had Larry, the hired man, who took the pledge once a year and kept it faithfully. When the year was over he drank long and pleasurably for a few weeks and then took the pledge again. Minnie tried to get him to take it for two years at a time but Larry refused.

General Sherman sent them directions for making a grape arbor, an asparagus and a strawberry bed, and Minnie promised him the first bottle of wine from their own grapes.

Ellen did not occupy the house which General Sherman had rented in Washington until the beginning of 1879. First she felt she must go to Chicago where the Catholics of the city were giving a fair in honor of Archbishop Purcell. She wished to show by her presence her great esteem for this old man whose last years had been made unhappy by financial misfortunes beyond his control. She took with her three hundred dollars, the General's gift, to be spent at the fair, and, as her husband had been certain she would, she used it all. Then she went on to St. Louis to be with Minnie when her fourth child was born. The baby, a girl, was born on Christmas Day and was, the other children agreed, a very fine Christmas present. She was named Catherine, a name promptly shortened to Katy, but was often referred to as "the Christmas baby."

Ellen told Cump of this very busy Christmas Day when she finally reached Washington. There had been the tree in the morning and presents for the children. At five in the afternoon there had been a small party of which Ellen and Will took charge. At seven in the evening the baby was born and at eight she was brought in, in a pink shawl and fast asleep, to be presented to the company by her proud grandmother.

The new Sherman home in Washington was on 15th Street just back of St. Matthew's Church. Next to them lived General Van Vliet, an old West Point classmate, and two doors away James Blaine; next came Admiral Sands, another old friend, and across the way lived Charles Ewing and his family.

Several former Confederate generals came often to the Shermans'.

General Joseph Johnston lived a short distance away and was a frequent caller. Mrs. Johnston often came with him to visit with Ellen and General Sherman always enjoyed her sparkling talk. Once when he found her in the parlor waiting for Ellen, she greeted him with, "Well, General, during the war I spent all my time running away from you. But now it looks as if I am spending my time running after you." General Longstreet was another welcome caller. He was one general whose strategy Sherman had always upheld, claiming that he had been blamed for General Lee's blunders. General Joe Wheeler, then a member of Congress, came sometimes and the two generals argued on each other's tactics in the past conflict. General Sherman always complained that General Wheeler ought to have been blamed for at least half the destruction in Georgia: "You did that by your own burning and destruction of supplies," he said.

Young Cumpy was glad to be back in Washington. It was a clean city, and besides he found many old friends. Life was simple for the young in the capital. They went barefoot all summer long except on formal occasions, and these were few. They fished and went frog-hunting in the swamps that lay between the White House and the river. Cumpy was a proud boy when he could take home to his father a good mess of frogs' legs, a favorite dish.

The General had promised Ellen there would be very little entertaining, since at any time he might retire and give his place to General Sheridan. But with three girls to take over the entertaining, Ellen did not worry. She continued her church work, as chairman of the Ladies of Charity in Washington, and as working member on the altar guild at St. Matthew's. During the famine in Ireland she agreed to act as chairman of various entertainments designed to raise funds for the starving children. She herself helped generously, and pleaded warmly for aid for the poor souls who were living on a meal a day, of meal and water, in a land where the commonest staple of food — potatoes — had almost vanished.

One day the General found her looking over her assets with troubled eyes. On examining them he found they were almost nil.

"Ellen, Ellen, is your money gone again — all I gave you?"

"I've used some of my own too," she retorted. "The Christmas presents cost a good deal, and with Elly's getting married this spring and these Irish benefits I have to spend it. But I'm not wasteful, Cump — truly I'm not."

"Tell me, Ellen," he asked her, "do you and the children consider me close?"

"Of course not," she said indignantly, "I think you have always been most liberal and the children feel the same way."

She and her husband agreed on most matters but not about entertaining. On this they never did, for General Sherman insisted she had no more right to avoid the incidents of public office than she had to complain of the weather.

"But no public duties devolve on me," said Ellen tranquilly. So the General filled his days with engagements which sometimes lasted into the morning hours, and Ellen lived as quietly as she wished. She felt that what she had had to do in the past she had fulfilled faithfully. Now all she wanted was the children and her friends and her work in the church. These contented her and filled her life.

In the spring of 1880, Elly Sherman was married to Lieutenant Thackara. It was a small wedding but attended by distinguished guests — among them the President and the Cabinet members. Elly carried the silver filagreed flower holder which Henry Clay had given to her mother at her own wedding.

In the early summer of 1880 Tom took his first vows at Manresa, and on that day Ellen and Lizzie went to Mass and received Communion for his perseverance and greater sanctity. When he came home from England soon afterward he went straight to Washington to see his father. The meeting was a happy one. The General did cast a look of repugnance at the strange dress his son was wearing, but affection quickly gained the upper hand. "Papa has let his grand heart get the better of past disappointments," Tom wrote Minnie, "and received me most affectionately and showed no resentment."

He went on to Woodstock near Baltimore, to continue his studies, but on the way he stopped at Altoona where his mother and Rachel were spending a week, and told them the news of the reconciliation. He had taken his meals with the General and stayed at the house; he had gone to the Smithsonian with him and would have gone with him to the circus that same evening — "were he not taking a party of young girls with whom, of course, a young religious could hardly go. But best of all, we are good friends again," he told his mother. "I prayed for it, I craved it, and my keenest earthly desire is satisfied."

Ellen felt deeply content after he had gone: Tom was in his own country again, continuing his life's work; Cump had grown gentle towards their son.

## 18. *The Fitch Children*

### [1878–1885]

THE years began to follow a regular pattern for Ellen Sherman. Summers at mountain resorts — Altoona or Berkeley — a brief visit in Woodstock with Tom. Winters in Washington. Visits to Minnie in St. Louis.

The General, returning from a Western trip one year, had brought Willy Fitch back with him to spend a winter. Ellen was very proud of this grandson, and after a few weeks in Washington she wrote reassuringly to Minnie that he was a very good child and no trouble at all: "All we have to do is to read to him, and there are plenty of us to do that."

When Willy went home — "but I'll come again and stay till I'm

sixteen years old" — Eleanor Fitch took his place. It was her turn
to visit her grandparents, said Minnie, and besides she could not
spare Willy any longer. Willy had taken Washington very quietly,
but Eleanor came home putting on great airs because she was the
only little girl in the neighborhood who had lived in the capital.
After she had gone back to St. Louis her grandmother met a Quaker
lady with whom she was slightly acquainted who said, "I have been
invited by thy grandchild to visit when the spare room at thy home
becomes empty." Young Eleanor had also invited little Lizzie Thackara to come to see them — "because our cradle is empty." She
returned home to find a new baby occupying it. "Now what will we
do when Lizzie gets here?" she asked in distress.

Willy had resented this new baby, born in the autumn of 1881,
although he had been devoted to Katy from the day she was born.
"This new baby is mine because she looks like me," he had said and
it was true he and Katy were very alike. But Maria aroused in him
no enthusiasm. "We will not have any more babies," he said to his
mother with decision, "but if we do the next one will have to be a
boy and then we will stop."

By the summer of 1882, Ellen Sherman had six grandchildren:
Minnie's five children and Elly's one. But Ellen Sherman's own family circle had grown very small. Minnie was gone and Tom and
Elly. Rachel was in Europe with friends. Only Cumpy and Lizzie
remained — and Cump who was still the one, as she always said,
whom she loved most of all.

That spring Ellen worked on a long cherished plan for a summer
reunion of all her children and grandchildren. The house in Washington was too small for such a meeting but in Oakland, Maryland,
she found a comfortable, roomy house that would be big enough for
everyone, including Cump and the sons-in-law whenever they could
manage to come. Perhaps even Tom could come down for a while.

Early in June she went to Oakland with Lizzie and they selected
the rooms for each of the expected guests. Minnie and her children,
it was decided, were to have the two downstairs rooms on one side

of the wide hall, so that she need not always be climbing stairs. Ellen was especially anxious to have Minnie with her, feeling that she should have not only a change of air but a good rest from house-keeping.

After plans for provisioning and for arranging the rooms, Ellen and Lizzie settled down to await the arrivals. One afternoon, as they sat on the shady veranda and looked out at the fields of buckwheat flowering beside the house, Ellen began to talk of the dream she had never quite given up — the dream of a permanent home for the Shermans, or at least for what remained of them. The General was again talking about retiring. If he did, a small house in St. Louis would be best for them. "A quiet chimney corner where I can keep my papers and small possessions," she said to Lizzie. "I have lived in a crowd so much and so long."

She drew her plan for such a house that evening; it must have rooms for guests and it ought not to be too far away from Minnie's home. Perhaps a corner of Sherman Place would do nicely. A frame cottage would be nicest with growing and blooming things about.

"I cannot have such a quiet chimney-corner in Washington," she wrote Cump and enclosed her sketches in the letter. "Your rank and acquaintance preclude it, as do the habits of visiting and the customs of the place."

In a few days a reply came from the General, and Ellen looked with alarm at the result of her simple suggestion. For he was most interested in the idea and countered her plan with much more ambitious ones. She realized she had started Cump on something far beyond her small desires. As a result she feared she would find herself in a mansion that would be as much trouble as any house in Washington had been.

On the first of July, Will Fitch arrived with Minnie and her five children and two nurses. The next day Elly came with her little girl and a nurse. The General had promised to come in time for the Fourth and sent all sorts of things ahead — fireworks of every kind, big boxes of dry toast and the hardtack which the children loved.

Minnie was very willing to do nothing but rest. To get five small children ready for this trip had been no easy task. "I made four hundred button holes," she told her mother. "That left about three hundred to do, and those I had the Sisters of the Good Shepherd finish for me."

Katy was the special darling of them all. She was just three, a pretty curly-haired little girl who, as her grandmother said, had the light of Heaven in her blue eyes. She adored her grandmother and followed her everywhere, or sat in a little chair beside her big one, her doll in her arms.

The "Sherman bummers" had never had a happier Fourth of July than this one although Lancaster had seen some gay celebrations. The children played through the long day and the older people, in comfortable chairs on the veranda, watched them and talked. At dinner time they gathered — twenty-one of them at the long table. At one end General Sherman carved the great ham which had been roasted with an entire bottle of wine. At the other end the children were grouped about their grandmother. It was a very merry and happy meal. At night all the children but the two babies stayed up to see the fireworks, even small Katy. She fell asleep now and then, awaking only at an unusually loud noise from the lawn. At last she fell completely out of her little rocking-chair and the General picked her up and carried her to her bed.

A few days later the men went back again to their offices, and the women and children prepared to spend two happy, carefree months. Everyone liked the house, the grown-ups because it was so light and well arranged, the children because it was a wonderful place to run and play. Minnie had one small fear: her rooms, though large and well lighted, were damp. In the closet mould formed on the children's shoes, and one wall felt wet to the touch. But the children seemed very well and were outdoors a great deal, so Minnie said nothing of the matter to her mother who had gone to so much trouble to bring the family together.

One morning Minnie was sewing on the veranda, worried because Katy had a slight fever. She intended to speak to her mother about it when she came from a walk. But when Ellen came in, she herself looked white and worried. "Minnie, I had the oddest thing happen to me just now. I saw your Grandmother Boyle go up the walk in front of me. She was walking in that quick way she had and she went up the walk into the house."

Minnie put her mother into a chair, amazed to see her so upset; gradually Ellen became her normal self. "It was silly of me to act like that. But, Minnie, if I were superstitious I'd say, the way old people did in Lancaster, that she was coming for her namesake."

Both women glanced at the floor where Maria lay on a large blanket, curling her hands around a rattle, cooing and smiling when she saw them looking at her. She looked a picture of blooming health and both women laughed and forgot their apprehensions.

On the 1st of August, Tom came from Woodstock for a short vacation and found, instead of a happy holiday group, a very distracted family. Katy had not recovered from her illness and Maria was showing traces of it. The doctor said he was afraid it was *cholera infantum*.

Tom immediately sent a wire to the General in Washington who promptly sent his own doctor to Oakland. By the time he arrived, Maria, the baby, was as sick as Katy, and after a hurried consultation it was decided to take them both to Washington for treatment. After a hurried packing, everyone went along on the train, except Tom who had to return to Woodstock.

As the train sped along it seemed to Minnie that Katy was a little better, and she gave her full attention to Maria, holding her in her arms and hardly taking her eyes from the flushed little face. Once she thought the baby was smiling and with a sense of hope told the doctor so. The latter said nothing, and a moment later she realized the reason: it was not a smile that had crossed the baby's face but the beginning of a convulsion. The doctor took her until she was quiet. When he brought her back to her mother, Minnie asked, "Do you think she will live till we get to Washington?"

There was no use in evading her question. "I am afraid not," he said gently. He was right, for just as the train pulled into Washington, Maria died on the pillow on which she lay in her mother's arms. It was dusk and the street lights were glowing when the family came off the train. The General was waiting for them, and when Minnie came from the train with the dead baby in her arms, he put his arms around them both and wept with her. There was a cradle still at the Sherman house and they put the baby in it, the signs of suffering still clear on the little face. After Father Boland came to bless the body, Minnie sat for a long time beside the cradle, and no one dared to disturb her. The General sent Will a wire, and a return message said he was on the way, adding — "carefully watch Minnie for she is worn out and will become seriously ill." Next day Colonel Bacon, the General's aide, taking Maria's body to St. Louis to be put in the vault there, reached the Washington station just as Will Fitch arrived from St. Louis.

Minnie had to forget her grief for Katy was no better — was in fact worse, and was delirious most of the time. On the 17th she seemed a little better and recognized some of those about her. Once she threw her arms around her mother when she bent over her, and Minnie's heart leaped with joy. But when she looked at the little face again it was empty of reason. The next day she was very cold and could breathe only with difficulty. Once they heard her talking, but the only word they could distinguish was "Mama." And suddenly she was gone.

When Minnie realized it she stared at her father and mother, at the nurse Emma, her face stained with tears, at Will, white and silent. "Both my babies," she said, and Will caught her as she fell.

Eleanor Fitch and her brothers were playing with Bessie O'Hare, the daughter of the sexton of nearby St. Matthew's, under a big rose of Sharon in full bloom, when Katy's nurse came over to them and said gently, "Katy will not suffer any more." That evening they all went to bed happy, thinking that she was well again. Even at the funeral when the children sat stiffly on the hard little chairs they were still scarcely aware of what had happened. They thought Katy looked very pretty in her best white dress with blue ribbons and with rosebuds in her hands.

The funeral service took place in the Sherman parlor. The little casket was surrounded with white flowers — roses, jasmine, lilies, carnations. Candles burned at her head and feet. Her grandmother had dressed the little girl's body, as years ago she had dressed her own baby for his grave at Notre Dame. And when Minnie saw Katy again, it was her own little girl, not the weary sick child with suffering in her eyes and hands wandering over the sheet.

Not until the funeral was over did the other children realize what had happened, and then it was Tommy who was first to say anything. "I didn't want them to die," he sobbed. "I liked them best of all."

In the train in which they all went home, the little casket was placed on one seat of their private car and always someone sat beside it. The Sherman lot was ready when they reached St. Louis. Maria's casket was brought from the vault and the two children were buried side by side.

The homecoming was a dreadful ordeal for Minnie, for every object reminded her of the babies. Her heart was desolate as her arms were empty. The house was so full of them; their small belongings, their toys, their clothes were everywhere. "Tate" and "Ria" she used to call them in fun; now those two playful names seemed written on a heart that ached without ceasing. When she passed the nursery she remembered how Maria used to coo and smile in her cradle. When she saw flowers in the yard, she remembered how Katy picked them and played with them. She remembered her in the little chair beside her grandmother reassuring her doll when the noise of the fireworks was very loud.

Minnie was not a sentimental woman. Nor was she despairing. The

Ewing women were Catholics, and their faith did not allow despair to come to a woman who believed in a hereafter. But she did permit herself one small sentimentality. The little pillow, on which both babies had been lying when they died, she had embroidered with their names — Katy and Maria — and every night she slept with it under her head.

There was Will to help her through the worst hours of those first days at home, and there was her mother; but both were almost as overcome as she by the double tragedy. Perhaps the one thing that helped her most was the entirely unheralded visit of Kit Phillips, her school friend from Cincinnati and her bridesmaid, who came with her own three young children and a nurse, a wire preceding her by only a few hours.

It was an experiment but it turned out most successfully, for in the confusion of a houseful of youngsters, Minnie was kept so busy that the worst days passed far more easily than if she had been alone with her loss. Kit's children had not been brought up under such discipline as the young Fitches, and the latter responded to their independence and saucy talk. It was a lively fortnight and it brought Minnie safely through her first hard weeks.

Ellen stayed in St. Louis for some time after Kit had gone home. Back in Washington again, she told the General how worried she was about Minnie. She went too much to the cemetery to visit the little girls' graves, always taking the other three children with her. They, however, were fascinated by the tombstones of their young uncles — Charley's with its marble angels and Willy's with its marble drum and flags — and the two new little graves did not affect them as they did Minnie.

Sorrow and loss had greatly changed Minnie; she felt she was definitely at the end of her youth. One other sign of change in her was her much greater indulgence toward the children left to her.

A great comfort to her during those hard days was Bishop Ryan, who came often to Sherman Place and who made the house happier for his coming. The children loved him, and on his visits their laughter was mingled with his.

The first time he called, Minnie had gone to the city. When, on her return, she drove up to the gate the children came tumbling down the path, all talking at once. She managed to understand that the "dandiest man" had come to visit. She asked who it was, but they did not know.

When the four reached the parlor Minnie found it in utter confusion. Chairs were in a row, all but the big armchair which stood at one end with its back to the rest. They had played a wonderful game, they told her and the man had planned it. Tom stood up in the big chair which was the pulpit and then the man put a big ring on Tom's finger from his own, and told Tom to preach a sermon.

"And he did," said Eleanor proudly, "and it was a good one. The rest of us were the congregation." Not until then did Minnie realize that the visitor and originator of the game was the Right Reverend Bishop.

On May 28, 1883, a daughter was born to the Fitches and named Mary Elizabeth, after Minnie's sister, Lizzie. She was baptized in the little frame church recently built on the King's Highway by Father Edward Fenwick, the pastor. Later Minnie took the baby to the same Jesuit church, where in May, 1853, Ellen Sherman had taken her own baby daughter and had her dedicated to the Blessed Virgin. The three older children knelt in the front pew and watched interestedly.

Minnie took the baby to the altar rail in her arms, and when the brief ceremony was over, her brother Tom Sherman, now a scholastic in St. Louis, took the child from her arms and laid her for a moment on the altar while he knelt and said a brief prayer. As Minnie watched she had a fleeting moment of fear that Our Lady might take this child to herself by such a direct offering. When Tom brought the baby back she looked up tremulously at him, and he reassured her with a smile, although he had not realized her passing fear.

That same year General Charles Ewing died suddenly, at the age of only forty-eight years, leaving a family of seven children. At least a part of his illness had been brought about by overwork, some of it in connection with the Indian Bureau. He had been appointed Catholic Commissioner of Indian Affairs by Archbishop Bayley in 1873, when the thirty Indian agencies which had been in Catholic hands had been transferred by the government to Protestant denominations. At the end of years of unremitting legal proceedings, the right to freedom of worship was granted these wards of the government. In 1878 General Ewing had been given the first Papal decoration ever bestowed on an American layman — the Order of Saint Gregory the Great.

The Shermans were planning to move to St. Louis. In February of 1884, the General would be sixty-four years old, the official age for retirement; he intended to retire a little earlier, an intention which greatly pleased Ellen.

Before they left, Tom came to Washington for a brief visit and Ellen rejoiced to see that the old relationship with his father had been re-established. They even discussed amicably Tom's chosen life work. "With no family of my own," he told the General, "I shall remain more strictly a member of your little circle than if I were to marry and be absorbed in other interests." And his father, though it was evident he did not wholly agree with this sentiment, said nothing against it. When Tom left, the General embraced him tenderly and when Tom kissed his mother good-bye, he whispered to her, "we are not so far apart after all."

So in November of 1883 the Shermans were again at home in St. Louis, and Ellen rejoiced in the good news that Tom would remain there all that winter, teaching in the Jesuit college. They would see each other now oftener than in the past.

One reason the General had hurried his return to St. Louis was that Ellen's health was failing and he hoped the change would benefit her. He was always offering suggestions regarding her health, although he never wanted her to take much medicine. "Rather I'd trust to natural laws," he would say. "Medicine can't create good health; it may only modify or alleviate decay."

But he was certain she would get better, and he was right. Back in the Garrison Street house she was her old busy self, having the woodwork washed, the chimneys swept, carpets shaken, the beloved pictures rehung in their old places. And she evolved a plan for Minnie to go with Will to New York for a month. Billy was to board with the Christian Brothers, Eleanor with the Sisters of Charity in St. Louis, and they would spend their weekends with their grandparents.

The plan was good, but events spoiled it. On her first Sunday with her grandmother, Eleanor was taken ill with scarlet fever; and a dinner which was to be given as a welcome home for the General was hurriedly cancelled, since the house was quarantined. Katherine and Edith Healy were visiting Rachel Sherman, and had expected a gay month, but they too were placed under quarantine.

Ellen, greatly worried over the sickness of another of Minnie's children, and while their mother was absent, gave great care to the nursing, putting the little girl in her own bed. One day when Eleanor was better, she felt a hard object under the pillow next to hers and asked her grandmother what it was.

Ellen hesitated a moment and then drew out a blue package and unrolled it. It was a faded little uniform. "It belonged to your Uncle Willy," she said, and told Eleanor the story of the little sergeant. "I have kept it under my pillow ever since he died," she told the awed little girl.

Later, when Billy came to the house, his grandmother called him into her room and locked the door. "I want to try a suit on you," she said, and put on him the faded blue uniform of the little sergeant. She walked a little distance from him and Billy stood straight for her inspection.

"May I keep it, Grandma?" he asked eagerly.

She shook her head. "No, Billy, but I want to tell you this. You are just the same age as the little boy who wore it and you have the very same name."

The Sherman family was now more united than it had been for a long time. At Garrison Avenue were the older Shermans, and Lizzie, Rachel, and Cumpy; three miles away was the Fitch family; and not much farther was the college where Tom taught. Cumpy had finished at the Christian Brothers school and was now at the Jesuit college. He had made his first Communion in May in the college chapel, where his brother Tom served the Mass and the whole family received Communion.

Ellen was thoroughly happy. When occasionally the General was away, her letters to him bore the simple heading, "Home."

They led a pleasant, simple life. Evenings they often gathered around the piano, and Ellen sang the old songs — Foster melodies or Scotch ballads. Sometimes they read together — Shakespeare or Scott, Thackeray or Dickens.

The Shermans liked the theater and on Sunday evenings, the actors and actresses who were playing in the city during the week were often their guests — John McCullough, Mary Anderson, Laurence Barrett or Edwin Booth. Sometimes they entertained literary notables from their own or other lands. When Matthew Arnold was on a lecture tour in the United States, he came to visit the Shermans.

During their first year back in St. Louis there was a family reunion on the General's birthday, and Tom wrote these verses in honor of the occasion:

> "What crown shall deck his brow?
> Wears he the laurel now?
> Weave we the holly bough,
> With myrtle entwine him.
>
> Spray of the staunch old yew,
> Sprigs of the oak so true,
> Broad beech and buckeye too
> Bud to enshrine him.

Gone are his days of war,
Danger and strife are o'er;
Comes now the autumn hoar,
Sweet peace, enfold him!"

In those happy days Ellen hoped only for one thing: that she and Cump could end their days in peace in this their own home.

Ellen's generosity was as wide as ever. Sometimes Cump thought it went a little too far, and even Minnie had occasion to think so. For one day when Eleanor had come for a visit with her grandmother, a woman came to the door with a little girl to ask for some clothing for the child. Mrs. Sherman, seeing that the little girl was blue with cold, impulsively took Eleanor's coat and bonnet from the hall and put them on her, while the astonished mother stammered her thanks.

Eleanor looked aghast at her grandmother. She loved her coat and bonnet and they were quite new. And there was additional reason for worry. "What will Mama say?" she said, half weeping.

Mrs. Sherman brushed this aside. "She'll understand. I'll buy you another. You see, darling, there was no child's clothing in this house except your coat and the poor little girl had to be warmed up right away." Eleanor was still dubious, and rightly so, for her mother was much annoyed when Eleanor returned in the evening in the Sherman carriage, wrapped in her grandmother's best shawl. Next day Mrs. Sherman bought a new coat and hat for Eleanor and her daughter perforce accepted them. "The others were a prettier color," she said, with great restraint.

Her grandchildren all loved their Grandmother Sherman. Her lovely hair, of which she was very proud, was still brown and shining. She wore night caps to keep it glossy and unbroken, very pretty ones, made of fine lawn and lace and tied with ribbons. She always wore snowy collars and cuffs of linen by day and of lace in the evening. The children loved to linger near her dressing table and sniff the crystal bottles of bay rum and cologne.

The youngest member of the Fitch family was everyone's pet.

Mary Elizabeth was nearly two before she began to talk, but her grandfather insisted her smile said more than any words. To her own father she was an answer to prayer, for it was this baby who had brought Minnie back from the anguish of her loss.

Minnie at Côte Brilliante was now as happy as Ellen at Garrison Avenue. The children were flourishing, and thought the farm the most exciting place in the world to live. During the summer gypsies often camped in the grove next to theirs, and when the children saw their covered wagons lumbering up they dashed out to watch them from behind their hedge. They were thrilled by the bright clothing, the chattering voices, the dark faces, the big black kettles on the open fires — usually filled, said Larry, the hired man, with Fitch chickens.

When General Cody brought his Wild West Show to the city, the General took his grandchildren to a matinee. To their great pride, Buffalo Bill came over to talk to them, fascinating in his buckskin trousers, flowing red neckcloth and big high hat.

The finale of the show was a stage-coach attack by Indians on ponies. Special spectators were invited to ride in the coach, and Colonel Cody asked Billy to come. He was reluctant, but Eleanor would gladly have taken his place. "Let me, Grandfather, let me," she begged. But she was told that little girls couldn't do such things and watched sadly as Billy stepped gingerly into the coach.

Will Fitch was as contented as his wife with their home and their life in St. Louis, but as the years went by he realized more and more that his future did not lie in that city. The wire works to which he had devoted so much time and labor failed entirely in 1885. An opportunity was offered him to build, with the financial backing of John Gates, the Braddock Wire Company in Pittsburgh. He went there to erect a plant, coming back to St. Louis to see his family at frequent intervals. He felt that eventually they must move to Pittsburgh, but he did not want to suggest it until he was sure of success in his new position.

An unfortunate event crystallized his plans. On St. Joseph's Day the family had come home from early Mass. After breakfast the boys went to the playroom, and Minnie was bathing the baby, with Eleanor helping. Josie, the nursemaid, and the governess were sewing. Suddenly Minnie saw a rain of bricks fall past the window, and called Josie to go to the attic and see what was wrong.

Josie quickly clattered down the stairs. "The roof's on fire," she shouted.

Minnie did not wait to hear more. She wrapped the baby in an afghan and called to the boys, "Put on your hats and coats and go outdoors."

She handed the baby to Josie and put the other children in charge of the governess. Then she went back in the house, got her silver together, took as many photographs from the walls as she could carry in a waste basket, and ran out to join the rest. The fire had made great headway in that short time.

Fire companies were summoned, but they had to come the three miles from the city, and unfortunately the men had mistaken "Sherman Place" for the General's house on Garrison Avenue and had stopped there first. They arrived just as the General himself dashed up on horseback.

They were able to save the downstairs furniture, but nothing on the other floors. One piece of furniture which had many family associations was completely burned — it was the chest of drawers that Eleanor Gillespie Boyle had taken from Brownsville, and which had been inherited by Eleanor Fitch because it had always been passed to an Eleanor ever since Eleanor Dougherty Gillespie brought it from Ireland.

Now, with the house gone, and the realization that his position in Pittsburgh was permanent, Will decided to move his family there. General Sherman was opposed to the move, but this time his son-in-law stood firm. He had agreed to leave the Navy when he married Minnie, and he had not regretted it, but this time he knew he would have to act as he himself felt best. He was certain that Pittsburgh would become the center of the steel industry even though the General thought it would remain in the Middle West.

# 19. The Older Shermans

[1885–1888]

Early in the summer of 1885, Minnie and the children left St. Louis to join Will in Pittsburgh. He had rented a large roomy house in Edgewood, six miles from town. The wire company itself was at Rankin, on the banks of the Monongahela, five miles from the house. Steel was becoming the big industry in the city and both banks of the Monongahela were lined with mills. Next to Will's plant was the furnace of Captain Jones and his able young assistant Charles Schwab; across the river were the Carnegie Mills.

Will's place of business was a considerable distance from his home, for it was considered unhealthy to live in the river valley, and those who could had their homes in the hills back of the river. Each day he took the train from Edgewood to Braddock and made the long walk over the hill to his mill. He often reached home very late, but he was too absorbed in his work to care.

The children loved Edgewood, their new home, from the first moment they saw it. The sprawling grounds contained a ravine through which ran a little brook. The house was large and rambling, and had a big porch; the wide windows opened on lawns and flowerbeds and an old orchard with many kinds of fruit trees.

The young Fitches were introduced to the joys of apple-butter making. They all helped bring the fruit from the orchard and with the peeling which went on all day. Sometimes one or other of the children was allowed to stir the dark pungent mass in the great kettle. Even at night when they were in bed the stirring went on by the light of lanterns.

The neighbors' children made the Fitch place their favorite playground. A baseball team was formed, and to her joy Eleanor was allowed to be a member, the one restriction being that she must stay on home grounds.

The children had liked Sherman Place but this old estate was far better. Their accumulation of pets was remarkable, and Mary had three of her own: a little black kitten, a canary and a rabbit.

For the young Fitches the world was bounded by their father and mother, especially their mother. They learned from her reserve and dignity and the New England reticence which was a Sherman trait. They learned to find pleasure in small ceremonial actions. In the parlor the children always rose when she entered, although upstairs in their mother's room, where they all met to read and sew and live a happy family life, there was no such formality. Eleanor was shocked when on a visit to her cousins she saw them lounging in their living-room and never rising when their mother came in.

In the long parlor, which ran the whole length of the house, the children put on theatrical performances. It lent itself admirably to the purpose, they felt, for the doors at front and back made it like a real stage. At first they were allowed to play without grown-up supervision the stories they dramatized, but one day, when a gladiatorial combat was being staged, Tommy and Billy filled hot water bottles with red ink and water and wore them under their shirts. In the ensuing fight both were pierced and blood spurted generously over boys, rugs, and audience of little girls. After that the properties were carefully scrutinized by higher authority before the show went on.

Their favorite ceremony was one connected with the big wooden box, still in its black oilcloth cover, in which Minnie's wedding gown had come from Paris. With great ceremony the box was brought from the hall closet, and they would take from it a wonderful array of Minnie's most treasured possessions. There was the exquisite rose-point handkerchief, still in its case, which Mr. Stewart had given her when she was married. There was the black ostrich-feather fan she had bought in Paris after her meeting with the Empress Eu-

génie, a story that was often retold to the young audience. There
was the black veil she had worn at her audience with Pius IX, another story the children heard over and over, and other incidents of her
visit to Europe were illustrated by the books of photographs which
young Minnie Sherman had collected.

Then there was the tiny parasol, hinged in the middle, which, in
Grandmother Sherman's day, ladies held in their carriages to keep
off the sun. There was the handkerchief which their mother had
made as an engagement gift for their father, its monogram embroidered with her own hair, and their father's Navy chapeau and
his epaulets. Best of all was Minnie's wedding gown and the corded
slippers with big rosettes she had worn, the petticoats with long
ruffled trains, the fine white lisle stockings. Sometimes they were
allowed to dress up in the contents of the trunk, Eleanor the bride
and Billy the groom, their mother meticulously adjusting the frills
for her daughter and showing them the slow pace at which a wedding
party must move.

In St. Louis, the whole pattern of the older Shermans' lives was
changed, for both Minnie and Elly lived in the East now and the
beloved grandchildren were seldom seen. Cumpy was at Yale; Tom
had been transferred to a college in Detroit — "where," he wrote
his mother, "everything is on runners and Russian in magnificence."
Except for the two girls still with them, there was no one of the
family left in the West any longer.

The General grew bored with life in St. Louis. Eventually the
house on Garrison Avenue was rented, and late in 1885 the Shermans
moved to New York City, where for several years the Fifth Avenue
Hotel was home for the General, his wife and his two daughters.

The change suited him well. He had liked the city since he first
came there as a boy of sixteen. He loved the theater; he loved dining
out — but for the company, rather than the food; he ate little and
drank only a glass of sauterne or sherry.

Ellen herself seldom went anywhere, except to church, an occasional matinee, or shopping, and one of the real delights of New York to her was to be so close to the great stores; Best's, Altman's and Putnam's were all on Fifth Avenue and easy of access. She had many visitors during the afternoon and evening. "I see more people here in a week than I saw in St. Louis in a month," she told the General. One constant visitor was their grandson Billy, who came very frequently to the Fifth Avenue Hotel because it offered a fine relief from school life at Fordham.

Sometimes Ellen left New York to visit Minnie at Edgeworth, or Elly in her home in Rosemont. Occasionally the General came to Pittsburgh and if he were passing through to attend a convention or a G.A.R. reunion in another city he would wire ahead. On those occasions the whole Fitch family came down to the little station to watch for his train. The dusky, smiling porter always opened the door so that the General could stand on the steps and receive the children's enthusiastic welcome which continued until the train disappeared from sight.

Sometimes the train stopped long enough for a short talk, and occasionally the General stayed overnight. Once a proud Eleanor was given the task of being his nurse; his fingers were bruised and bleeding from the cordial handclasps of old soldiers at a G.A.R. meeting, and at his direction Eleanor heated bread and milk and poulticed his hands. That night she proudly served him a dinner cooked entirely by herself — fried chicken, mashed potatoes, corn pudding and hot biscuits. "I never had a better cooked dinner," he said to the little girl, "nor anywhere in the world a better cup of coffee."

Ever since coming to Pittsburgh to live, Minnie had planned a pilgrimage: since she was now so near the old home of the Gillespies, she wanted to go to Brownsville, the cradle of her ancestors in the New World. But each year something prevented her from going, and not until June of 1887 was the plan finally carried out. The group which set forth was composed of the Fitches and their children and Mr. Edenborn, a business friend of Will's, who brought his wife and their small daughter along.

The trip by river boat was a grand adventure; the children slept at night in staterooms, watched the boat's wake from the stern until they were black with cinders; they even listened politely to such boring talk as a discussion between their father and the captain as to how best to get coke down the river to the steel mills.

Mr. Edenborn spoke often of German scenery, especially of the Rhine River, its green slopes, its castles and ruins. He even quoted poetry about the river and a mermaid called Lorelei. The Fitch children were not overpleased at his enthusiasm about the Rhine when their Monongahela was so lovely, and they were relieved when their father began to speak of the river up which they were sailing — of General Washington and the redcoats who met here in battle, of the Indians who lived along its banks. "Perhaps young maidens like Nettie and Eleanor," he said, "here paddled canoes which their fathers made for them."

The party landed at Brownsville and walked up the high bank of the river until they found the carriages in which the ladies and little girls were driven into the town. The men and boys walked and met them at the town's center. The church their mother thought very nice, and in the little graveyard adjoining it they found the gravestones of Neal Gillespie and his wife. Minnie told them some of the family stories about these early settlers in the town when it had been an outpost and trading village, stories she had heard from her Grandmother Ewing. And she told them about her brief visit to Donegal, whence had once come some of those now buried there.

The children enjoyed the trip back down the river, romping about the boat until they were weary and then sitting quietly listening to their father tell more tales of the country through which they were passing. Minnie sat on deck beside him, sometimes listening, sometimes remembering herself as a child, rocking in her little chair beside her grandmother as she told her about the men and women who had lived in Brownsville and whose descendants they were. She felt

as disappointed as the children when the trip was over and they were
back again in prosaic Pittsburgh.

Ellen Sherman was at Rosemont in May of 1887, when a son was
born to Elly and named William Tecumseh Thackara. Later she
went on to Edgewood where Minnie told her of a visit she had made
the month before to the Sisters of Mercy Academy in Latrobe, Pennsylvania, close to the great Archabbey of St. Vincent's. She had taken
all the children with her, but her chief reason for going was that
Eleanor was to make her First Communion there. Sister Veronica,
Hugh Ewing's daughter, and now a Sister of Mercy, prepared the
little girl for the great occasion.

Her Uncle Tom Sherman had sent his niece a message in a letter
to Minnie, and Eleanor listened with pride while her mother read
it aloud to her grandmother. "Tell Eleanor," it ran, "that I send her
as a special token a whisper from my Guardian Angel. He can speak
to her and she will hear it tonight when she says her prayers. If the
angel does not make her hear I will keep it until I meet her for I
can't be with her now."

The rest of the letter was for his little niece's mother: "How much
Communion grows on us as we mature. Deeper ever as a mystery,
appalling as a divine condescension, it is the link to bind earth and
heaven; the only thing here worth living for. Like all good works it
is gradual and slow in its workings but a sure remedy for every
spiritual disease. In the long run it conquers the most subtle evils of
our nature. You have a beautiful task in explaining to your little
ones what the good Lord has done for us in a thousand ways. And
don't worry over trifles, except salvation — 'the one thing necessary.' "

Later when Ellen visited Tom, she spoke to him of this letter. He
laughed and said, "You see I am constitutionally a preacher. Even my
letters are apt to be little sermons."

Ellen went occasionally to Detroit to visit her son, as he neared
the goal of the priesthood. Once, when Rachel went with her, they

were invited to stay at Governor Alger's house, and she accepted for Rachel, who had a wonderful time, dancing, riding, and as guest of honor at a ball. But Ellen stayed at a lodging-house close to Tom's college, for he had permission to come to see her several times a day and she wanted to be close by.

She had asked to be excused from social duties while in Detroit, but there were certain demands from which she never shrank at any time. When a committee of veterans came to see her to ask if she would persuade General Sherman to come to their reunion, she gladly received them and promised to put the request before him.

Governor Alger had placed his carriage at Mrs. Sherman's disposal, and she and Tom went out in it when they could — "doing all the things we can do," Tom said, "with three score years on one side and a cassock on the other."

They often talked of the General and of his slowness in accepting Tom's choice of a way of life. "It takes a deal of softening to take the kinks out of some natures," said Tom, "and I'm not sure we Shermans are the most malleable individuals in the world."

"If only he would come into the Church," said Ellen wistfully.

"Well," said Tom, "of that I saw no sign when last we met. He seems no nearer than he ever was. Still one must pray and trust and wait."

This visit and the long talks together were a great joy to Tom and his mother. When she and Rachel went back East, he kissed his mother with deep affection, saying, "My heart and spirit have gained from this visit."

"And mine too," she said.

"Two years from this summer, Mother, I shall be a priest," he reminded her.

"God grant I am there to see you," said Ellen.

On the way home she drew from her purse a little prayer he had written for her: "Let me be Thy child and burn out my life in Thy love and service. Amen."

"How like him that is," she thought, and put it carefully away.

Christmas of 1887 was set as a reunion date for the Shermans, this time to be held at Elly's house in Rosemont. The General and Ellen were the first to arrive and helped Elly receive the rest. Minnie was ill and she and Will sent Billy to represent the family, proud in his blue Fordham uniform and dashing cape with red lining. Tom came. Cumpy arrived from New Haven. Lizzie and Rachel were there.

The Thackaras were building a new house, which at that time was not quite ready for occupancy. But on Christmas Day they all went to look over the new home and held a little ceremony at which General Sherman kindled the first fire in the main hall.

Ellen greatly enjoyed every moment of the Rosemont party, but it had wearied her greatly. She was glad she was going back to Edgewood before she returned to the New York hotel, for a little peace and quiet. The older Fitch children were at school now, Eleanor at Eden Hall in Philadelphia, Billy still at Fordham. But Tommy was at home and Mary, now five years old, was Mrs. Sherman's delight. She shared all her pets with her grandmother and was disappointed when she could not persuade her to take the black kitten to New York with her.

During her stay at Edgewood the Fitches celebrated Minnie's birthday, and in her honor Will brewed a punch made according to Ellen's recipe and under her direction. The children watched fascinatedly as their father ground loaf-sugar with a muddler and added cold tea, lemon rind and other ingredients from the bottles lined up on the marble-topped table.

In the center of the table stood Maria Boyle Ewing's punch bowl of delicate china in which the whisky punch was mixed. The grownups had big glasses; the children were given little champagne glasses of the punch and they alternated small sips with big bites of cake. Rachel played her banjo while the rest sang and the children gave recitations. The pleasant and homelike surroundings made Ellen long for a home instead of hotel life in New York. "This is peace," she said to Minnie. "I feel like a bird freed from a cage." She was indeed far from well, and Will Fitch was so solicitous about her that he thought he should himself bring her back to New York.

Back in the Fifth Avenue Hotel, living very quietly in her rooms and seeing only Cump and the girls and Cumpy on his visits from New Haven, Ellen grew better. She took her meals there too, sitting in the comfortable rocker she liked best. When the General dined out, he always came to her afterward, no matter how late the hour, to tell her about the dinners and the clever things the guests had said. "I have to tell them to her now," he said once to Rachel, who thought her mother ought to sleep, "for the jokes might grow stale overnight."

The General always read to his wife the occasional contributions he made to the magazines. Once as he finished reading an article on Cardinal Wolsey which he had written for *The Century,* Ellen said: "Cump, you ought not to let the Rebs have the entire field. Your reminiscences of the times after the war ought to be written, and if you did not want to bring them out now, you could leave them to be published after your death. They would be interesting and entertaining, as well as of use for later compilers of history. And," she added practically, "it would mean money for the children."

"Perhaps it will be you who will publish them for me," he said.

"No, Cump, I think you are going to outlive me. And I want to tell you one thing — money for the children made me think of it. I think you have always been very, very generous in money matters, even if you always have thought I gave too much away. You have never held me to strict account. And you aren't saying anything now when you know mine is all gone."

For Ellen Sherman had given all her money away, the seventeen thousand her father had left her, in addition to the generous sums he had given her in his lifetime. Nothing was left to her but a few lots in St. Louis. "And what they bring," she said to Cump firmly, "will go for gifts to the family or to the Church. Right now I would like to outfit Eleanor Fitch for school." And she began to persuade him to buy the lots from her, or at least let her have the money they would bring when they were sold, so that she might have immediate use of it.

In June of 1888 the Shermans were waiting for news from Edgewood: the Fitches were expecting another child. But when word came, it was to tell the grandparents that the baby had lived only a few hours, long enough to be baptized Hugh Ewing. Will cut off a lock of the dead baby's bright hair, put it in a locket engraved "Hugh," and brought it to Minnie, spent and heartbroken with another loss. She put it around her neck and told him she would always wear it. The little body was sent to St. Louis to be buried beside the others.

In August, Ellen went to pay a short visit to Tom, now at Woodstock. "I have brought you a gift," she told him. "Some day you are to have my prie-dieu, and Rachel and I are making you a set of vestments from Elly's wedding dress for your ordination, but this I want to give you now," and she put in his hand the gold rosary with its relic of the True Cross which Pope Pius IX had sent her.

One day while Ellen was at Woodstock Tom came to her lodgings to find her face alight with joy as she waved a letter at him. "Oh, Tom, I have wonderful news from your father. He has bought a house for us in New York. It is an entire surprise to me; I never knew he was even planning it. It is on Seventy-first Street and he is having it fitted up so that when I go back I can go to my own home. Oh, Tom, how wonderful to go to a home and not to a hotel!"

She spent the following weeks visiting her daughters, for the General wanted their new home entirely ready before she returned to New York in mid-September. Minnie had gone to see the house, and sent her mother a favorable report as well as a detailed description of all the rooms. There was much to be done — painting, papering, carpentering — and her father was having Cumpy help with the needed work during his vacation. Ellen spent the time in joyful anticipation of being "in our own home" and among her old possessions, for the furniture long stored in St. Louis had been sent for, to be put in the new home.

There was no doubt as to who worked hardest to get the house ready. It was Cumpy, called by his father from his vacation at Lake George to come immediately to New York. When he reached the Fifth Avenue Hotel, the General told him he had bought a new house; the family baggage was on its way; the household furniture was coming from St. Louis; a cook and butler were already in the house, and were complaining because they had only a few cots, a few blankets and very few dishes. Last of all the General told Cumpy that he himself was leaving immediately for Toledo to attend a meeting of the Army of Tennessee and would be gone three weeks.

A very dazed young man was left in sole charge on 71st Street. In the new house he found a drunken cook whom he managed to fire with the aid of the police, and a butler who was a jewel, being willing even to scrub floors when he learned that Cumpy intended to help with the job. He bought everything the butler said was needed from the large expense account his father had opened for him at the bank.

The furniture arrived, was uncrated and set in place. By midnight of the 24th of September the pictures were hung, the books in place. Ellen's secretary was placed where a hurried note from the General had directed, and her favorite statue of the Immaculate Conception was in its place above the secretary. By four o'clock on the next day the painters were out of the house, the workmen had cleared up their debris, and the carpets were laid. At five Ellen was to arrive. The General had returned that morning, and when he saw pictures hung, books in place and even a borrowed cook in the kitchen, he was as pleased as his son was weary.

Ellen had written him a little note: "Lizzie and I shall drive up to the door of 75 Seventy-first Street on Monday afternoon. We shall be in no haste for dinner. Do not let Cumpy lift or carry too much in his efforts to have things just so for my arrival."

On this one note the General did not put the date and his usual

memo — "ans," — as with the hundreds of other letters from her
written during their separations over the years. On this he noted:
"Ellen arrived in New York, today, September 24." There was no
need to answer it.

When the carriage stopped at the door of the new home and Ellen
stepped out, there seemed to her to be an actual glow around the
house before her. It was only one in a row of ordinary New York
brownstone fronts, but even without seeing the number she knew it
instantly as hers. She would have known it, she assured herself, even
without the smiling face of her husband at the door, welcoming her
home.

She was too tired to have her dinner downstairs, so, according to
their old habit, the General ate with her in her room. They sat companionably together while he told her of his trip to Toledo, and she
gave him reports of their children and grandchildren.

Ellen's room was a large sunny one on the second floor. It ran the
width of the house, and was filled with all her loved familiar things.
Cumpy had put chairs and tables and pictures in their places, having
a good memory of just how her room had been arranged in St. Louis.
"It is almost as though the whole room had been moved from Garrison Avenue and placed here," she said gratefully.

The next day she was taken on a tour of inspection and to see the
General's room in the basement — a war office in miniature, Ellen
said, as she looked at the walls covered with military pictures, old
flags and maps, and the three portraits of Grant, Sheridan and Sherman hung together in a group. The General soon became greatly attached to his study; there and in Ellen's room all his time at home
was spent. His desk faced the windows and here he could be seen by
those who passed the house sitting in his old smoking-jacket, horn-
rimmed glasses on his nose, answering the interminable mass of
letters which came to him, or consulting one of the old maps that detailed his campaigns.

The office was a rendezvous for military men, for research writers,
and for the soldiers of his old army who came in to see "Uncle Billy"

for advice or old clothes or a little money, as in the days in St. Louis. Every morning he took a walk in Central Park with one of his children or a visiting grandchild.

There were three children living at home. Lizzie was acting housekeeper. Rachel was her father's secretary. Cumpy was going to law school at Columbia.

On October 4, 1888, Ellen Sherman celebrated her sixty-fourth birthday. She received many congratulatory letters and gifts and loving messages from the absent members of the family. But her best gift was this house which — it was a thought which came to her every day — she need not leave again. She was not well enough to trouble with the details of housekeeping, but she planned for many things to do when she was better — entertaining the married children, giving dinner parties, and resuming her church work. But sometimes, even while planning, she felt a small fear in her heart. How long would she be allowed to enjoy this home, so long desired? For even the small exertions of her day were growing more and more difficult for her.

Early in November she had a heart attack, and Cump called a new doctor who gave her some relief. But it was only temporary, and two weeks later she had another and more severe attack. Doctors summoned in consultation gave the General little hope, and that evening Father Taylor from the nearby Church of the Blessed Sacrament gave Ellen the last rites. Even yet the General refused to believe she was beyond recovery. "Her father's heart acted exactly like that and he lived to eighty years," he said stoutly.

Dr. Smith, the army physician whom the General had called in, remained at the house, while Lizzie and Rachel and Cumpy helped the two nurses take care of their mother. The General spent all his time on a sofa in her room, taking an occasional nap when he became too weary with watching. When Ellen's brother, Thomas Ewing, came and saw how haggard he was getting, he said to him, "You must think of yourself, Cump."

The General looked at him with tragic eyes. "Tom, all I can think of is Ellen."

On the day before Thanksgiving, those in the room realized that Ellen, who had been for some time in a coma, was wide awake. She looked around the room, at her children, at Cump by her bed. Father Taylor was called, and began to recite the prayers for the dying while her brother and her children knelt about her bed and Cump sat very close beside her.

Several times they thought they heard a response from her. Several times a faint smile crossed her face as her eyes rested on one or the other kneeling there or on Cump. But before the prayers were ended she was unconscious again.

An hour later, the General, who had gone to his office for a few moments, heard the nurse come running down the stairs. "General Sherman, quick, your wife is dying," she called.

Suddenly the General realized that what he had refused to admit was really true. He ran upstairs calling, "Wait for me, Ellen, wait for me. No one has ever loved you as I love you." And just as he came into her room he heard a little sigh and knew it was her last.

He stood beside the bed for a long time looking at the quiet face, the still hands. It did not seem possible that his Ellen would not open her eyes again and smile at him in the old loving way.

The children's first and deepest concern was for their father who was prostrated by his grief. When in the afternoon Lizzie went to him to see if he would be able to attend to some of the details of Ellen's burial, she found him sitting quietly in his office. Going up to him, she put her cheek against his sleeve and said nothing until he spoke. "I expected to go first, Lizzie," he said almost in bewilderment. "I was so much older and I have been so much more severely tried." And then, as if to comfort himself, "but I shall resume my place at her side some day." And then he said he was ready to help with the funeral arrangements.

Ellen had left a note of instructions to be carried out after her death: "Have a Mass said which will not keep the family very long in the church. Impress this on the priest who makes the arrangements. Do not have many carriages and have no flowers, but beg that prayers be offered for the welfare of my soul. . . . Use no mourning paper for letters — pray for me, pray for me. Have Masses offered and get good humble people to remember me in their prayers. Do not give up the time to gloomy mourning. Make the homes cheerful . . . but not given up to frivolous people who care nothing for you and have no faith in your best and holiest sentiment and belief."

The General read every word carefully, and then he wrote on the back: "Ellen's directions for her death and burial — all anticipated. W. T. Sherman." He had placed a notice in the papers, with directions regarding the funeral route and its ending in St. Louis — "in our lot in Calvary Cemetery, long ago secured . . . there to deposit her coffin to await mine."

That Thanksgiving morning, at Edgewood, Will Fitch had gone to his office at the mill for a few hours and Minnie was resting. The odors of dinner — turkey, celery, roasting sweet potatoes — pervaded the house when Will came back from his office and hurried to Minnie's room.

Five-year-old Mary and her brother Tommy came in from playing when they head that their father was at home and stopped in the living room to find him, but he was not there.

"Listen," Mary said, "they're laughing in Mama's room."

But Tommy looked scared. "No, she's not laughing, Mary. She's crying."

Will had found a telegram at his office, announcing Ellen's death the day before. Minnie was not to come to New York, it read, but the train with Ellen's body, the General and the other children, would stop at Edgewood on its way to St. Louis two days later.

When on November 29th, the private car with its passengers reached Edgewood, the General got slowly out of the train as it pulled into the little station. He and Minnie wept in each other's arms as he repeated over and over his remark to Lizzie in New York, "I always thought I would go first."

All that night in the train General Sherman sat beside the coffin, careworn and weary, but refusing to leave his wife's side. At the head of the coffin were two crossed palms tied with purple ribbon. At the foot rested a wreath of hyacinths and lilies of the valley.

Father Tom Sherman met the train in St. Louis in the early morning, and many friends of the family were also waiting at the station. With masses of flowers in two cars, the procession started for St. Xavier's Church. As Ellen had asked, there was only a simple low Mass, and the choir sang the Gregorian chant. There was a brief sermon by Father Bronsgesst, who took for his text the "valiant woman" of the Bible. Ellen's daughters and sons followed the service closely, but her husband sat upright throughout, hardly taking his eyes from the coffin before him.

In the cemetery Ellen was buried close to the graves of Charley and Willy, and close to her little grandchildren, Katy and Maria and Hugh. It seemed very fitting that she, who loved children so much, should have them about her now.

# 20. General Sherman's Later Years

### [1888–1891]

GENERAL SHERMAN recovered very slowly from the shock of his wife's death. The children tried to help, to assure him in every way of their affection, but it was with him as it had been with Ellen herself when she had written him that much as she loved the children she loved him "best of all." As with Thomas Ewing after the death of his Maria, so a part of Tecumseh Sherman died when Ellen was gone.

Rachel and Cumpy and Lizzie stayed with him in the New York house. Mr. Barret, his secretary, and Rachel helped him with his letters and the series of articles he was writing for the *North American Review*. They knew that it was better for him to be busy. When he was not he felt ill, and, as he told Lizzie, "I haven't the patience to become an invalid."

Minnie and Elly who had come to New York to be with their father, returned to their homes, promising to come often for visits. Tom went back to Woodstock, leaving with his father verses he had written in his mother's room after they all returned from St. Louis, and called *In Advent*.

> The nest is empty; flown the mother bird,
> Yet warm the down that lines its cozy walls,
> And soft as down the whisper nightly heard,
> Upon the wounded spirit soothing falls.

Is it the flutter of departing wing
That upward darts to greet eternal day?
Is it the murmur of the saints that sing
To greet her soul and waft it on its way?

I know not, but I feel her room as sweet
As April blossoms burgeoning in pride
Or incense, prayer commingled, when they meet
The tuneful voice and organ's swelling pride.

Yes, 'tis a chapel, holy, pure, serene,
Her spirit is its patron saint to me;
This advent season lit with heavenly sheen,
I seek the shore of the eternal sea.

Here, where she battled last with storms of earth,
Whence sailed to win the Islands of the Blest;
Our tears are dried by the thrill of angel mirth —
The loss, the cross — 'tis but the shore of rest.

The General put the verses with the many letters sent him after
Ellen's death, pasting them all carefully in a large scrapbook. There
were hundreds of these messages of sympathy. John Hay, Cardinal
Gibbons, the Blaines, Augustin Daly, Bishop Chatard of Vincennes,
among many others, wrote to him. Letters came from those who had
known Ellen's love and her charity, from friends of old days in St.
Louis and California, even from Ireland where she was remembered
for her efforts for famine relief in 1879.

One veteran in Toledo sent the General his sympathy: "I could
not rest till I sent you this message," he wrote. And there was a
postscript: "I followed you through to the sea." From San Francisco
a dealer in, according to his letterhead, "groceries, boots and shoes"
wrote: "You have lost your partner and the whole U.S. has lost, and
keenly feels it, a leading woman." The old Thirteenth Infantry,
which had been with General Sherman from its formation when he
was its colonel and had followed him in all the marches and battles
of the Civil War, sent messages of sympathy, some official, but many
from the pens of the old soldiers themselves.

The letters and telegrams were not placed in the scrapbook in any special order. Bishop was next to veteran, simple Ohio friends next to ex-Presidents, in the way Ellen Ewing Sherman held in her heart all her friends, the world's important and God's needy.

One thing the General treasured above all else: his wife's japanned tin box which had gone everywhere with her since the California days. Opening it he and the girls had found it filled with all manner of mementos — small envelopes, labelled, "Father's hair," "Baby Charley's curl." There were pressed flowers in some — "from Charley and Willy's graves." There was the jubilee medal of Pope Pius IX, and a tiny brown leather book, *Think Well On't,* by Bishop Challoner, with Father Vespre's name in the flyleaf.

Ellen had left no will. There was no reason for one because she had given everything away.

In the summer of 1889, Thomas Ewing Sherman, S.J., was to be ordained in the chapel of the Cathedral in Philadelphia. Some of the young priest's family were able to come — Tom's four sisters, still in deep mourning for their mother, Philemon Ewing and Cumpy — and classmates and friends.

Two were missing. Ellen, who had seen so many of her prayers granted, but not this one, that she see her son raised to the priesthood; and the General, who had found an excellent excuse for his absence in important meetings in Denver. Tom had written his father asking if he would find it convenient to be present, and he had answered that duties in the West prevented his coming. But he added that he wanted to see Tom afterward in New York, and then they would have a good talk. Tom wrote back agreeing: "After all it is the being together," he said, "and not anything else which is such a happiness."

There was one other matter he told his father he wanted to attend to when he came to New York: he had given what he possessed to his sister Lizzie when he joined the Society, and now he wanted to make to her a deed of gift of anything to which he might be entitled in the future.

Years before Ellen had asked Archbishop Ryan to officiate at her son's ordination, and he had not forgotten his promise to her. Father Van Rensselaer, who had been with Tom during his year in England, and Father Haven Richard of Georgetown assisted the Archbishop. On the two days previous Tom had received the first two major orders. On Sunday morning, July 5, 1889, he was ordained priest.

At the beginning of the ceremony, after the exhortation, the candidate prostrated himself before the altar and the Litany of the Saints was chanted. The Mass continued until the time came for the imposition of hands of the Archbishop on the candidate. He drew the candidate's stole over his right shoulder and crossed it on his breast: "Receive the priestly vestment by which is signified charity." Then followed the *Veni Creator,* the anointing of the hands, the giving of the chalice and paten, the kiss of peace. Then at the end of the Mass the celebrant and the newly ordained priest said the final prayers together.

After his ordination, when the Archbishop and the clergy had gone from the sanctuary, Father Thomas Sherman knelt for some time absorbed in prayer, his face in his hands, until Father Van Rensselaer went to him and reminded him that all were waiting for his blessing. He rose quickly to his feet; he was very pale and his eyes had a faraway look. But when he became aware of the waiting people he went quickly to the altar rail, and beckoned to Minnie who went up alone. It was clear to all that she was representing his mother. After her the others came to receive the young priest's blessing.

Two who came were long ago residents of the Sherman household. There was Effie, once Tom's nurse, an old lady now, who sat proudly with the family during the ceremonies; and another nurse of early days, Emily, stout and motherly in contrast to the austere looking Effie. Both wore new black silk dresses and bonnets and there was equal happiness in both faces as they watched the child they had cared for become a priest.

After a time there were still so many who came forward that Father Tom had to stop and give a general blessing. The next day, when he celebrated his first Mass in the Church of St. Joseph, he wore the white and gold vestments made from Elly's wedding dress, and his lace alb was one his mother had given him.

In November of the same year the Fitches attended another religious ceremony which interested them deeply, this time the clothing of Katherine Drexel in the Convent of the Sisters of Mercy in Pittsburgh, the same convent which Nellie Ewing, Minnie's cousin and Ellen's godchild, and the daughter of Hugh Ewing, had entered some years ago.

The clothing was a dazzling affair. The altar in the chapel was a mass of flowers; the Sisters sat in the front rows and behind them the postulants; relatives and friends filled the remaining seats. Miss Drexel entered in a very lovely white satin wedding dress, wearing a diamond necklace and gold bracelets; diamond rings gleamed on her fingers. Back of her came eight little girls in white satin dresses and white veils, exact copies of her own.

Archbishop Ryan awaited her at the altar, accompanied by three bishops and a score of priests.

"My child, what dost thou demand?" asked the Archbishop.

"The mercy of God and the habit of religion," she answered in her firm sweet voice.

After he had blessed her habit and given it to her she left the altar. A few minutes later she came back. The jewels were gone, so was the glistening satin robe. Up the aisle, walking softly, came a nun in black habit and white veil.

Later, when Will read about the ceremony in the newspaper and came to the statement, "the most beautiful wedding dress ever seen in Philadelphia," Minnie said emphatically, "Oh, it was!" And when he went on to read that the event had caused great excitement in society, Minnie smiled. "And in the Mercy Convent too," she said.

Those of his children who lived away from New York knew that General Sherman was well taken care of by Cumpy and Rachel and Lizzie, who still lived with him. Minnie and Elly managed to come to see him fairly often, and the General himself was always eager to have them visit him. "We will keep this hotel open for all summer," he wrote Minnie and Elly. "You and your husband can always without notice find bed and board here."

During a visit to Edgewood he admitted to Will that the latter had been right when he had moved his family and his business to Pittsburgh. "It was a wise move. All transportation is by rail, east and west, and the Mississippi has ceased to be the controlling agent in the commerce of America which it was in my day. You are now in the very channel of the new stream of commerce."

Will had resigned a short time before as superintendent of the Braddock Wire Company and had sold his stock, making plans for a new company to be called the Pittsburgh Wire Company. When they heard that he was leaving the firm the Braddock employees, some five hundred of them, sent word they were coming to bring him a farewell gift, and Will had invited them to a party on the lawn at Edgewood.

In the morning he had a large rain barrel brought on the porch and into it the children helped him put the juice of a whole crate of lemons and pounds of sugar and ice. To stir it a long stick, cut from the handle of a broom, was used, and, the children thought, this was what their father meant when he told their mother that the men must have a "stick" in their lemonade. After the stirring, Will brought out several bottles and poured the contents into the barrel. Beside it were tables piled high with glasses which were to be filled from a long-handled dipper. There was a huge tray of cookies and cake and these the children were to serve.

The men arrived, headed by the St. Thomas Band of Braddock, and assembled on the lawn in front of the house. Farewell speeches were made and Mrs. Fitch was presented with a case of silver. Mr. Fitch was given a fine gold watch, to which was attached a charm made of a coil of wire and drawing tongs. Then the guests came up, one by one, to the porch to shake hands and partake of the refreshments. The children were kept very busy helping serve, and the men, who knew them, talked to them while they ate and drank. Everyone of the Fitches was very tired when the reception was over.

On the evening of February 9, 1891, Will and Minnie Fitch were in their sitting-room quietly reading when a telegram arrived from Lizzie: "Papa's condition such you had better be here. Come at once."

They knew that the General had not been very well, but there had been no hint of danger, and during the past months he had been very active socially, quite in his old way. He had attended various functions, from a dinner to John Sherman on his sixty-seventh birthday to a Grand Army meeting in Boston, had made a speech in Philadelphia on Decoration Day, had gone to West Point for graduation, to Cincinnati for a meeting of the Army of the Potomac.

She looked at Will bewildered. "Just a week ago in a letter to me he noted that he would be seventy-one on February 8th, and said he felt no different in strength than he did twenty years ago."

Minnie hurried to take the train for New York. Lizzie met her at the door of the 71st Street house and told her that Elly had already come. "Papa is a little better, but he is all excited at seeing everybody. Oh, Minnie, I'm terribly worried! Just last week he came home one evening feeling very well, but all of a sudden he said, 'Do you know, Lizzie, sometimes when I come home like this I feel death reaching out for me!'"

However, when on her arrival Minnie spoke to Dr. Alexander, he seemed not greatly alarmed. "I don't believe it is serious, Mrs. Fitch. We will have him around in a day or two and you can go home."

Minnie sat all day in the room next to her father's and heard his continuous and incoherent talk. Once he actually rose from his bed, came to her door and looked in. "Why, it's — " and Minnie thought he recognized her, but he turned back to his bed again with no more word.

Next morning — Ash Wednesday — she went to the Church of the Blessed Sacrament and after Mass asked Father Taylor to request prayers for her father. Returning to the house she learned that there had been a change for the worse, and another doctor had been summoned. During the night the General had crept from his bed before the nurse could stop him. "Tom, I want Tom," they heard him say as he wandered about the room.

When Minnie came in he was lying with his eyes closed, but suddenly he opened them and looked at her. "I know you — Minnie," he said weakly. Then he turned to the nurse. "Where are the girls? I have four, you know," he said with a little smile.

Later he spoke to Minnie of the inscription he wanted placed on his monument. "Put 'faithful and honorable.' Only that — 'faithful and honorable.'" He repeated the words once more as if to make sure she had heard correctly, and she promised it would be done.

By night there was little hope; the General was sinking. His children thought it was time to send for Father Taylor.

"Is there any objection to administering the sacraments?" the priest asked. The doctor shook his head and said, "No, nothing will make any difference now." So the General was anointed as his children gathered around his bed. Only Tom was missing from the group, but word had come that he was speeding home from the Jesuit Seminary on the Isle of Jersey as fast as the ship could bring him.

The General was unconscious and did not once open his eyes during the rite. When Father Taylor was leaving the house a carriage drove up, from which John Sherman sprang and hurried into the house to join the rest of the family in his brother's room.

In the morning Will Fitch arrived. Only Tom was still missing, and all were praying that his ship would reach port in time. The General lay very quietly, and only his clear eyes showed he was now conscious.

Suddenly, just before noon, those around him heard a long-drawn-

out breath and a quick sigh, and they realized that General Sherman
was dead.

On February 15th, all the flags in New York were at half mast,
on the buildings, on the river tugs and the English ships in the harbor, and black rosettes were placed on the harnesses of the horses.
From end to end, West 71st Street was filled with black-bordered
flags.

In the hallway of the General's home a military guard was placed.
The family had decided there was to be no lying in state, but when
veterans began calling at the house for a last look at their old Commander and were turned away bitterly disappointed, it was decided that all who came could see him.

From ten in the morning until ten at night, they came in an unbroken line — crippled veterans, able-bodied ones, some in old uniforms, most of them in faded work-clothes — and filed past the still
form in the flag-draped coffin. The General's face was indistinct in
the gloom of drawn shades; he was in full uniform, the one he had
worn last in the field; his right hand lay on his breast. On the casket
was his sword with its hilt of gold and the diamond monogram.

At the head of the coffin was a tall crucifix of bronze with seven
tapering candles burning. Late that night when the last of the visitors
had gone, Saint Gaudens and Daniel Chester French came to the
house to make a death mask. But when Saint Gaudens looked down
at the dead man, his emotions overcame him. Remembering the
pleasant days he had spent with the General not long before while
he was working on a bust of him, he could not go on with the task.
So French carried out the work alone.

In the long procession of visitors who came on the second day,
Minnie saw one old man break down and weep. She took him to
the General's study and let him look at the old maps until he had
regained control of himself. He held his coon-skin cap in his hands
as he thanked her. "I saw him last under fire at Atlanta, ma'am. I
was worried he was hit, but he came out safe. Thank you, ma'am."

The newspapers were filled with long columns on General Sherman's life and death. The Southern papers had kindly headlines: "His long march finished" . . . "Death removes last of great commanders" . . . "The final roll call." One paper commented on what was perhaps the true secret of Sherman's popularity with his men: "He saw no difference in rank, simply because there is none and has been none since 1865."

One paper quoted his farewell to his armies on May 30, 1865: "Your general now bids you farewell with the full belief that as in war you have been good soldiers so in peace you will make good citizens; and if unfortunately new wars should arise in our country, Sherman's army will be the first to buckle on its old armor and come forth to defend and to maintain the government of our inheritance."

There was only one unpleasant note: the *New York Times* carried an editorial implying that the final rites of the Catholic Church had been forced upon the General. When Minnie showed it to John Sherman he was very angry. "We are both Christians," he said, "and he was far too good a Christian and too humane a man to deny his children the consolation of their religion. I'll write and tell them that whether one calls it prayer or extreme unction, uttered by priest or preacher, it doesn't matter. As for me, I am a Protestant, but I would not care who prayed over me if only the man were honest and had faith in his creed."

"After all, Papa was baptized in the Catholic Church, married according to its rites, and went to Mass with us often," said Minnie.

"Of course he did," said John Sherman comfortingly and went off to write his letter of protest to the *Times*.

On the 18th, Tom arrived at two in the morning. He had already learned of his father's death from the men on the revenue cutter. The coffin had been sealed, but it was opened for him. "Bring the lights closer," he told Cumpy, "I want to see Father's face." He remained beside the body for a while, and then himself put down the lid. A few hours later he said a Mass for his father's soul in St. Francis Xavier's Church on 16th Street. He then returned home, and at noon, in surplice and black stole, he read the prayers of the Church for his father. His brothers and sisters knelt about him; John Sherman and his wife were there, the Blaines, Mrs. Grant, relatives and friends, some hundred and fifty people. The boy choir from St. Francis Xavier's sang the *Miserere* and *Pie Jesu*. Then the coffin was resealed and the funeral procession to the station began.

The caisson was draped in black and drawn by five black horses. Behind it a man led another horse, on its back an empty saddle; in the stirrups were the General's boots — old, wrinkled, rusty. The marshal of the procession was General Butterfield; a long line of generals followed, among them Sherman's old enemy and likewise his old friend, General Joseph E. Johnston, wearing a tall black hat with a mourning band. Not long ago he and his dead friend had followed General Grant's body to the grave.

Crowds stood hatless, church bells tolled, as the coffin went by, followed by a long line of carriages filled with family and friends. President Harrison was there, ex-President Hayes and ex-President Cleveland, Carl Schurz, Chauncey Depew, Archbishop Corrigan, Cyrus Field, Augustin Daly — leaders from many walks of life.

Insistent demands had been made that General Sherman be buried at Arlington or at West Point, but he had himself given positive orders in that regard: he wished to be buried beside his wife in St. Louis.

The funeral train went slowly out of New York, stopping in Edgewood to pick up the Fitch children. In those towns which had G.A.R. posts, people were gathered at the station. There was a rolling of drums and gun-fire as the train passed slowly by. Every town was draped in mourning and every flag was at half mast.

In St. Louis the depot was draped in black and crowds lined the streets. There was to be another funeral procession there, this one at the special request of the General himself. "Omit the military part in New York, if you wish," he had told the children some months before his death, "but don't omit it in St. Louis." On his seventieth birthday he had said he would always keep his membership in Ransom Post — "and it is to deposit my body in Calvary Cemetery some day."

It was a four-mile procession of well over twelve thousand people; it passed, as in New York, through a city in mourning. In it were soldiers, many of them marching in groups; one unit was made up of only twenty-four men, members of the Ransom Army Post, ten of them in blue uniforms, a feeble white-haired remnant, all who were left alive of the Old Thirteenth which had followed "Uncle Billy" through Vicksburg and Arkansas Pass and Missionary Ridge. Not far behind them came two hundred members of the ex-Confederate Association of Missouri, with crepe armbands on their faded gray uniforms.

The bier was placed before Willy's grave, with its monument of crossed flags and its inscription "Our Little Sergeant," presented by the very men who stood about it now. To the right was Ellen's grave; to the left that of little Charley.

Father Tom Sherman, pale and agitated, came up with Lizzie on his arm, Minnie and the rest of the family behind them. He went quickly behind his mother's monument and there donned surplice and cassock; as he came forward a boy walked beside him carrying incense and holy water. He paused by the coffin for a moment to console John Sherman who was weeping bitterly. Then in a clear strong voice he read the burial prayers in Latin and in English, his voice unshaken until he read the words of St. John: "I am the resurrection and the Life," and then he had to wait for a moment to regain his own composure.

After he stopped speaking, the infantry fired three volleys, followed by a twelve-gun salute from the battery. Then came the sweet music of taps, and the last of the great Northern generals of the Civil War was at rest.

## 21. Minnie Fitch

[1891–1913]

AFTER the death of General Sherman the house which Ellen had lived to enjoy for only a few months, and where the General had spent the three years he survived her, was sold. Lizzie, with Rachel and Cump, took an apartment in Waverly Place. At the year's end even this small remainder of a once large family became smaller: Rachel married Dr. Paul Thorndike and went to live in Boston. Her Uncle John Sherman insisted he must take her father's place and that she must come to Washington to be married from his home. Among the four hundred guests were President Harrison, his wife and his Cabinet members. Rachel's brother Tom performed the marriage ceremony. Among the members of the family who came were Billy and Eleanor Fitch, representing their mother who was ill. In Washington the two stayed with their Aunt Virginia Ewing. Eleanor and her three cousins — Virginia, Eleanor and Maria, who were near her age — had a glorious time. It was an especially notable occasion for Eleanor, for she was wearing her first silk dress — a pale lavender, very stylishly made.

In the spring of 1892 Minnie spent a few weeks at St. Vincent's Hospital in New York City; although not actually ill, she was badly in need of a rest. In the room next to hers was a patient who came from South Carolina; the two often talked together of the fears and agonies of the war years. Minnie realized how fortunate the Ewings and Shermans had been to have their husbands and sons return to them when this Southern woman told her that she had lost her husband and sons in the conflict. She showed Minnie a leaf from a branch of the palmetto tree under which the edict of secession had been signed and said it was one of her greatest treasures. General Sherman, she said, had been very kind to her family and she felt indebted to him for personal attention and protection during the war. Later, however, she said, "Let me tell you that when a Georgia child heard the awful words, 'Sherman is coming,' it shook with fear."

"Well," said Minnie, "let me tell you that a Northern child certainly shook with fear when *she* heard the awful words, 'Morgan is coming.' "

Back in her own room, she tried to down a rising indignation. It was so difficult to think that anyone had ever used her father as a bugaboo to frighten children — her father who had never in his life been anything but kind and gentle to them, whether in the North or in the South.

In October, 1892, the Fitch family left the big old house in Edgewood and moved to Wilkinsburg to a smaller one. It was a greatly reduced family: Billy was at West Point and Tom at Holy Cross College in Massachusetts. Only the two girls were left at home.

Nine-year-old Mary felt saddest at leaving Edgewood, for she had come there as a baby, and ever since had played in the ravine and the big yard, climbed the trees and grape-vines; it was the only home she had ever known. It took the excitement of helping with the moving and the promise of dancing-school to console her.

The new house was close to a church, which pleased Minnie, and she soon became head of the altar society. It was a poor parish, whose congregation was made up of miners and their families. Eleanor was the chief church worker, for her mother was not well enough to do a great deal, but between them they managed a parish fair that netted the church a new altar, and to which many old friends sent gifts, among them Mrs. Andrew Carnegie whose offering bought new altar candlesticks.

The next few years passed quietly. Will was hard at work with his new company. Mary was at school with the Ursulines and Eleanor was studying with private tutors. Minnie herself was still frail in health but as eager as ever to have a share in all that the family did. The devotion between her and Will was as deep as ever and their children's greatest hope was that their own lives would be as filled with love as their parents' had always been. Will Fitch always continued, even in smaller ways, the affectionate observances of their early married years. Each Saturday he brought Minnie a box of Reymer's candy; each Saturday night the two had a small celebration of their own: they drank the Navy toast together "to sweethearts and wives."

In 1896 a financial panic swept the country, but Will Fitch's firm weathered it. He was very anxious about Bryan and his silver platform, so much so that when, in the autumn before the elections, an excited Eleanor was leaving for a year of school in Paris, her father told her, "If McKinley is not elected, I may not have the money to bring you home." Eleanor did not worry much at this warning: she was more interested in getting to Paris than in any plans for getting back. But later when she read that McKinley had been elected, she felt a certain relief to know that she could get home again. She returned the following year, to find a great improvement in financial affairs: steel was booming and so was her father's business. Billy was out of school and had a position in the Pittsburgh Wire Company.

Two years later Will and Minnie took Mary with them on a brief visit to Europe, leaving on July 16th and planning to return early in September. The boys stayed at home and Eleanor and her friend Myra Hancock kept house for them.

On July 24th they landed at Havre where they visited Elly Thackara and her husband, who was now United States consul there. Then they went on to Paris where they made a tour of the shops, drove to the cemetery of Père la Chaise and attended Mass at the Madeleine — a high Mass which greatly impressed Will who had never seen the ceremony of the blessing of bread. At Versailles they breakfasted in a courtyard under great trees while two musicians played for them.

Mid-August found them in London, and they made this visit a celebration of their meeting of twenty-five years before — a "silver meeting anniversary" Will called it. They went to Sunday Mass at the Jesuit church in Farm Street, and called on Mr. Stevens, still in his old office at the American Embassy. He told them how happy he had been to receive their wedding invitation and to learn that his introduction had led to such a romance.

Mary was taken to all the historic spots her father and mother visited on their first meeting: to the old Cheshire Cheese, where she sat in Samuel Johnson's chair, to Simpson's-on-the-Strand, where Will showed his daughter the rose her mother had given him at their first meeting, carefully preserved in his prayerbook. They even walked past the house in Craven Street where Minnie and her French maid had lodged. If Mary sometimes grew weary of being regaled with the past, of revisiting all the places where her parents had gone, and hearing detailed descriptions of the dresses her mother had worn, she managed to conceal it politely.

In late August they went to Ireland. Will hired a jaunting car from a Mr. Dillon and in this they visited the cities of Dublin and Cork, the Lakes of Killarney and Blarney Castle. Sightseeing by jaunting car sometimes made Minnie's head ache, though her husband and her daughter enjoyed it greatly, but on the whole she was as sorry as they were when it came time to leave Ireland.

After a pleasant trip home on the *Britannic,* and back in New York at the Fifth Avenue Hotel, Will gave a sigh of relief, and said he wanted to stay there a long time: it was so unlike the French and English hotels. Even Mary and Minnie preferred shopping in the familiar stores — Sterns and Wanamakers, Huylers for sodas, Brentanos for new books and Deans for candy and cakes.

Immediately on his return to Pittsburgh, Will carried to completion negotiations which were begun before the Fitches went on their brief tour. The Pittsburgh Wire Company, in which he held the largest interest, was sold to the American Steel and Wire Company, soon to become the United States Steel Corporation. Will himself then began to organize and build a new company which was named the Pittsburgh Steel Shafting Company.

In 1899 Billy Fitch married the granddaughter of General Hancock and the entire family attended the wedding which was celebrated on the big plantation in Clarksdale, Mississippi. Father Tom Sherman performed the ceremony.

The following year Tom Fitch was married to Gray Emery of Sewickley. A year later Minnie Fitch's first grandchild was born and called Coleman Morrison. Minnie was distressed by this name, for she wanted the baby called for a saint. But Tom had promised his wife that she could name the children if she would consent to their being brought up in the Catholic faith.

When Minnie spoke of the matter to Tom's pastor, Father Tobin laughed at her. "It's a good name. There are at least six saints called Coleman and it is a fine Irish name to have."

The baby was baptized on Easter Sunday; since the weather was too stormy to take him to church, the ceremony took place at home. It was followed by an old-fashioned christening party; many of the family were present; there were toasts and merriment galore. The baby, his grandmother's pride and delight, remained the center of it all.

In 1903 Will, finding he was too busy to take the long vacation he had promised Minnie, decided to spend a brief month at sea. They would take Mary with them to Europe, leave her at school there for a year, and return almost immediately. Going by slow French liner, they would stay one night at Havre, and sail the next day for New York.

It proved a gay trip. Minnie had a twenty-four hour reunion with Elly and Lizzie at Havre. Will had the sea trip he wanted. "And besides," Minnie announced proudly, back at home, "I did quite a lot of shopping in France."

In October of that year, most of the family attended the unveiling of the statue of General Sherman in Washington. This memorial had been planned for many years, and officers and soldiers had contributed funds; a committee of army officers had finally selected a design from over twenty submitted.

On this occasion Will and Minnie and their children stayed with General Miles, now General of the Army, and Rachel was invited to the White House with her son Sherman who was to unveil the statue.

Many army corps were represented in the parade before the unveiling, and places in the reviewing stands were reserved for old soldiers. Each wore the badge of his own corps and many their wide brimmed campaign hats. There were men in gray as well as men in blue, as if in exemplification of Sherman's words, carved on the base of the statue: "War's legitimate object is more perfect peace."

The sun shone warmly over the long parade. Forty years had gone by since the war's end, and not many of the old soldiers were able to march; younger men filled the ranks of the parade. President Roosevelt and his Cabinet, escorted by a detachment of the First Regiment, walked from the White House to the reviewing stand facing the statue.

When all the troops had passed in review, an invocation was given by Father Stafford of Saint Patrick's Church; then the President spoke, as did one general from each of the four armies of the Tennessee, Cumberland, Ohio and Potomac. After Bishop Satterlee gave the benediction, the unveiling took place.

The next night a banquet was held at which addresses were given by the Civil War generals. Another speech was made by General Sherman's son, Father Tom, who spoke of the victories which had been won for one cause, under one flag, in the one war. "But there is a greater triumph for you," he said to the veterans, "than your conquests in battles, and that is the absolute triumph of the principles you battled to maintain. Today this country is one because you have so welded and united us that we are in perfect accord with your principles everywhere. I hope you will always conquer by the strength of your principles as you did in the war."

For Minnie the occasion was a nostalgic one; it carried her back to the days of the '60's. Many of the officers had been with her father, and the old soldiers came crowding up when they heard that she was "Uncle Billy's" daughter who had been in camp with him on the Big Black River. They talked about that long ago day in '65 when in tattered weary ranks they had marched up the same Pennsylvania Avenue and General Sherman had reviewed them.

Billy's marriage ended unhappily, and a year later he was at home again with his parents, living now in a house on Clyde Street in Pittsburgh. It was close to the Church of the Sacred Heart where that year the Passionist Father Fidelis of the Cross preached each Sunday evening during Lent. When Billy came home, his brief wedded life over, he would go to hear Father Fidelis preach when he would go nowhere else, and he often went to talk to him in his monastery high up on the hill overlooking the grimy city — the monastery to the building of which little Minnie Sherman had years ago given one of her gold dollars from San Francisco. Father Fidelis was the force, Will and Minnie knew, which brought their son back from the despair into which his wrecked marriage had plunged him.

That year Minnie's health was poor. She went out very little, but she kept busy at home with sewing and reading, and spent many hours at her piano. "We can tell of whom she is thinking by listening to the tune she plays," her children declared. Her grandson Morrison came often to visit her, and sometimes he was left with her for days at a time. In him she took great delight, and he was devoted to his lovely grandmother in her lavender dresses, the red hair now softly blended with gray.

In 1906 Philemon Ewing died in Lancaster; two of his nephews took part in the funeral Mass, Father Sherman as deacon and Father Hugh Ewing as sub-deacon. In that same year Father Tom preached a Lenten mission in New York at Saint Patrick's Cathedral and attracted great crowds, many non-Catholics among them. He was well known as a fine speaker, and many said his delivery and his bearing greatly resembled that of the famous orator and preacher, Bishop Spaulding. And in that year Mary became engaged to Daniel Webster Armisted, greatgrandson of Thomas Ewing's friend, Daniel Webster, and grandson of General Armisted of the Confederate Army who had led Pickett's gallant charge at Gettysburg.

In 1907 Will Fitch fell ill, and his family persuaded him to take a long rest. He was sixty-three years old and had worked hard all his life. He hated to think of giving up, but it was the year of a great panic when many firms were failing and, knowing that his health prevented him from giving his business his full time, he turned it over to his son Tom. With so few left at home, it was decided to give up the Pittsburgh house entirely. Eleanor was living in New York with her Uncle Cump and studying at the Art League, Billy was working in Detroit, and Mary was to be married.

Her wedding was a simple one, taking place in early autumn in a small house overlooking the little town of Sharon, Connecticut, which her cousin Ann Hoyt had loaned the Fitches for the summer. The rooms were decorated with autumn leaves; Eleanor was her sister's bridesmaid and Dan's brother his best man, his cousin Jerome Bonaparte the one usher. Mary wore her mother's wedding dress, somewhat modernized and with a yoke made of the beautiful and costly handkerchief which had been the wedding gift of Mr. Stewart to Minnie Sherman.

Father Torrance Smith, the white-haired pastor of the Sharon church, married them, before the wide open door of the house, with the tall trees shading the wedding party and the sun of early September shining on them.

After the ceremony the bride's cake was cut and toasts were given. Through it all, Father Smith and Will had been sitting together, talking quietly. Suddenly their voices rose: they had made the discovery that they were related through Will's Grandmother Smith of Roscommon. Father Smith laid claim to being one of the kinsmen present. "And now the marriage is bound to be doubly happy," he declared, "because it has been blessed by a relative."

After a while the bride and groom rode away in the early sunset light, in an old-fashioned runabout bedecked with flowers. The bride's brother Tom sang "So Long Mary," after them through a megaphone until the runabout and horse and young couple passed out of sight down the valley road.

When all the guests were gone, Will and the children looked anxiously at Minnie. They knew how difficult it was to let this child go from her, even though she was glad to have her happily married. For through the years Mary had filled for her the place left so empty by the deaths of Maria and Katy and the baby Hugh.

During the next years there was little change in the pattern of the lives of the older Fitches. In 1908, Will insisted on going back to work, this time with the Columbia Steel and Shafting Company. Minnie spent much of the time with him in Pittsburgh in the comfortable rooms they had rented and where much of their own furniture had been brought. Sometimes she stayed with Billy in Detroit, or with Tom and his family in Sewickley where there was now another grandchild — Philemon Tecumseh — or with Mary Armisted, who lived with her husband in Bethlehem, Pennsylvania.

At Christmas time in 1911, four of the Fitches managed to celebrate the day together in Detroit. Minnie had been staying there with Billy. Will came on from Pittsburgh and Eleanor came from New York. The talk was of old times, of those of the family who could not be with them, of plans for the future. Then Billy spoke up suddenly. "I'm tired of business," he told the others. "I'm going to give it up as soon as I can break away and buy a farm to run myself."

He did not want a farm in the East he said or even in the State to which all with Ewing blood were apt to gravitate — Ohio. He wanted to settle somewhere in the South.

"Why not take your mother with you?" suggested his father, and the others agreed, for they all knew how the cold northern winters were weakening Minnie's resistance.

Billy's plan was already well formed. He even had in mind the place — "and it once was family land too," he said. He wanted to go to Bay Manette, Alabama, a great tract long ago acquired by Thomas Ewing, which some of his descendants were now forming into a land company and selling off in farm sites. The cover of the prospectus which advertised it had been drawn by Thomas Ewing's great-granddaughter, Eleanor, at her art school in New York. It was an elaborate drawing, which contrasted snow-capped mountains with a horn of plenty from which flowed bright fruits and multicolored flowers, and it bore the words: "While you are shoveling snow we are gathering roses." Perhaps it was the gay drawing, perhaps the thought of Ewing land to live on, perhaps the thought of warm sunlight — at any event, Minnie decided to go with her son and within a month the pioneers were on their way.

But, after all, Billy and his mother did not settle at Bay Manette. When they reached the place it had grown into such a boom town that they sought a quieter spot nearby and found the small settlement of Magnolia Springs near Mobile. Minnie wrote home that she loved it all, and that the warm and flower-laden breezes made her feel ten years younger.

As for Billy, there was no doubt that he had found exactly the work he wanted to do and that he was perfectly happy on the land. Evidently Father Fidelis had been right when he said that Billy would be reconciled to life only when he had completely accepted his loss and had begun a new life.

The following summer Eleanor came to Magnolia Springs to visit, and spent quiet months with her mother, reading aloud and sewing. She also spent much time copying in long-hand the letters of General Sherman which her mother dictated from the contents of the old brown sheets. On Sundays the three Fitches went by row-boat to Mass in a small church where they were the only white people in the congregation.

Eleanor went back to New York in September, feeling that her mother was much better, but early in January, 1913, Billy wired from Mobile that Minnie had been taken to a hospital and was in need of an immediate operation. Eleanor was to come immediately. Her father had also been sent for.

Eleanor found her mother at Providence Hospital, content and smiling in a comfortable, sunny room, but there was evidence of suffering in her eyes and she had grown very thin. Nevertheless she was happy, and she chronicled some of the reasons to Eleanor: at the hospital she had Mass and daily Communion, and the Sisters of Charity to care for her; the Jesuit Fathers from Spring Hill College, some of whom had made their studies with her brother Tom in Woodstock, came often to see her. And there were the friends she had made in Mobile, who kept her room full of flowers and fruit.

Eleanor had intended to persuade her mother to return with her to New York to consult a competent surgeon there. But Minnie said pleadingly that she trusted the doctor who was taking care of her, and she did not want to go back to the cold North. "I don't want to see snow ever again," she declared with her old vigor.

Will came to Mobile and so did Tom and Mary. When Minnie's operation was performed, her family learned it had been delayed too long: the trouble was malignant. However, the doctors assured her husband and children that she would live for an indefinite time. The others went North again, but Eleanor stayed with her mother.

As Minnie grew stronger there were visitors. One of them was the Jesuit Father Guyol, nephew of the Southern General Beauregard. In the summer of 1863, when little Tom Sherman was visiting his father on the Big Black River Camp at Vicksburg, young Guyol had been there too, but on the Confederate side of the river visiting his uncle. Another visitor was Father de la Moninieres, the noted Shakespearean scholar, who sometimes recited to Minnie in his deep musical voice. Especially there was young Father Doherty who talked to Mrs. Fitch about his own mother in England. From the day he first saw her in the hospital he adopted her as his own and called her his *Mater Americana*. Each afternoon after his classes at Spring Hill, he came on horseback for a short visit with Mrs. Fitch. She opened her heart to him and told him her joys and sufferings, her anxiety about her children, her worry about her grandchildren's religious upbringing. A strong bond grew between the elderly invalid and the young Jesuit.

In early March her children took Minnie to the hotel at Biloxi, a lovely spot on the Mississippi coast close by the water; there she sat for hours on the veranda, sewing while her children read to her. The days passed quietly and they rejoiced at the invalid's improvement. Then in late March, Minnie had a setback due to shock: the hotel caught fire and she had to be carried out on the beach in her chair while Billy and Eleanor went back into the building to try to save their possessions. When they returned they found their mother looking very haggard in the light of the burning building, but she smiled at them and they saw she was saying her beads quietly.

After a brief stay at a nearby hotel, Billy took his mother and sister to a new farm he had recently bought, a beautiful site on the Mississippi coast not far from Biloxi with a wide view across the Gulf. It contained twenty-five acres of land and a white house overrun with roses, back of it a grove of tall dark pines.

"What shall we name it?" Billy wondered.

"I always said that any place I lived must be called Sherman Place," said Minnie, "but it really doesn't fit this one."

The others agreed that it was hardly the name to give the new home, especially since Jefferson Davis' old house "Beaurevoir," not a mile away, was now a haven for Confederate veterans.

Billy had an inspiration. "We'll call it Côte Brillante," he said.

The Fitch furniture, long in storage in Pittsburgh, was sent for, and Minnie made plans for the blessing of the house by young Father Doherty. On June 22nd he said Mass in the front room where a little altar had been set up; Minnie herself arranged the flowers. Vestments and Mass cards had been borrowed from the parish church nearby and on that day, to her great joy, Minnie was able to receive Communion with the others.

Minnie did not know that the Mass and the blessing were for something more than the new home where she hoped to spend a few happy years. Father Doherty's intention was for a happy death for Minnie Fitch.

All that summer she sat for hours at a time on her big screened porch with its four windows overlooking the water. Often the Sisters of Mercy came from Biloxi and played for her on the little Steinway piano which Will had given her when she was a bride in St. Louis.

Billy had planted flowers all around his mother's side of the house. He had smoothed the paths so that he could wheel her about the grounds and show her his flourishing vegetable garden, the rose bushes and japonica, the jasmine and oleander, the pecan, persimmon and fig trees.

In September 1913 the family was warned that Minnie had only a short time to live. Tom came with his wife and three children; Morrison was eleven now, Tecumseh five and the little granddaughter, Rosamound Thomas was three. To his grandmother's delight, Morrison remembered her well; he was a quiet, gentle boy who looked and acted much like Minnie herself, and she talked to him sometimes of the Faith in which he had been baptized and taught him little prayers to recite in the hope that he might keep something of that Faith.

All that summer Will and Minnie had written to each other every day, and he knew just how she spent her time. He thought he knew Minnie's condition from Eleanor's letters as well, but he was utterly unprepared for the change in her appearance in the few months since he had seen her. He had not expected to find her so thin, so evidently ready to leave the earth. Sometimes he left her to go on

ren and her husband joined them. Billy had that morning brought
his mother a little bunch of violets with a rose in the center; she had
it tucked under her cheek when, just before noon, she sighed gently
and was gone.

She lay on her bed, looking serene and happy, on her features
the gentle dignity which had been hers all her life. Around her neck
was the chain with the locket that held a curl from her baby Hugh's
head; under her head was the little pillow.

She died on November 22nd, the Feast of Saint Cecilia. "What a
lovely day to enter Heaven," said Sister Neri. "It will be so full of
music."

Will was very silent after his wife's death, and spent hours walking up and down in her room, pausing now and then to look at her
peaceful face. Once he spoke to Eleanor and Tom about his first
meeting with their mother in London. "When I saw her my heart
just stopped. I loved her from that minute," and then for the first
time he broke down and wept.

Very early the next morning her brother Cump arrived to accompany the funeral party to St. Louis. The train coming from Biloxi
paused for a ten-minute stop at Mobile, long enough to allow Father
Doherty to enter the car where the coffin had been placed, and to bless
Minnie in death as he had so often blessed her in life.

In St. Louis, Father Tom Sherman met the train. He was accompanied by two old friends, Henry Hitchcock and Theophile Papin.
The coffin was taken to the home of Mrs. Samuel Reber, Minnie's
cousin. In the morning Mass was sung in the Jesuit University
Church of Saint Francis Xavier, where twenty-five years before the
requiem Mass had been said for Ellen Sherman. The celebrant was
the president of St. Louis University, Father Bernard Otting. Father
Tom Sherman, just recovering from an illness, said he was emotion-
ally unable to say his sister's mass.

Many Shermans and Ewings were there. Minnie's sister Lizzie had
come from Boston with Rachel; Sissy's son, Sherman Steele, was

imaginary errands until he had full control of him
go back to her with a calm face and a smile.

When in late October Mary arrived, she too was
change in her mother. It was evident from Minnie's f
she was to have this child with her. "You filled the p
of my lost ones," she told Mary one day, and she sai
to have the heavy silver rosary, one of her most tr
sions, which Archbishop Ryan gave her long ago.

Though she said little about it her family knew he
increasing. One day, she said suddenly to Eleanor,
I can't stand it any longer. And I will see my babie
for a moment, and then a worried look came over h
will have to leave you four alone. What will become
She seemed to think her husband and children were
care.

She asked to see Father Doherty again, and when h
her that she was near death and that he wanted to
was dusk when the rite was begun and the only ligh
came from the fire on the hearth, from the little re
the statue of Our Lady of Lourdes, and the candles
laden table-altar on which Father Doherty had placed
and holy oils.

Minnie lay propped on the big high-backed bed, the
her mother, Ellen Sherman, had died. Under her hea
low embroidered with the names of Katy and Maria v
carried with her everywhere since their deaths.

Will knelt beside her on her prie-dieu and the othe
her bed. When Father Doherty put both hands on
smiled at him and he returned the smile. "And now
ceived more sacraments than I have," he said to her.

After that her mind began to wander and one day a
was evident that she was dying. All day two Sisters o
up continuous prayer at her bedside and from time to

there and Philemon Ewing's son, John Gillespie. Every branch of both families had sent at least one representative.

When, after the service, Will came down the aisle, for the first time he saw a group of old soldiers, veterans of Ransom Post and the Old Thirteenth. In their old blue uniforms and campaign hats they were lined up at attention on each side of a pathway leading down the high steps of the church to pay a last tribute to their old leader by honoring his daughter.

At Calvary Cemetery the same guard of honor waited, and one of the members stepped forward to put a silk flag on the coffin, saying, "This flag is in memory of her honored father."

Another old soldier came forward and, with dignity and military precision, placed a long-stemmed red rose across the flag. "And this rose is for our General's daughter," he said.

Then Father Otting read the burial service and the coffin was lowered into the grave, the flag and the rose still on it.

# Afterword

THE CIRCLE of pure gold which holds the Host in the monstrance given to the Convent of Mary Reparatrix, in memory of the three women whose story has been told here, was collected from their possessions and those of their families. The cross which Maria Ewing always wore, and Thomas Ewing's cuff links are there. There is gold from watches and rings, from lockets and chains that belonged to their children, from a clasp of Hugh Ewing's daughter who became a nun, from medals which Father Hugh Ewing and Father Tom Sherman won at school. Ellen Ewing's wedding ring is there and something that belonged to each of her children. There is the gold chain which Minnie Fitch wore when she died, and her husband's scarf pin, and a small medal which belonged to Katy, "the Christmas baby."

Out of these transitory personal possessions was made the golden circlet that holds the Love that is not transitory, the everlasting gold of the Love of God.

# Acknowledgements

I wish to acknowledge the kindness of those who have given me or sent me material for this book. Much of it came to me directly through Miss Eleanor Sherman Fitch, the direct descendant of the women with whom this book deals, who wrote and made inquiries with indefatigable zeal, who answered for me patiently the many inquiries I directed to her and who gave me all the material regarding her own mother's later life. In addition, she loaned me all the diaries and letters needed for this book, as well as scrapbooks and newspaper clippings. Without her continuous aid this book could not have been written as it is. It could have been statements of fact woven into biography, but it could not have been an intimate chronicle of the three lives.

My thanks go to Reverend Thomas McAvoy, C.S.C., archivist at Notre Dame University, who has been unfailingly kind in supplying copies of letters and with advice whenever he has been approached during the several years this book has been in the writing. He kindly consented to read the proofs, a valuable aid, since he is widely read in early Ohio history.

To Mrs. Charles M. Montgomery of Newark, Ohio; to Neal H. Ewing of Roselle, N.J.; to Eleanor Sherman Ewing of Silver Springs, Md., and to Maria Ewing of Washington, D.C.; to Mrs. Daniel Webster Armisted of Bethlehem, Pa.; to Helen Grace Smith of Torresdale, Pa. and to Miss Victoria Janson, I offer my thanks for assistance.

Miss Dorothy Breck, of the New York Historical Society, was helpful in showing me scrapbooks of the families, which are kept there, and Dr. St. George L. Sioussat, chief of the Division of Manuscripts at the Library of Congress, sent photostated copies of Ewing letters from the archives. Mr. Arthur Maynard of the Genealogical and Biographical Society of New York, also gave me valuable information.

My grateful acknowledgments are offered for letters sent me by Sister Monica, of the Brown County Ursulines; Sister Mary Mercedes, of the Sisters of the Blessed Sacrament; Mother Ann McCabe, R.C.; Mother M. Rose Elizabeth, C.S.C.; and to Mother Williams of the Religious of the Sacred Heart.

For other assistance with letters and research my thanks go also to Most Reverend John F. O'Hara, C.S.C.; to Right Reverend Monsignor Edward B. Jordan, vice rector of Catholic University; to the Reverend Hugh J. Wilt, O.S.B., of St. Vincent's Archabbey, Latrobe, Pa.; to the Very Reverend Francis A. McQuade, S.J.; to Reverend V. F. O'Daniel, O.P.; and to Reverend Laurence J. Kenny, of St. Louis University.

# Bibliography

"Autobiography of Thomas Ewing," edited by Clement L. Martzolff, *Ohio Archeological and Historical Quarterly,* January, 1913.

BYERS, S. H. M. *Twenty Years in Europe.* New York: Rand, McNally, 1900.

DE CHAMBRUN, CLARA LONGWORTH. *Cincinnati.* New York: Scribner's, 1939.

*Charles Ewing,* by his Youngest Corporal (Thomas E. Sherman, S.J.). Philadelphia: J. B. Lippincott, 1886.

DALE, EDWARD and LITTLE, GASTON. *Cherokee Cavaliers.* Norman, Okla.: University of Oklahoma Press, 1939.

EWING, THOMAS, JR. *Honorable Thomas Ewing and General Thomas Ewing.* Pamphlet. Chicago: Century Publishing & Engraving Co. 1897.

FITCH, MINNIE SHERMAN. *Recollections of My Mother.* Mss.

———. *Memory Book for My Children.* Mss.

FLEMING, WALTER L. *General Sherman as a College President.* Cleveland: Arthur H. Clarke Company, 1912.

FLOWER, MILTON AND LENORE. *This is Carlisle.* Pamphlet. Harrisburg: J. Horace McFarland Co., 1924.

*General Sherman in the Last Year of the Civil War.* Pamphlet privately printed by P. Tecumseh Sherman. 1908.

*George Ewing, Gentleman, a Soldier of Valley Forge.* Privately printed, 1928.

*Historic Church of St. Peter.* Brownsville Diocese of Pittsburgh. Privately printed, 1936.

*Hitchcock, Henry. Letters.* Edited by M. A. de Wolfe Howe. New Haven: Yale University Press, 1927.

HOWE, M. A. DE WOLFE. *Home Letters of General Sherman.* New York: Scribner's, 1909.

———. *Letters of Sherman.* New Haven: Yale University Press, 1927.

LASSERRE, HENRI. *Our Lady of Lourdes.* New York: D. J. Sadlier, 1873.

McALLISTER, ANNA SHANNON. *Flame in the Wilderness.* Notre Dame, Ind.: Sisters of Holy Cross, 1944.

————. *Ellen Ewing, Wife of General Sherman.* New York: Benziger Brothers, 1936.

MONICA, SISTER, O.S.U. *The Cross in the Wilderness.* New York: Longmans, Green, 1930.

MOORE, FRANK. *Women in the War.* Hartford: S. S. Scranton Co., 1867.

MUZZEY, DAVID S. *James G. Blaine.* New York: Dodd, Mead & Co., 1934.

O'DANIEL, V. F., O.P. *Rt. Rev. Edward D. Fenwick, O.P.* New York: Frederick Pustet, 1920.

SHANE, LESLIE. *Letters of Herbert Cardinal Vaughan to Lady Herbert of Lea.* London: Burns Oates, 1942.

SHERMAN, ELLEN EWING. *Recollections for My Children.* Mss.

SHERMAN, W. TECUMSEH. *Reminiscences of Early Days.* Mss.

————. *Memoirs.* 2 vols. New York: D. Appleton, 1875.

DE SMET, P. I., S.J. *Western Missions and Missionaries.* New York: James Kerker, 1863.

SULLIVAN, A. M. *General History of Ireland.* New York: Murphy & McCarthy, 1914.

*Thomas Ewing of Ohio, a Memorial.* New York: Catholic Publication Society, 1873.

WISEMAN, C.M.L. *History of Lancaster, Ohio, and the Lancaster People.* Columbus, Ohio: C.M.L. Wiseman, Tranger Co., 1898.

Scrapbooks of Sherman Family, 1870 to 1914.

Letters: Maria Ewing, Thomas Ewing, Ellen Ewing Sherman, William T. Sherman, Minnie Sherman Fitch, Thomas William Fitch.

# Index